ADOBE® DREAMWEAVER® CS3
HOW-TOs

100 ESSENTIAL TECHNIQUES

DAVID KARLINS

Adobe Dreamweaver CS3 How-Tos
100 Essential Techniques

David Karlins

Adobe Press books are published by
Peachpit
1249 Eighth Street
Berkeley, CA 94710
510/524-2178
800/283-9444
510/524-2221 (fax)

For the latest on Adobe Press books, go to www.adobepress.com
Find us on the World Wide Web at: www.peachpit.com
To report errors, pleae send a note to errata@peachpit.com

Peachpit Press is a division of Pearson Education

Project Editor: Rebecca Gulick
Editor: Ellen Cavalli
Proofreader: Liz Welch
Production Editor: Connie Jeung-Mills
Compositor: ICC Macmillan
Indexer: James Minkin
Cover and Interior Design: Mimi Heft

ISBN-13: 978-0-321-50893-5
ISBN-10: 0-321-50893-9

9 8 7 6 5 4 3 2

Printed and bound in the United States of America

Dedicated to Brad and the BlackKoffee café in Chitown for hosting my late-night writing sessions with green tea, jazz, and cookies. You'll definitely feel the vibes in this book!

Acknowledgments

Thanks to the entire editorial and production crew at Adobe Press, including Rebecca Gulick. Special thanks to my editor, Ellen Cavalli, to Virginia DeBolt for expert and vigilant technical editing, and to illustrator and advisor Bruce K. Hopkins. Extra special thanks to my agent-enabler Margot Maley Hutchison.

Contents

Chapter One: Creating a Web Site 1

#1   Collecting Site Content 2

#2   Defining a Local Site 6

#3   Organizing a Local Site 8

#4   Managing Site Views 10

#5   Managing Sites 14

#6   Defining a Remote Server Connection 16

#7   Connecting to a Remote Server 19

#8   Transferring Files Between Remote and Local Sites 22

#9   Synchronizing Local and Remote Content 26

Chapter Two: Working in the Document Window 29

#10   Exploring the Document Window 30

#11   Viewing Panels and the Property Inspector 34

#12   Editing Page Content in Three Views 37

#13   Examining Dreamweaver Toolbars 39

#14   Using the Insert Toolbar 42

#15   Using the Insert Menu Bar 44

#16   Creating a New Page from Scratch 48

#17   Defining Links 52

#18   Creating Pages from Blank Templates 55

#19   Creating Pages from Sample Starter Pages 58

#20   Creating Pages from Sample Style Sheets and Framesets 61

Chapter Three: Designing Pages with Tables and Frames 65

#21   Creating a Table in Standard Mode 66

#22   Creating a Table in Layout Mode 70

#23   Creating Fixed and Flexible Columns 73

#24   Embedding Tables Within Tables 77

#25   Defining Table Properties 80

#26   Defining Cell Properties 82

#27 Generating a Frameset from Samples 84

#28 Formatting Framesets 87

#29 Defining Links Between Frames. 91

Chapter Four: Designing Pages with Absolute Placement Objects **93**

#30 Defining Absolute Placement Objects 95

#31 Formatting AP Divs in the Property Inspector 102

#32 Managing AP Divs in the AP Elements Panel 104

#33 Defining Div Tags. 106

#34 Using Rulers, Guides, and Grids 112

Chapter Five: Working with Text and Images **115**

#35 Formatting Text with HTML Attributes 116

#36 Applying Colors to Fonts. 119

#37 Defining Inline Text Attributes with CSS. 121

#38 Preparing Images for the Web 126

#39 Embedding Images in a Web Page. 130

#40 Making Images Accessible with Alt Tags 132

#41 Editing Images in Dreamweaver 135

#42 Aligning Text and Images. 139

#43 Defining Image Maps. 142

#44 Placing Photoshop Files in Web Pages 145

Chapter Six: Planning and Embedding Site Elements **151**

#45 Creating Template Pages 152

#46 Generating New Pages from Templates 157

#47 Updating Templates 159

#48 Creating and Placing Library Items. 161

#49 Updating Library Items 165

#50 Including Navigation in Templates and Library Items. 167

#51 Uploading Templates and Library Items. 169

Chapter Seven: Formatting Page Elements with CSS. **171**

#52 Formatting Page Elements with Style Sheets. 172

#53 Defining Page Style Using the Body Tag. 178

#54 Formatting HTML Text Tags with CSS. 181

#55   Formatting Image and Page Styles............................ 184

#56   Applying CSS to Links 186

#57   Defining CSS for Printable Pages............................ 189

Chapter Eight: Collecting Data in Forms.................................... 193

#58   Creating Jump Menus 194

#59   Embedding Forms Linked to Server Databases............... 198

#60   Defining a Form in Dreamweaver 200

#61   Defining a Form Fieldset.................................... 203

#62   Placing Text Fields and Text Areas........................... 205

#63   Placing Check Boxes.. 207

#64   Placing Radio Buttons 208

#65   Placing Lists/Menus and File Fields.......................... 210

#66   Using Hidden Fields 212

#67   Placing Form Buttons...................................... 213

#68   Defining Form Actions...................................... 214

#69   Defining a Spry Validation Text Field Widget 215

#70   Defining a Spry Validation Textarea Widget 218

#71   Defining a Spry Validation Checkbox Widget................. 221

#72   Defining a Spry Validation Select Widget..................... 223

Chapter Nine: Embedding Media 225

#73   Creating Flash Text in Dreamweaver 226

#74   Creating Flash Buttons in Dreamweaver 228

#75   Embedding Flash and Flash Video Files 230

#76   Embedding QuickTime Media 233

#77   Embedding Windows Media................................ 235

Chapter Ten: Adding Effects and Interactivity with Spry 237

#78   Inserting Tabbed Panels 238

#79   Inserting a Spry Menu Bar Widget 240

#80   Formatting Spry Menu Bar Widgets.......................... 241

#81   Inserting a Spry Accordion Widget........................... 242

#82   Inserting a Spry Collapsible Panel Widget.................... 243

#83   Deleting Spry Widgets...................................... 244

#84 Attaching Effects to Page Elements 245

#85 Defining Effect Events 246

#86 Editing and Deleting Effects 248

Chapter Eleven: Adding Interactivity with Behaviors **249**

#87 Defining Browsers for Behaviors 250

#88 Opening a Browser Window 251

#89 Designing a Pop-up Message 253

#90 Creating a Timeline 254

#91 Deleting Behaviors 257

#92 Designing a Rollover. 258

#93 Creating an Interactive Navigation Bar 260

#94 Editing a Navigation Bar 262

Chapter Twelve: Testing and Maintaining Sites **263**

#95 Checking Browser Compatibility 264

#96 Previewing Web Pages in Device Central 266

#97 Testing Links Sitewide 267

#98 Cleaning Up Word HTML. 268

#99 Adding Design Notes 270

#100 Testing Browsers for Media Support 271

Index **273**

CHAPTER ONE

Creating a Web Site

Many people think of Web design in terms of simply creating a Web *page*. However, before you start designing Web pages, you should define a Dreamweaver CS3 Web *site*. Defining a Web site *before* you create pages allows Dreamweaver to connect your Web pages to each other with links. It makes it possible to embed images or other nontext content in pages. When you move or rename a Web page (or any file in your site), Dreamweaver updates any links that are affected by that change. And, your Dreamweaver Web site can manage (usually one, but sometimes more) style sheet files that control the formatting of multiple pages across a site.

Defining a Dreamweaver Web site is necessary to manage your files and make them all work together. It is also necessary when you get ready to transfer your site content from your local computer to a remote server—where others can access your content.

Dreamweaver CS3 has essentially two work environments—the Document window and the Files window. The bulk of this book is devoted to using the Document window, and most of your time creating Web sites will be spent in the Document window. This is where you create and edit Web pages. But before you do that, you should understand how Dreamweaver manages Web sites and files in the Files window. The Files window provides tools to control your Web site. The Files window also has tools that allow you to manage your files once you define your site.

This chapter will help you understand how to manage files in your Web site. In it, you will learn how to define a *remote* Web site and transfer files from your local Web site (your computer) to your remote site, where they will be accessible to everyone over the Internet.

#1 Collecting Site Content

The most basic elements of Web site content are text and images. But the Web is rapidly becoming more accessible and friendly to other types of content; media files, Adobe PDF files, FlashPaper files, and other types of content are increasingly moving to the "accessible" list. Content beyond text and images, however, requires plug-in software—programs like Adobe Flash Player, Apple QuickTime Player, Microsoft Windows Media Player, Adobe Reader, and other programs that *add* capacity to browsers.

Web browsers can interpret and display text and images without plug-ins. For this reason, and because a large percentage of Web site content remains text and images, this How-To will focus on preparing text and images for your site.

The *most accessible* Web content is HTML text. HTML stands for Hyper-text Markup Language—the "hyper" referring not to drinking too many caffeinated beverages, but to the fact that Web text includes *links*, click-able text (or images).

Not all formatting features work the same way on a Web page as they do on a printed page. This poses a challenge when you copy or import text into Dreamweaver.

Note
Technically speaking, bringing text intended for a printed page into a Web page involves translating the formatting from PostScript (the coding language used for most printing) into HTML (the markup language used for formatting Web text).

Preparing text for Web pages requires bridging the gap between formatting markup language that translates into print formatting (usually PostScript), and formatting markup language that is supported by Web pages. There are several ways to move text to a Web page, but none of them is completely satisfactory. This is because type formatting in a word processor, like Microsoft Word, has features that are not available in Web formatting, and vice versa.

There are three basic options for bringing type to a Web page:

- Copying relatively unformatted text into Dreamweaver, and formatting it in Dreamweaver

- Using export tools in your word processor and import tools in Dreamweaver to translate the markup language from PostScript to HTML

- Saving the text file as an Adobe PDF or FlashPaper file, opening the file in a browser using plug-in software, and defining links to the file in a Dreamweaver Web page

There are important advantages to using the first two options. If you copy and paste text from your word processor into Dreamweaver, you can avail yourself of all the formatting tools provided by Dreamweaver. These tools are designed to apply formatting that can be interpreted well and consistently by browsers. The downside of this method is that you'll need to reapply formatting in Dreamweaver.

On the other hand, saving your word processing file as an HTML file (some word processors have a Save As Web Page option) allows you to bring as much formatting as possible with the text as you move it into Dreamweaver. The downside of this method is that the formatting generated by your word processor is unlikely to hold up as consistently in browsers as text formatted in Dreamweaver.

Tip

If you're not using Microsoft Word, other word processors like TextEdit, WordPerfect, and OpenOffice all save to Word format. Or, you can copy and paste text from any source (including a Web page that is open in a Web browser) into a Dreamweaver page in the Design window. If you copy and paste, you will lose most or all of your formatting.

Importing Spreadsheets and Word Documents in Dreamweaver CS3 for Windows

The Windows version of Dreamweaver allows you to import Microsoft Word (and Excel) files directly to Web pages. This saves the step of opening the file in a word processor and saving it as an HTML file. To import a Word or Excel file, open the Web page to which you are importing the file, and choose File > Import > Word Document (or Excel Document). The Import Document dialog opens, and you can choose a few options for importing, ranging from Text Only (no formatting) to Text with Structure Plus Full Formatting (which retains the most formatting).

4

If you save a Word file as an HTML page, or if you use the Windows-only option for importing a Word file into a Dreamweaver Web page, you can clean up the HTML that results by choosing Commands > Clean Up Word HTML. From the Clean Up HTML from pop-up menu, choose a version of Word. Then accept the default check box settings. Doing this will strip from the generated HTML any coding that would confuse browsers (**Figure 1a**).

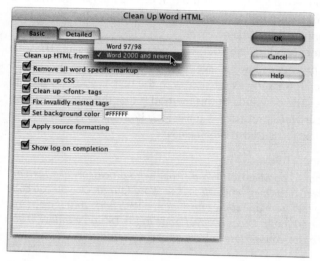

Figure 1a Cleaning up imported HTML code.

Many programs (Adobe Photoshop and Photoshop Elements among the most prominent) allow you to export image files to JPEG, GIF, or PNG format. These programs provide you with advice on when to use which format. Here, I'll list a few basic attributes of the various formats:

- JPEG images support millions of colors and are best for photographs. *Progressive* JPEG files "fade in" as they download, rather than appearing line by line.

- GIF images support far fewer colors than the JPEG format, and are not usually used for photos. But GIF images support *transparency*, which allows the background of a Web page to show through empty spots in the image. GIF images can be defined as *interlaced*. Interlacing, like the progressive attribute in JPEG images, allows the image to fade in as it downloads.

- PNG images support more colors, like JPEG, and allow you to define a transparent color, like GIF files. However, PNG format is generally not acceptable for photos because it lacks the JPEG format's capacity to manage colors and photo detail.

Programs like Photoshop allow you to preview how images will look in all three formats, with different settings for quality. Higher quality preserves color and image quality. But higher-quality images (and larger ones) take longer to download than small or lower-quality images.

Programs like Adobe Illustrator, Photoshop, and Photoshop Elements have Save for Web features that can assist you in preparing images for the Web.

Lower-quality images are generated using *compression*. Compression "looks for" pixels in an image that do not need to be saved as part of the file information, and it reduces file size by saving less of the image definition.

Differences Between Print and Web Images

Preparing images for the Web presents a separate set of challenges than preparing images for print. There are several major differences between images on the Web and images prepared for print documents. These differences include these parameters:

- Web images are usually saved at 72 dpi (dots per inch), while print images are routinely saved at 300 dpi and higher resolution.

- Web images are saved using the RGB (Red, Green, Blue) color system, while print images usually use CMYK (Cyan, Magenta, Yellow, Black) color mode.

- Web images are saved to JPEG, GIF, or PNG format, while print images are often saved in the TIFF format.

#2 Defining a Local Site

"I'm a designer, not a file manager!" I hear this protest each time I teach Dreamweaver, and I sympathize. But you need a *basic* understanding of how Web sites manage and organize files, or your site will fall apart. Links won't work; embedded images won't appear in pages; media files won't open; and style sheets, which control page format, won't attach.

The good news is that Dreamweaver will manage all your file connection issues, as long as you play by a few simple rules. The first of these rules is *always start by defining a Dreamweaver Web site*. This Web site will manage your files for you. If you change a filename, Dreamweaver will update links throughout your site. If you go on an organizing binge and decide to move all your images into appropriate file folders, Dreamweaver will update links throughout your Web site. Again, to emphasize: This works as long as you 1) set up a Dreamweaver Web site, and 2) do *all* your file management (renaming or moving files) in the Dreamweaver Site panel.

Now that I've emphasized the importance of creating a local site, here's how you do it:

1. Start by collecting your entire site content in a single folder. You can create subfolders (subdirectories) for images, media, Web pages, and so on. But all these folders must be within the folder that will serve as your local site folder.

2. From the Document window menu, choose Site > New Site. The Site Definition dialog opens.

3. At the top of the dialog, click the Advanced tab to see all options at once, instead of a wizard that reveals only one element of the site at a time. In the Category list, choose Local Info (**Figure 2a**).

Figure 2a Defining a local site.

4. In the Site name box, enter any text you wish. Nobody will see this but you and other developers; it is simply descriptive information to help you remember which Web site this is.

5. In the Local root folder area, click the folder icon at the right and navigate to the folder in which you saved all your files.

6. If you want Dreamweaver to automatically save images to one folder on your local storage system (usually a hard drive), you can navigate to a folder using the folder icon next to the Default images folder field. This is not a particularly essential option, and it can get in your way if you want to make conscious decisions on where files are stored.

7. Choose the Links relative to Document radio button; this is the most efficient and reliable way to generate and update links between files, and to define links for embedded images.

8. The only other important option is the Enable cache check box. This activates the Asset panel that displays all site content.

9. With your local site defined, click OK. Dreamweaver is now ready to organize your files for you.

#3 Organizing a Local Site

When it's time for housekeeping and moving files from one folder to another, you can also rely on the Dreamweaver Files panel. You can display the Files panel by choosing Window > File, or pressing the F8 function key (to toggle between displaying and hiding the Files panel).

The Files panel menu has options for typical file management actions, like creating new files or folders, renaming files, copying or pasting files, deleting files, and so on (**Figure 3a**).

Figure 3a Using the Files panel menu to create a new file.

The theme of this technique is as essential as it is simple: *Never* change filenames or move files between folders using your operating system's file management tools. Instead, *always* rely on Dreamweaver's Files panel to manage filenames and to move files between folders. The Site folder looks and works like the Finder (for Mac) and Windows Explorer (for Windows) utilities. It allows you to drag files between folders, copy and paste files, rename files, and delete files, just as you would do in Finder or Explorer.

Why should you use Dreamweaver's Files panel? Because in a Web site, files are almost always connected to other files. You might have an image embedded in a page. If you change the name of that image file or move it to another folder, the link between that image and the page in which it is embedded becomes corrupted.

However, if you do all your file management in Dreamweaver, Dreamweaver will *fix* the problems caused by moving or renaming a file by redefining links that involve that file. For instance, if files in your Web site contain links to a file and that filename is changed, Dreamweaver will prompt you to change those links in an Update Files dialog (**Figure 3b**).

Figure 3b Dreamweaver redefining links to match a changed filename.

When you define your local Web site in Dreamweaver, you define a local site folder. Dreamweaver knows that this folder is where all your site files *should be* kept. If you open a file from another folder or copy or move a file from another folder, Dreamweaver will prompt you to save a copy of that file in your Web folder. For example, if you embed an image in a Web page, Dreamweaver will prompt you to save that image to your site root or image folder when you place it on the page.

#4 Managing Site Views

Skilled Web designers create Web pages with a clear plan for how those pages will be accessed. From which page will they be linked? To which pages will they link? The system of links between pages defines a site navigation structure. Such a structure is like the blueprint for a building—it defines how visitors will enter and move around the site.

Dreamweaver CS3's expanded Files window provides three ways to look at your site. The default view is the Site Files view. Here, you can see a list of all files at your local site, and if you have defined a remote site, you can see all files there as well. The Testing Server view is for data-driven Web sites, where data from a database at a remote server is embedded in Web pages. That advanced approach to building Web sites relies on extensive server scripting and database programming, and is beyond the scope of this book. The third view is the Site Map view. You select an expanded Files window view using the group of three view icons in the expanded Files window toolbar (**Figure 4a**).

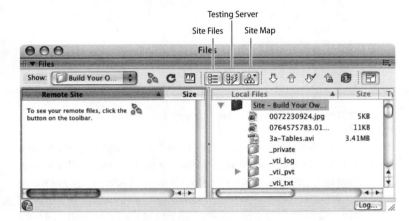

Figure 4a Three view options in the expanded Files window.

The Site Map view in the expanded Files window provides a flowchart of your Web site links. You can draw a Web site navigation diagram in a program like Adobe Illustrator or Microsoft Visio. But Dreamweaver allows you to generate site navigation while you create Web pages.

When you *prototype* site navigation, or sketch out a flowchart representing site links in Dreamweaver, you generate bare-bones pages that contain *only* links to other pages. The navigation bars that get generated are simple (**Figure 4b**).

Tip
Once you prototype a site, you can save a graphical map of the links you create, and print or display that.

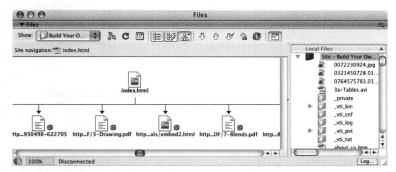

Figure 4b Links generated by Dreamweaver.

You can also use the Site Map view to prototype a Web site, and in the process generate pages with links.

To design a Web site using Site Map view, follow these steps:

1. From the Files panel menu, choose File > New File.

2. In the Files panel, rename the new file you created as index.htm.

3. Control-click (Mac) or right-click (Windows) the file you created and named index.htm. From the context menu, choose Set as Home Page.

(*continued on next page*)

4. From the Files panel menu, choose View > Site Map. The home page appears as an icon (**Figure 4c**).

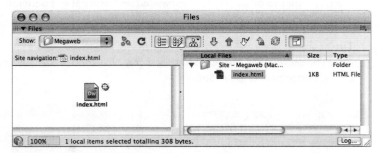

Figure 4c Viewing a home page in Site Map view.

5. Expand the Files panel by clicking the Expand icon (**Figure 4d**).

Figure 4d Expanding the Files panel.

6. Choose File > New File from the Files panel menu. Create several new files, and assign filenames (with no special characters like $, ^, or #). Add an .htm or .html filename extension to each file.

Note

Almost all Web servers and browsing environments support both .htm or .html as a filename extension for Web pages. Which option you select is basically a matter of taste. However, it is best to be consistent, and either use .htm or .html. If you create both an index.htm and an index.html page, it will be very confusing to figure out which one of these is actually your home page, and which one will open in a browser when a visitor comes to your site.

7. Click the link icon next to the home page, and click and drag to create a connection to one of the files you created. You can draw links from the home page to other pages, from other pages to the home page, or between any two pages. The page you draw a link *from* has a link placed on it to the page you draw a link *to*.

8. Select any page icon and click and drag to another page icon to create links. As you do, a site map schematic appears in the Files panel (**Figure 4e**).

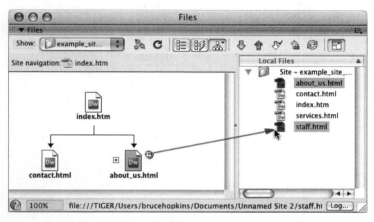

Figure 4e Generating links in the Files panel.

9. To see one of your pages with the generated link bar, double-click the page to open it in Page view.

Index.htm or Index.html Is Your Home Page

Different servers have different rules for home pages, but generally the index.htm or index.html file serves as a Web site home page. The home page is the file that opens when a visitor comes to your site. This has more significance when your site is transferred to a remote server and made accessible to visitors. But even when you are only working with a local site, defining a home page is necessary to generate a site map or prototype navigation links using the Dreamweaver Files panel.

#5 Managing Sites

In addition to creating new sites, you can edit site properties, duplicate a site (to create a copy of that site), remove a Web site from your computer, or export and import sites using the Manage Sites dialog.

To access the Manage Sites dialog, choose Site > Manage Sites. If you have multiple Web sites on your computer, choose the site you wish to edit from the list on the left side of the dialog (**Figure 5a**).

Figure 5a Selecting a site to edit.

Duplicate, Export, and Import . . .

The Export and Import options in the Manage Sites dialog do not, as one might readily assume, export or import *Web sites*. Instead, they export and import *Web site settings*. These settings are valuable because they define things like login information and paths where files are stored. But again, they are not a way to back up an entire Web site. To do that, use the Copy option. Duplicating a Web site creates a backup of that site.

Note
You might well manage many Web sites from a single computer. A professional Web designer, for example, will likely work on the sites of many clients from his or her computer.

With a site selected, choose from the set of options on the right side of the dialog.

Use the Edit option to reopen the Site Definition dialog. Here, you can revise any of the information that defines the local or remote sites. So, for example, if you change your remote Web host provider, you can enter new Web host information this way.

The Copy option is sometimes useful in creating an experimental site. Or, if you are using one site as a "template" to create other sites, you can copy the original site, and then edit the definition of the new site and make changes to customize it.

The Export feature in the Manage Sites dialog allows you to save site settings as a distinct STE file. This file can then be used to restore the site settings on another computer.

You can export your site settings as an XML file that you can import into Dreamweaver later. This enables you to move sites between machines and product versions or to share settings with other users.

To export site settings, follow these steps:

1. Select Site > Manage Sites, and select a site from the list on the left side of the Manage Sites dialog. With the site selected, click the Export button on the right side of the dialog. The Exporting Site dialog opens.

2. To back up your site settings, including user name and password as well as local path information, choose the first option. To back up site settings *without* user name and password so you can give the password to other users, select the second option (**Figure 5b**).

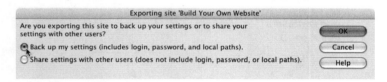

Figure 5b Backing up site information, including user name and password.

3. Click OK, and then click Done in the Manage Sites dialog.

When you back up site information, you create an XML file to which Dreamweaver CS3 attaches an .ste filename extension. This file can be opened using the Import feature in the Manage Sites dialog to install Web site settings for a site that has already been exported.

Warning! Removal Is Permanent

Choosing to remove a site in the Manage Sites dialog *permanently removes* that site from the computer, and cannot be "undone."

#6 Defining a Remote Server Connection

Local vs. Remote Sites

Normally, there are two versions of your Web site. The local site, on your computer, is where you create content. When that content is ready for the public, you upload it to the remote server.

In order for the remote (publicly accessible) site to match the content on your local site, all files must be transferred correctly, maintaining the same filenames and folder structure as exists on the local site. Dreamweaver provides the Files panel to manage your local site content, and you use the same Files panel to manage your *remote* site.

Normally, a remote server reflects content developed on a local site. In other words, most developers first create and test their Web pages on their own computer and then upload that content to a remote server once it has been tested, proofread, vetted and approved, and deemed ready to share.

When you launch Dreamweaver, the site you had open at the end of your last session will open. Your open site is indicated in the Files panel, but if that panel is not displayed, there is nothing that indicates which site is open. To determine which site is open, choose Site > Manage Sites. The Manage Sites dialog opens, and the current open site is highlighted (**Figure 6a**).

Figure 6a Identifying the open site in the Manage Sites dialog.

With a site selected in the Manage Sites dialog, click Edit to open the Site Definition dialog. In the Site Definition dialog, choose the Advanced tab.

Tip
Both the Basic and Advanced tabs provide access to the tools necessary to define a remote server connection, but the Basic tab marches you through multiple wizard-type screens, while the Advanced tab provides easier access to an overview of your connection options.

In the Advanced tab of the Site Definition dialog, click the Remote Info category. Then, follow these steps to define your remote server (**Figure 6b**):

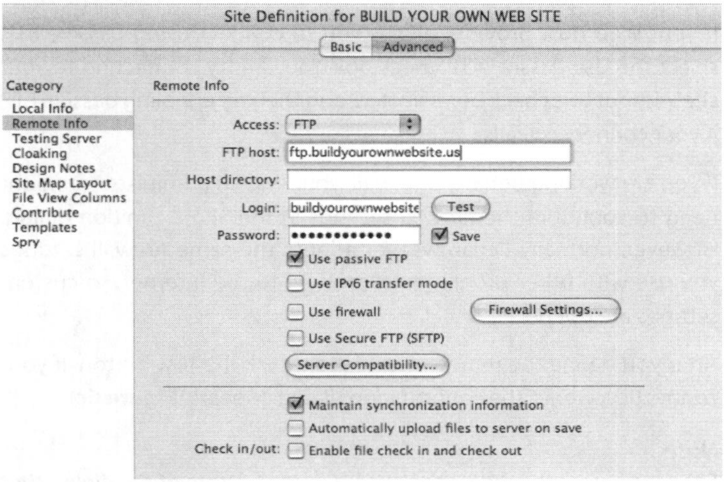

Figure 6b Defining FTP location, login, and password.

1. From the Access drop-down menu, choose FTP to define a connection to a remote server, or Local/Network if the remote site will be on another computer on your internal network.

2. In the FTP host field, enter the FTP location provided by your Web host provider.

3. In the Host directory field, enter the server folder information provided by your Web hosting company, if needed.

4. If your Web hosting company requires a host directory, enter the information the hosting company provided in the Host directory field.

5. In the Login field, enter the login or user name provided by your Web host provider.

6. In the Password field, enter the password provided by your Web host provider.

(continued on next page)

Note
Password and login information is case-sensitive and must be entered exactly as provided. Once you have entered an FTP location, a login, and a password, you have defined the essentials of your connection.

7. If your Web host provider allows you to connect using passive FTP, select the Use passive FTP check box. You can try connecting to your site without this check box selected, and then try enabling passive FTP if your connection fails.

8. If you are working behind a firewall, your system administrator might need to configure the firewall settings in the Site Definition dialog. However, normally Dreamweaver adopts the same firewall settings you use with other programs to connect to the Internet, so custom settings are not necessary.

9. After you define the remote connection, click the Test button. If your connection works, the confirmation dialog appears (**Figure 6c**).

Note
For now, ignore the three check boxes at the bottom of the dialog that define synchronized, automatic, and shared file management options. The check-in feature is for large sites with multiple developers. Synchronization is examined in #9, "Synchronizing Local and Remote Content."

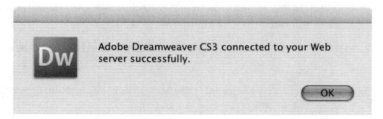

Figure 6c A successful server connection test.

#7 Connecting to a Remote Server

Simply defining a remote server connection does not automatically *connect* you to that server. When you open a Web site in Dreamweaver, you normally open only the local site.

Only after you actually *connect* to your remote site can you see what files are on that site and manage files at the remote server.

When you define your remote site, you can add a URL for the site to the local site panel in the HTTP Address field of the Site Definition dialog. But this information is not necessary to begin designing your Web site.

After you pay for your remote server space, your Web host provider will give you three essential pieces of information: the FTP address, your login (user name), and your password. Some Web host providers also assign a host directory. If you didn't get that information, you can probably assume it is not necessary, but you might confirm with your site provider that there is no host directory.

Can You Have a Remote Server with No Local Site?

It is *possible*—though generally not a good idea—to work on *just* a remote server. In this case, as soon as page content is edited and saved, it appears immediately on the remote server. There are two major dangers to this "remote-only" approach: There is no backup of your content if your server crashes. And there is no buffer between saving content on a page and making it available to the world; there's no chance to review, check, test, or supervise content before it becomes public.

In short, any site content worth developing is worth first developing on a local site, and then transferring to a remote site.

Signing Up for a Remote Server

Shopping for a Web host can be simple if you are creating a small site with small files and not expecting a lot of traffic. Yahoo!, for instance, offers a deal for about five dollars a month, and often throws in a free domain name (the name people type in their Web browser to get to your site—like davidkarlins. com).

If you plan to include large files (like video) or expect a lot of visitors (over 100 a day), or both, you'll want to do some comparison shopping before choosing a Web host. The site www. buildyourownwebsite.us has useful resources and articles for finding Web hosting and obtaining domain names.

With a site open, you connect to your remote server by clicking the Connects to remote host icon in the Files panel (in either expanded or collapsed view) (**Figure 7a**).

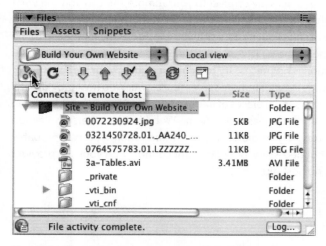

Figure 7a Connecting to a remote server via the Files panel.

Once you connect to a remote server, you can see either local or remote server content using the View pop-up menu in the Files panel (**Figure 7b**).

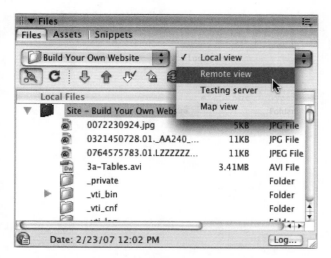

Figure 7b Viewing the content of the remote site.

To see the content of both the local and remote sites at the same time, click the Expand icon in the Files panel toolbar. In expanded mode, click the Site Files icon in the Files panel toolbar (**Figure 7c**).

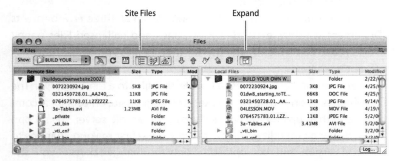

Figure 7c Comparing local and remote site content.

Note

If you choose Site Map view, you can't see the remote site. The third view option, Testing Server, *displays connections to live data—a topic that is beyond the scope of this book. The topic is covered in excellent detail in* Macromedia Dreamweaver 8 Advanced for Windows and Macintosh: Visual QuickPro Guide, *by Lucinda Dykes (Peachpit Press).*

#8 Transferring Files Between Remote and Local Sites

Coordinating Local and Remote Sites

As a general rule, avoid editing filenames, folder locations, and so on at your remote server. If you stick to a protocol of creating and managing files on your local site, and then transferring those files to the remote site, you'll ensure that both sites match, and what you see on your local site will match what visitors see at your remote site.

The Dreamweaver Files panel provides tools for managing files at both the local *and* remote servers. That is a potentially scary power to have. It means that you can rename, move, and delete files from your remote server and, in the process, corrupt your remote server files so they no longer match the files on your local server. This is part of the reason why standard procedure is to edit files on a local site before uploading to a server.

You can transfer files from the local site to the remote site, or vice versa, in the expanded Files panel. You can *upload* files to the remote site directly in the Document window. And you can view both the local and remote sites in the collapsed Files panel.

Getting comfortable with transferring files in all three environments (Document window, expanded Files panel, and collapsed Files panel) allows you to conveniently and quickly transfer files and easily keep track of what is where.

There are two basic phases to transferring files to a remote server. The first phase is when you design and test the original site on your local computer, and then upload the whole site to your remote server. The second phase is when you edit elements of your site—first making changes to the local version, and then uploading only the changed parts of your site to the remote server.

Although you can edit Web pages while files transfer to (or from) a remote server, you cannot do other file management activity on the server while files are in transit. This means, for example, that you cannot edit your site in the Site Definition dialog while you are transferring files. But you can open a Web page on your local site and edit it.

To upload an entire site from your local folder to the remote server, click the root folder of your local site in the Files panel—either in expanded or collapsed view. With the root folder selected, click the Put File(s) icon in the Files panel toolbar (**Figure 8a**).

Put File(s)

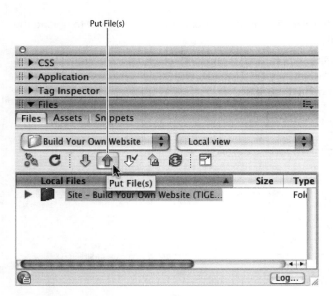

Figure 8a Uploading an entire Web site.

Background File Transfer

Dreamweaver CS3 allows you to continue editing Web pages while files are being transferred from local to remote sites (or from remote to local sites).

This is a huge relief for those of us who have twiddled our thumbs for hours, waiting for Dreamweaver to become functional only after file transfer was complete.

Dreamweaver will prompt you to confirm the action by clicking OK, and then it will upload your entire Web site. The Background File Activity dialog will track the progress of uploading your site (**Figure 8b**).

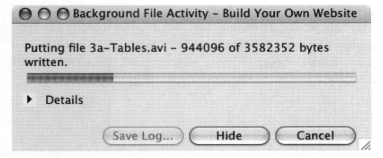

Figure 8b Transferring files in the background—you can continue editing pages in Dreamweaver while files transfer.

Once you have uploaded your site, you won't want to waste time re-uploading the entire site each time you change a file. Instead, you can upload selected files. Use Shift-click or Command-click (Mac) or Ctrl-click

Dependent Files

If you transfer a Web page with an embedded image to a remote server, a dialog opens asking if you want to also upload *dependent files*. These are files that open along with the page. An embedded image, for example, appears when a page is opened in a browser. The page won't work correctly without the photo being uploaded to the server along with the page. Therefore, you need to include dependent files if you are uploading a page with an image. The next time you upload that page, however, you

(continued on next page)

(Windows) to select files in the Files panel, and choose Put to upload the selected files.

You can also upload open pages directly from the Document window. Do this by clicking the File Management tool in the Document toolbar and choosing Put (**Figure 8c**).

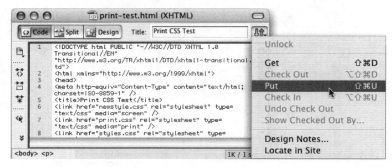

Figure 8c Uploading an open Web page.

In addition to putting (uploading) files to your server, you can also download files from your server. If you are working on a Web site by yourself (you are the only person who places files on the server in Dreamweaver), you will rarely need to transfer files from the remote server to your local computer, since all files originate on your local computer, and you can overwrite files on the server by uploading the matching file from your local computer. However, if you are working with other developers on a site, you might well need to download a file that was updated *by someone else*. In that case, click the file in the server, and click the Get File(s) icon in the Files panel toolbar (**Figure 8d**).

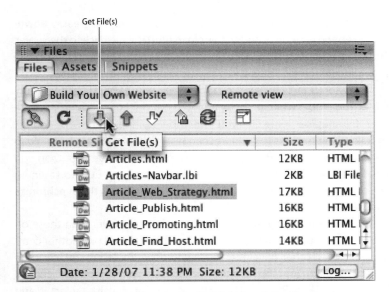

Get File(s)

Figure 8d Downloading a file using the Get File(s) icon in the Files panel.

do not need to re-upload the image file unless you have changed it.

Other files that Dreamweaver considers dependent are style sheets that define how a page looks. Embedded media files are also considered dependent files.

What is *not* considered a dependent file is any page or other file to which that page is *linked*. For instance, if you upload a page that links to another page, you *still need to manually upload* the page to which the uploaded page is linked (if the linked page is missing or has been changed).

#9 Synchronizing Local and Remote Content

If you are editing one or a few files at a time, you can fairly easily download (Get) the file, edit it, and then upload (Put) the file back to the server. Or, on the other hand, if you are uploading an entire site, you can click the root folder in the local site, and click Put to upload the entire site.

What about in-between scenarios, when you have edited too many files to remember what has been updated but you haven't done an entire site? If you upload only files you remember editing, you might neglect to upload important site content changes. If you play it safe and upload the entire site, you might end up transferring way more data than you need to, tying up Dreamweaver's site tools, and tying up and straining your Internet connection. Dreamweaver CS3 introduces the Synchronize feature.

To identify files on your remote server that are newer than those on your local computer (that is, files that have been edited on another computer, or by another developer since you downloaded them), click the Files panel menu (not the top menu bar, but the panel menu) and choose Edit > Select Newer Remote. Newer files on the server will be selected and can be easily downloaded (**Figure 9a**).

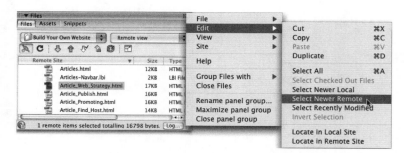

Figure 9a Selecting newer files at the remote server to download to a local site.

To synchronize files by updating the server with newer files from the currently open local site, follow these steps:

1. If you want to manually select files to synchronize, Shift-click or Command-click (Mac) or Ctrl-click (Windows) to select those files. Otherwise, by default, Dreamweaver will automatically detect changed files.

2. In the Files panel, choose either Remote view or Local view, depending on which direction you want to transfer files. Select Local view to transfer files to the remote server, and select Remote view to transfer files from the remote server to the local computer (**Figure 9b**).

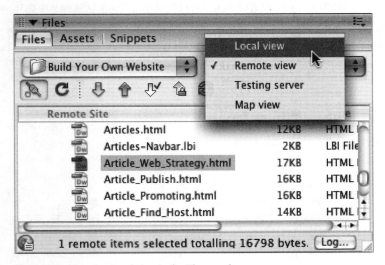

Figure 9b Choosing Local view in the Files panel.

3. Choose Window > Files to view the Files panel if it is not open. From the Files panel menu, choose Site > Synchronize. The Synchronize Files dialog appears. From the Synchronize pop-up menu in the Synchronize Files dialog, choose either selected files or the whole site.

4. In the Direction pop-up menu, choose from the options—get from server, put to server, or both—that allow you to transfer files from local site to server, server to local site, or both ways, replacing older files with more recent ones.

(continued on next page)

Automatic Check-out

If you enable automatic check-in and check-out in the Remote Info category of the Site Definition dialog for your site, then every time you open a file, that file is automatically downloaded from the server and locked for editing at the server.

The check-in and check-out feature is used to prevent multiple developers from editing a page at the same time.

5. In the Synchronize Files dialog, click the Preview button. Dreamweaver connects to your remote site and creates a list of files that meet your criteria (new at the remote site, newer at the local site, or both). The list is displayed in a dialog (again) called Synchronize. Click OK, and Dreamweaver will update all files according to the criteria you defined (**Figure 9c**).

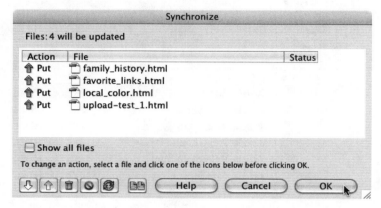

Figure 9c Synchronizing files.

CHAPTER TWO

Working in the Document Window

The Document window is the basic workspace in Dreamweaver. The Document window is where you design Web pages; you can create or paste text, embed images, define links, or place and sometimes create page elements like style sheets (that control the look of a page), input forms, embed animation, and create interactive objects (that react to actions by a visitor). In short, the Document window is where you will spend the bulk of your time in Dreamweaver. Even if you have some familiarity with creating pages in Dreamweaver, there are many features rooted within the various elements of the Document window, so it is worthwhile to explore them in some detail.

It is important to be aware of the fact that many features in the Document window, such as defining links, do not work properly unless you have already defined a Dreamweaver site. The whole process of defining a site in Dreamweaver is covered in Chapter 1, "Creating a Web Site," and you should make sure you have a properly defined site before creating and editing pages in the Document window.

#10 Exploring the Document Window

You work in the Document window when you open an existing Web page or when you create a new one. Use the File menu to open an existing Web page (File > Open, or File > Open Recent to access a list of recently opened pages) or to create a new Web page (File > New).

When you choose File > New, the New Document dialog opens. Throughout this book we will explore some of the more useful categories of new documents, but the first and main type of new document you'll create in the New Document dialog is a basic page, and the basic and main type of Web page you'll create is an HTML page (**Figure 10a**).

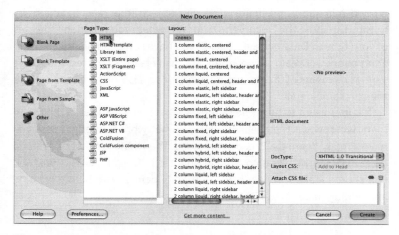

Figure 10a New Document dialog, with a new HTML Web page selected.

Clicking the Create button in the New Document dialog generates a new page, and opens that page in the Document window. The Document window is crammed with features. The objects floating around in the Document window are mainly panels, menus, and toolbars, which we'll explore in the following How-Tos in this chapter. But there are plenty of useful (and sometimes unintuitive) features in just the Document window that should be part of your design arsenal.

The Document window can display with three views: Code, Split, and Design. Code view displays *only* code, and is used by designers who wish to bypass Dreamweaver's ability to generate code. Design view hides most code, providing a graphical design interface. Split view displays code on the top of the Document window and a graphical design environment on the bottom (**Figure 10b**).

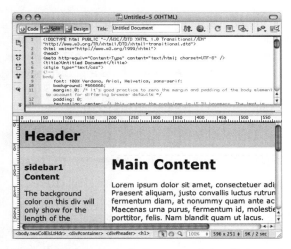

Figure 10b Split view in the Document window displays code on top and a graphical design interface on the bottom.

There are a number of advantages to working in Split view, both for designers who know how to write code, as well as for designers who are not comfortable or proficient in writing their own code. Split view is a way for proficient coders to see a graphical representation of the code they are writing. And Split view is a good way for designers who are not conversant in coding to become familiar with coding, since generated code appears as you create elements in the graphical design window. And, even though Dreamweaver is the best existing program for generating HTML and other page layout code, there are times when the only way to troubleshoot a design problem is to edit the code directly. If you edit code in Split view, you can see the effect by clicking in the lower (graphical) window.

Stripped of menus and panels, the main features available in the Document window are rulers, the tag selector, and the status bar. Horizontal and vertical rulers provide a quick way to judge the size of your page and objects on it. Hide or change ruler attributes by choosing View > Rulers from the menu. The View > Rulers submenu lets you show or hide rulers and change the unit of measurement from the default pixels to centimeters or inches.

The tag selector, on the left side of the status bar on the bottom of the Document window, allows you to select specific tags for editing in the Property inspector (the Property inspector is examined in #11, "Viewing Panels and the Property Inspector"). The tag selector is especially handy when you're working with objects like tables or embedded CSS (page design objects), and simply clicking an object in the Document window itself can be difficult (**Figure 10c**).

Figure 10c Selecting the Body tag in the tag selector section of the status bar.

The right side of the status bar has some handy and exciting tools that were introduced in Dreamweaver 8 and retained in CS3.

- The Select and Hand tools provide two ways to navigate around your document. The Select tool is the default mode; it allows you to click on objects, or click and drag to select text. The Hand tool works like similar tools in Adobe Photoshop or Illustrator—allowing you to grab a section of the page and drag it in or out of view.

- The Zoom tool is a way to draw a marquee and enlarge a section of a page.

- To exit either the Zoom or Hand tool mode and return to the default cursor, click the Select tool.

- The Set Magnification drop-down menu is another way to define magnification.

- The Window size display tells you the size of your design window—normally in pixels.

- The File Size/Download Time display estimates download time for the page parameters (**Figure 10d**).

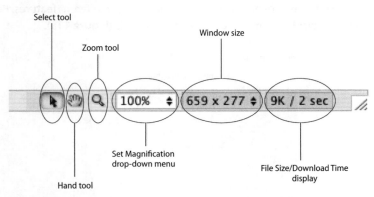

Select tool

Zoom tool

Window size

100% ⬍   659 x 277 ⬍   9K / 2 sec

Set Magnification drop-down menu

File Size/Download Time display

Hand tool

Figure 10d Tools in the status bar.

You can adjust the units displayed for window size, or the connection speed used to estimate download time in the Status Bar category of the Preferences dialog. On the Mac, choose Dreamweaver > Preferences, and in Windows choose Edit > Preferences, and then select the Status Bar category to edit these parameters.

Don't Make Visitors Wait Too Long

Having a sense of how long your page will take to open in a browser window is very handy. In general, it's useful to have a sense of how long you think your visitors will tolerate waiting for your page to open. Different designers have different theories on this, and different rules apply to different kinds of sites. But my general rule of thumb, based on my consulting and teaching experience, is that if visitors have to wait more than 10 seconds for a page to open, you'll lose many of them.

#11 Viewing Panels and the Property Inspector

Many of the features explored in other chapters and How-Tos in this book are available in *panels*—rectangular boxes that are normally aligned to the right of the Document window. While each panel obviously controls different features of your Web site or Web pages, panels have some features in common.

Dreamweaver panels all provide access to very different features. But there are display elements common to all panels (**Figure 11a**).

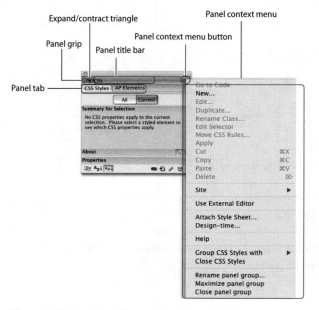

Figure 11a Elements of Dreamweaver panels.

You can drag panels from their default position on the right side of the Document window by dragging on the Panel grip.

You can separate tabbed panels by choosing Group [the name of the selected panel] with from the Panel context menu, and then choosing New panel group (**Figure 11b**).

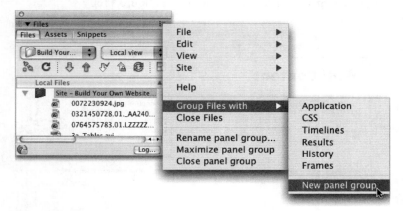

Figure 11b Separating a panel from a tabbed group.

Similarly, you can group panels with other panels as tabbed groups by choosing Group [the name of the selected panel] with from the Panel context menu and selecting another panel to which the selected panel will be grouped.

You can expand or contract panels using the Expand/contract triangle. To hide (or unhide) all open panels, press the F4 function key.

Display panels by selecting them from the Window menu. Active panels display with check marks next to them in the Window menu.

36

Other Uses of the Property Inspector

You will likely use the Property inspector mainly to apply attributes to text and images. But the Property inspector also adapts to and provides formatting options for other selected page elements.

If you select a table, you can define table size, number of columns, number of rows, cell padding (space between cell content and the edge of a cell), cell spacing (space between cells), table background color, and other attributes. If you select a table *cell*, you can define horizontal and vertical alignment, cell width and height, cell background color, and other alignment and color attributes.

Input forms and their embedded form fields have attributes that can be edited in the Property inspector as well.

More complex page design elements like AP Div elements or Div tags also have definable attributes that can be edited in the Property inspector.

The Properties panel—usually called the Property inspector—is a unique and special type of panel. It is adaptive in that it allows you to edit properties of a selected object, somewhat similar to the Object bar in many Adobe applications. For example, if you select text, the Property inspector makes available options for formatting type, including type size, type font, type style, and link attributes (**Figure 11c**).

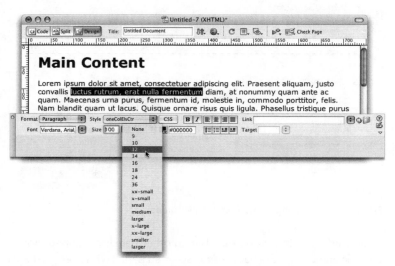

Figure 11c With text selected, the Property inspector allows you to define type attributes.

Or, if you select an image, the Property inspector makes available image-formatting attributes, like image size, ALT text (alternate text to make your image accessible to visitors or browsers who cannot view images), or hotspots (clickable linked areas within an image).

#12 Editing Page Content in Three Views

There are three ways to *edit* the content of a Web page in Dreamweaver's Document window: Code view, Split view, or Design view. Even if you never plan to enter a line of code, it is helpful to understand how these three views work and how to take advantage of them.

Most page designers do most of their work in Design view. Design view allows you to apply page design formatting and add content to your page in an environment that looks like a word processor. As you enter text, embed images, or apply formatting—using graphical design tools—Dreamweaver generates the necessary code (**Figure 12a**).

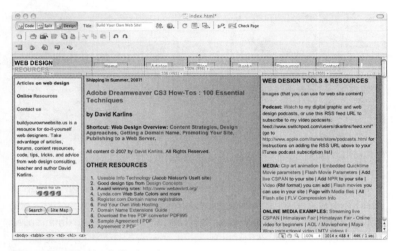

Figure 12a Working in Design view.

Designing Pages in Code View or the Code Inspector

Dreamweaver CS3's Document window provides three views: Code, Split, and Design. The Code and Split views are for developers who want to write their own markup code, rather than have Dreamweaver generate it. These views are covered in #10, "Exploring the Document Window."

Dreamweaver's Code Inspector window—available in both Windows and Mac versions—is accessed from the Window menu (Window > Code Inspector). The Code Inspector is a highly functional code-writing environment with a toolbar that provides prompts as you enter code, as well as prepackaged code snippets. The Code Inspector allows you to collapse or expand sections of coding, making it easier to focus on and edit sections of code.

The easiest way to see how this works is in Split view. In Split view, the top of the screen displays generated code, and the bottom of the screen displays the graphical design interface (**Figure 12b**).

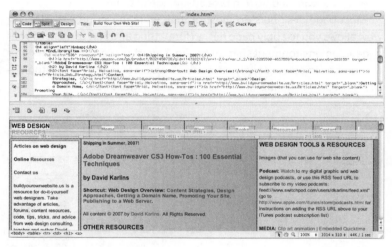

Figure 12b Working in Split view.

At the bottom of the screen in Split view (or on the entire screen in Design view), Dreamweaver displays a representation of how that code will be interpreted in a browser. This can only be an approximation, as different browsers and different versions of browsers display code differently. Dreamweaver CS3 provides two approaches to seeing more accurate previews of your page in different browsing environments; you can use the tools in the Style Rendering toolbar, or click the Preview/Debug in Browser button in the Document toolbar.

When you define page elements in Design view, your work is translated into code that is interpreted by browsers. When you enter code into Code view, that code is translated into a graphical display in Design view. If you enter code into the Code view of the Document window, the Design view updates when you switch to Design view. Or, if you are in Split view, changes to code update in the Design window when you click in the window.

#13 Examining Dreamweaver Toolbars

Many of Dreamweaver's page design tools are most easily accessed through toolbars. The Standard toolbar has some basic tools that are common to almost any application. The Document toolbar, on the other hand, provides access to an underappreciated set of rather powerful page design and management tools. The toolbars reside at the top of the Document window, and are displayed (if they are hidden) by choosing them from the View > Toolbars menu.

The tools in the Standard toolbar allow you to create new files, open existing files, print code, copy, cut, paste, and undo or redo an action. All these features are accessible from either the File or Edit menus (**Figure 13a**).

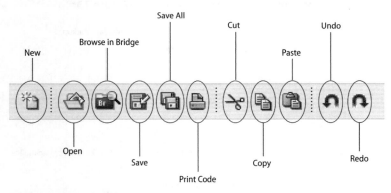

Figure 13a The Standard toolbar.

The Document toolbar collects some of the most frequently used tools for page design and management. The three buttons on the left allow you to toggle between Code, Split, and Design view (these views are discussed for both Mac and Windows users in #10, "Exploring the Document Window").

The Document toolbar also provides a convenient way to define a page *title*—the page "name" that displays in the title bar of a visitor's browser. You define a page title by typing the text to be displayed in the Title box in the Document toolbar.

The rest of the Document toolbar tools are used for managing documents, document display, and file management (**Figure 13b**).

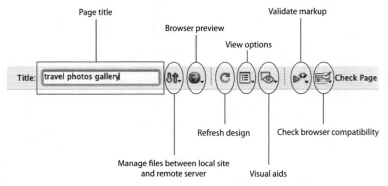

Page title

Browser preview

Validate markup

View options

Title: travel photos gallery

Check Page

Refresh design

Check browser compatibility

Manage files between local site and remote server

Visual aids

Figure 13b Entering a page title in the Document window.

The browser-compatibility check icon allows you choose from a variety of Web standards, and then choose actions (validating the open document, selected files, or all of the files in your site). Choose Settings from the pop-up menu associated with this icon to define the browsers, and versions of browsers, that your page will be tested for compatibility with (**Figure 13c**).

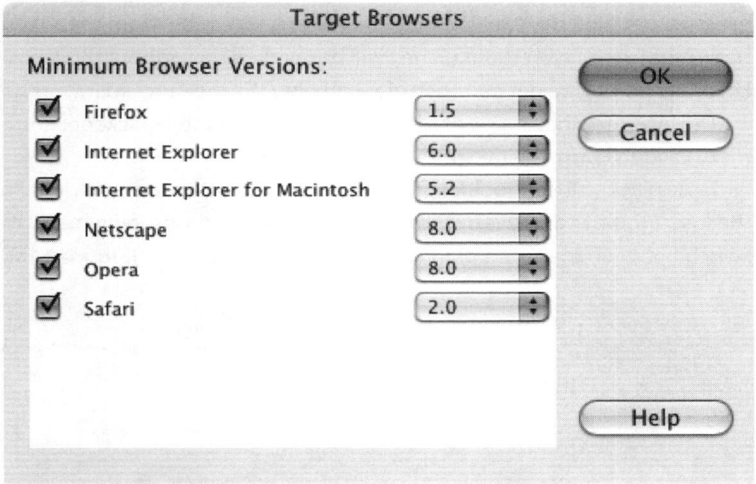

Target Browsers

Minimum Browser Versions:

☑ Firefox	1.5	
☑ Internet Explorer	6.0	OK
☑ Internet Explorer for Macintosh	5.2	Cancel
☑ Netscape	8.0	
☑ Opera	8.0	
☑ Safari	2.0	Help

Figure 13c Choosing browsers and browser versions that your page will be tested for compatibility with.

The Preview in Browser tool allows you to see how your page will look in a browser window. View options include displaying (or hiding) rulers, guides, and grids. Visual aids include displaying borders of tables, frames, and CSS objects—borders that are not displayed in browsers, but are handy for design purposes.

#14 Using the Insert Toolbar

The Insert toolbar, also referred to as the "Insert bar" for short, is the ubiquitous blue-collar power tool of Dreamweaver. As this toolbar provides access to the bulk of Dreamweaver's features, many developers keep it displayed at all times for quick access to features that can also be found, less conveniently, in Menu options or panels. Since a large percentage of Dreamweaver features, ranging from everyday (inserting images) to esoteric (detailed database management), are accessible from the seven basic tabs in the Insert toolbar, they will be invoked throughout this book. Here, the point is to get comfortable with how the Insert toolbar works.

The Insert toolbar is a *set* of toolbars. You get the whole package: Common, Layout, Forms, Data, Spry, Text, and Favorites.

To display the Insert toolbar, choose View > Toolbars > Insert. By default, the Insert toolbar displays in Menu form—you use a drop-down menu to switch between the seven different iterations of the toolbar (**Figure 14a**).

Figure 14a Choosing from the set of Insert toolbar display options.

To view all Insert toolbar tabs at once, choose Show as Tabs from the Insert pop-up menu in the Insert toolbar. In Tab view, you can easily switch between the seven different toolbars by clicking a tab (**Figure 14b**).

Figure 14b The Insert toolbar, displayed as tabs.

To get back to untabbed menu view, choose Show as Menu from the Insert bar context menu (**Figure 14c**).

Figure 14c Toggling from Tab view to Menu view.

While a full survey of the options in the Insert toolbar would amount to a documentation of most of the features available in Dreamweaver, I'll point you to some of the easy-to-access features:

- **Common:** Used to define links, e-mail links, page links (anchors), tables, and media

- **Layout:** Used to create the three main modes for page design in Dreamweaver—tables, Div tags, and Layers

- **Forms:** Used to define input forms, form fields, and form-handling buttons

- **Data:** Used to insert live data regions in Web sites linked to server-based databases. This method of building Web sites is beyond the scope of this book, but covered in *Macromedia Dreamweaver 8 Advanced for Windows and Macintosh*, by Lucinda Dykes (Peachpit Press).

- **Spry:** Used to place Spry widgets—JavaScript objects (some with CSS formatting attached) that can be inserted into Web pages to provide interactivity or animation

- **Text:** Used to apply HTML styles to text and insert special characters

- **Favorites:** A customizable bar; Ctrl-click adds features

The Spry Insert Tab

New with Dreamweaver CS3 is the Spry tab in the Insert menu. With the acquisition by Adobe of Dreamweaver comes the introduction of Spry as a library of effects and interactive scripts. These Spry "widgets," as Adobe has dubbed them, range from expandable/collapsible (accordion) regions, to scripts that validate form input. They are built with JavaScript and are highly compatible with a wide range of browsers and viewing devices. Using Spry to validate data form input is explained in Chapter 8, "Collecting Data in Forms." Chapter 10, "Adding Effects and Interactivity with Spry," explains how to generate various interactive objects with Spry.

#15 Using the Insert Menu Bar

The Insert menu in the main Dreamweaver CS3 menu bar provides an alternative to using the Insert bar. The Insert bar, explained in #14, "Using the Insert Toolbar," allows you to insert frequently used (and even some rarely used) elements like images or tables by clicking on icons. The Insert menu provides access to essentially the same set of options, but in a menu format. Which is better? It's a matter of taste.

Because the Insert menu accesses a wide range of often-used features in Dreamweaver, a quick survey of that menu will be useful. Many of the features in the Insert menu are, as noted, replicated in other forms (like the Insert toolbar). But some are not. Frequently used (or frequently looked-for) features like inserting links, e-mail links, and special characters (like the copyright symbol) are easily accessible from the Insert menu, but hard to find elsewhere.

Here, then, is a quick overview of frequently used page design elements accessible from the Insert menu:

Image: Use this menu option to insert images. See Chapter 5, "Working with Text and Images," for a full discussion of working with images in Dreamweaver.

Image Objects: Image objects include two frequently used design features: rollovers and navigation bars. These objects can be generated from this menu, but are better created, edited, and managed using the Behaviors panel. See Chapter 11, "Adding Interactivity with Behaviors," for an explanation of how this works.

Media: Use this menu option to add Flash, Flash Video, or other media files. See Chapter 9, "Embedding Media," for directions.

Table: Tables remain a useful tool for page layout or for displaying data. See Chapter 3, "Designing Pages with Tables and Frames," for instructions on page design with tables.

Table Objects: This menu option has features for editing tables, but also a useful tool for importing tabular data. Your spreadsheet program will export files to tabbed data for import into Dreamweaver.

Layout Objects: Dreamweaver CS3 incorporates new Advanced Placement (AP) page design elements based on CSS. See Chapter 4, "Designing Pages with Absolute Placement Objects," for instructions on how to use these design elements.

Form: The Form submenu includes tools for creating input forms and for placing a wide variety of form fields and objects (like buttons). Designing and implementing forms is explained in Chapter 8, "Collecting Data in Forms."

Hyperlink: Use this menu option to place links on your page.

Email Link: This menu option makes it easy to create links to e-mail addresses.

Named Anchor: Named anchors are links *within* a page that can be linked to.

Date: Use this menu option to insert today's date in a variety of formats. You can insert the date as text, or as an updatable field that will display the current date whenever the page is opened in a browser menu (**Figure 15a**).

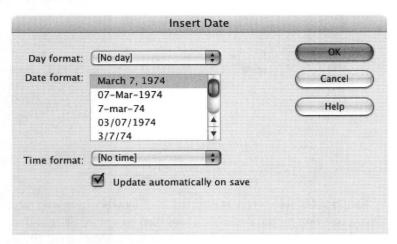

Figure 15a Inserting an updatable date field.

Server Side Include: This menu option inserts content from your Web server. Your Web-hosting server administrator can explain what content is available from your server, if any, and how to embed it into a page.

Comment: You can insert comments that are read by you and other developers working in Dreamweaver, but are not visible in a browser window.

HTML: This rather massive submenu allows you to insert a variety of objects accessible through other menus, but also has hidden within it a couple of unique and highly useful features. One is the Horizontal Rule, a design element going out of style but not yet obsolete that places a horizontal line on the page. The other is the Special Characters submenu that allows you to insert a set of often-used non-alphanumeric characters, including a line break, a non-breaking space, the copyright symbol, the em-dash symbol, and a whole set of symbols accessed by choosing Other in the Insert > Special Characters submenu (**Figure 15b**).

Figure 15b Viewing a set of insertable symbols.

Template Objects: Dreamweaver templates allow you to create a container page with universal elements, and then customize parts of that page. See Chapter 6, "Planning and Embedding Site Elements," for an explanation of how to create and update templates.

Recent Snippets: Designers who code by hand can create snippets of code in the Snippets panel, and then insert these snippets with this menu option.

Spry: Adobe has introduced a set of JavaScripts into Dreamweaver, organized under the umbrella of Spry. Chapter 8, "Collecting Data in Forms," explains how to invoke Spry objects to verify form data, and Chapter 10, "Adding Effects and Interactivity with Spry," surveys many available Spry tools.

You can also customize the Insert menu or get more objects to add to it. The Add More Objects menu option in the Insert menu launches Adobe's Dreamweaver Exchange site in your default browser. Here, you can download extensions—code that adds additional third-party designed elements to Dreamweaver.

The set of Dreamweaver extensions at Adobe's Dreamweaver Exchange site ranges from carefully tested, highly useful tools, to more esoteric and untested features. These features are explained at the Dreamweaver Exchange site (www.adobe.com/cfusion/exchange/index. cfm?view=sn120).

The Exchange site includes ratings for the reliability of each feature, as well as descriptions of the feature, notes on compatibility with different versions of Dreamweaver, and statistics on how many times an extension has been downloaded. Some extensions cost money. Some work only for the Windows or only for the Mac version of Dreamweaver. After you choose and download an extension, you install it using the Extension Manager, available—oddly enough—from the Help menu. Choose Help > Manage Extensions to open the Extension Manager dialog. You'll see a list of all the extensions you downloaded. You can enable an extension by clicking the On check box in the Extension Manager.

#16 Creating a New Page from Scratch

You can create a new Web page in Dreamweaver from either the Files panel or the Document window. Creating a new file in the Files panel simply generates an HTML page, while creating a new page in the Document window allows you to define the file type and automatically opens the file in the Document window for editing.

To create a new file from the Files panel, go to the Files panel menu and choose File > New File (**Figure 16a**).

Create a Site Before Creating a Document

While you will spend the vast majority of your time with Dreamweaver in the Document window designing Web pages, the first step in creating a Web site is to define the *site*. Defining a local Web site ensures that, as you embed files in your Web pages and as you define links between your Web pages, the connections between these linked files will be maintained.

Relying on Dreamweaver to manage links between your files becomes even more useful when you upload Web pages to an intranet or Internet site.

If you are starting a new Web site from scratch, you should define your site before saving Web pages. See Chapter 1, "Creating a Web Site," for information on how define a local Web site and connect it to a remote site.

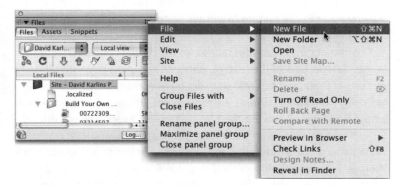

Figure 16a Generating a new file from the Files panel.

Files created from the Files panel menu are named untitled.html (or untitled2.htm, and so on). You can rename the file in the Files panel by choosing File > Rename from the Files panel menu, or by selecting the file in the Files panel and pressing the F2 function key. The Files panel is a good place to work in if you're generating lots of new Web pages and plan to open and edit them later.

Most often, you'll create new files from the Document window. From the Document window menu, choose File > New. The New Document dialog opens. When you create files from scratch, that is, without using predefined templates, you'll need to select the General tab of the New Document dialog.

From the far-left column in the New Document dialog, choose Blank Page. From the Page Type list, choose HTML. In the Layout column, select <none>. In the DocType (Document Type; DTD) field, choose the default document type, XHTML 1.0 Transitional. Then click Create to generate a new Web page (**Figure 16b**).

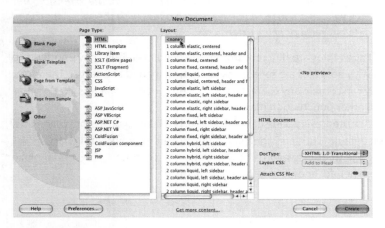

Figure 16b Defining a new file in the New Document dialog.

Once you create a new page, you need to *save* it with a *filename*, and you need to assign a page *title* to that page. Every Web page needs a filename and a title. The filename is mainly an internal element. It is used to locate the file in a Web site and to link the file to other files. As such, filenames don't have to be very creative, but they should avoid special characters like commas, ampersands (&), percent signs (%), spaces, and so on. You'll be safe if you stick to lowercase alphanumeric characters, plus the helpful dash (-) and underscore (_) characters.

There is a special requirement for filenames assigned to a site home page. A site home page is the page that opens when visitors enter your URL in the address bar of their browser. This URL does not specify a file, only a server location. Once the server location is open in a browser, browsers detect the home page by looking for a file named index.htm or index.html. *Never* create files named both index.htm and index.html; this will confuse your server, the browsers, and you. Instead, choose one or the other, and create a file called index.html (or index.htm). This will be your home page.

Choosing a Document Type Definition (DTD)

Dreamweaver CS3 uses XHTML 1.0 Transitional as the default document type for HTML Web pages. By generating XHTML-compatible coding for your Web page, you allow your Web page to integrate cutting-edge dynamic data content—content that is updated at a remote source and embedded (updated) in your Web page. Such dynamic data systems are issues that are decided at system-wide levels, not by a Web page designer. But again, by accepting Dreamweaver's default document type of XHTML 1.0 Transitional, you embed the ability to interact with and display dynamic data at any stage of system development.

Page Filename and Page Title

Every Web page has both a filename and a page title. The *filename* is the "internal" name—the way the file is identified and located within a Web site, and the way browsers find the file. Filenames must be supported by Web servers, and therefore developers often avoid special characters and stick to alphanumeric characters and lowercase in defining page filenames. While filenames are not the main or most obvious way visitors will identify a page, they're not hidden or secret, which should be kept in mind when assigning filenames.

Page *titles* are not part of the process of identifying or linking a file; they are an attribute of the page that describes or summarizes the page content for visitors. They *can* contain special characters, including punctuation and spaces.

Note

Every Web site generally needs one index file. This file is named "index" and has a filename extension of either .htm or .html. You can create files with the same name but with different filename extensions (like index.htm and index.html, for example). But don't! Web browsers will recognize either .htm or .html as a Web page filename extension, but they will get confused if you have Web pages with the same name and different versions of the extension.

Pages titles are different from page filenames. Titles have nothing to do with how files are saved, linked to, or managed at a server. Therefore, they can contain any characters, including special characters like commas and other punctuation marks.

As noted, *every* page has a page title, but unless you assign a page title, the default "Untitled Page" page title appears in browser title bars.

Page titles display in a browser title bar. Therefore, you should make them helpful and descriptive (**Figure 16c**).

Figure 16c A filename and page title displayed in a browser.

When you save a page for the first time, you name the page by entering a filename. With a file open in the Save As dialog of the Document window, choose File > Save, and enter a filename in the Save As field (**Figure 16d**).

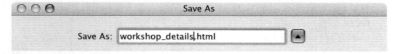

Figure 16d Saving and naming a Web page.

You can enter (or change) page title information in the Title field in the Document toolbar. If the Document toolbar is not visible in the Document window, choose View > Toolbars > Document (**Figure 16e**).

Figure 16e Entering a page title.

#17 Defining Links

Links are one of the most basic and dynamic elements of a Web page. In fact, hypertext, the "H" in HTML, refers to text that could have link properties (at least at the time the name was coined). Links can be associated with text or images.

Note

In this technique, we'll focus on assigning links to text. In Chapter 5, "Working with Text and Images," you'll learn about some additional link features that apply only to images, like image maps, which are clickable parts of a picture.

Links have three basic states: *unvisited, visited,* and *active.* Unvisited links display by default as underlined blue type. Visited links—links that have been visited in a browser (before the browser cache was cleared)—display by default as underlined and purple. And active links—links to pages that are currently open—display in red.

Note

You do not have to use the default colors or attributes (like underlining) for links. Also, you can define an additional link state (hovered) that displays when a link is rolled over by a mouse cursor. These changes to default link display are made with style sheets and are explained in Chapter 7, "Formatting Page Elements with CSS."

You will *not* see link status in the Dreamweaver Document window. All links display in unvisited mode. This is because you haven't actually followed these links in Dreamweaver. You can only view links in visited or active states if you preview your page in a browser (choose File > Preview in Browser).

Generally speaking, link targets can be one of two types: relative (internal to your site) or absolute (outside your site). Both are defined in the Property inspector for selected text (or a selected image).

To define an absolute link, start by selecting the text you want to link from. With the text selected, you can type an absolute link in the Link box in the Property inspector (**Figure 17a**).

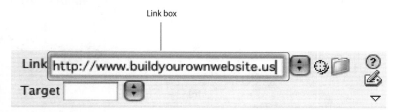

Figure 17a Entering an absolute-link target for selected text.

With relative links, you don't define where the link is found on the Internet; you define where the link is located relative to the current page—and at your Web site.

To define a relative link, with the link text selected, click the blue Browse for File icon next to the link box in the Property inspector. The Select File dialog opens. Navigate to the linked file, and click Choose to generate a link to that file. The relative link appears in the Link box in the Property inspector (**Figure 17b**).

Figure 17b Defining a relative link.

The other attribute that is important to define for a link is the Target window. By default, links open in the *same* browser window as the linking page, causing the linking page to disappear. A visitor can click the Back button on his or her browser to return to the original, linking page.

If you want a page to open in a *new* browser window, go to the Property inspector and choose the _blank attribute in the Target pop-up menu (**Figure 17c**).

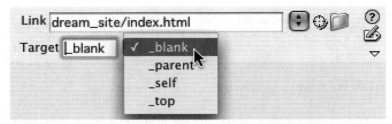

Figure 17c Defining the _blank link target that will open the link in a new browser window.

#18 Creating Pages from Blank Templates

Dreamweaver CS3's collection of blank templates provides more than 30 page designs. Blank templates use scripting code and Cascading Style Sheet (CSS) coding to define the look of a page.

Note
Blank templates do not provide template content. They just provide page designs, and you supply all the content. If you want help coming up with Web page content for a restaurant, a spa, a hotel, and so on, you can use a starter page. See #19, "Creating Pages from Sample Starter Pages," for instructions on how to use a starter page.

To select one of the blank templates, choose File > New, and choose Blank Template from the list of categories on the left side of the New Document dialog. In the Template Type column, choose ASP JavaScript template. The ASP and JavaScript templates are the most widely compatible with different hosting and browsing environments.

You can preview each of the page design ("blank") templates by choosing one in the Layout column of the New Document dialog, and inspecting the layout in the preview area in the upper-right corner of the dialog (**Figure 18a**).

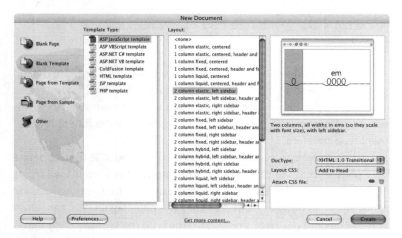

Figure 18a Previewing a blank template.

Templates . . . and *Blank* Templates

The term "template" has two distinct meanings in Dreamweaver CS3, so it will be helpful to sort out the distinction between templates and *blank* templates. Traditionally, Dreamweaver templates have been pages with fixed content, designed by a developer in Dreamweaver. That fixed content often includes page layout, along with some content elements that appear on every page. Dreamweaver templates have *editable regions* that allow developers (often lower-level developers) to insert content into pages where the

(continued on next page)

Once you select a blank template to use as a framework for your page design, you can accept the rest of the default settings in the New Document dialog, and click Create to generate a new page. That page still needs to be saved with a filename after you add your own content to it (**Figure 18b**).

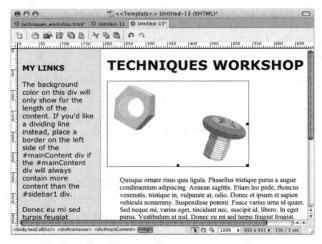

Figure 18b A page generated from the "2 column elastic, left sidebar" blank template.

When you generate a new page from a blank template, the default document type setting is XHTML 1.0 Transitional. This is a highly flexible, supported page format and generally you will not want to change this setting unless your Web administrator has mandated a different document type standard.

You also have options for how to handle the Layout CSS used to define your page layout. The CSS code for generated pages from blank layouts is, by default, added to the top of the Web page itself. Of course, this code is not visible in browsers, but it defines the page layout. You can, alternatively, elect to generate a *new* CSS page with the layout coding that is linked to your generated HTML page. This is more complex, but allows the CSS content to be attached to multiple pages. For a full discussion of embedding CSS in pages, or linking it via an external style sheet, see Chapter 7, "Formatting Page Elements with CSS."

You can choose the default option of adding CSS to the HTML page by choosing Add to Head from the Layout CSS pop-up menu in the New Document dialog. Or, you can elect to generate a separate, linked CSS page by choosing Create New File from the Layout CSS pop-up. The third option in that pop-up, Link to Existing File, is used if you already have a CSS file you wish to use to format the page (**Figure 18c**).

Figure 18c Saving blank page CSS as a separate, linked CSS file.

design and some content are automatically included and locked from editing. For a full exploration of creating and using templates in Dreamweaver, see Chapter 6, "Planning and Embedding Site Elements."

With Dreamweaver CS3, *blank* templates are not "templates" in the sense just explained. They are more like traditional templates in a word processing program that have some page elements already in place—usually design elements. Unlike Dreamweaver templates, *all* page elements in blank templates, including page layout, are editable by designers.

#19 Creating Pages from Sample Starter Pages

One of the reasons to use Dreamweaver to design your Web site, as opposed to using a cookie-cutter template supplied by a Web hosting service, is that you can create a unique style for your site. That doesn't mean, however, that you can't get some hints, inspiration, head starts, and expert design suggestions from Dreamweaver. Starter Pages (Basic) provide an option of bare-bones page designs for specific applications, ranging from journal entries to image slideshows to product catalog layouts. Starter Pages (Theme) provide fully formatted page layouts with selected color schemes and even template text that you can modify for your business, organization, or content theme.

To generate a page from a starter page, choose File > New, and choose Page from Sample from the category list on the left side of the New Document dialog. In the Sample Folder column, choose Starter Page (Theme) to see a list of fully finished sample pages, or Starter Page (Basic) to see page designs without color schemes or starter text and image content. When you select a page design from the Sample Page column, a thumbnail preview of the page appears in the upper-right corner of the New Document dialog (**Figure 19a**).

Home Page – A great starting point for your website. Include text, links and images to introduce yourself to the world. Layout is customizable.

Figure 19a Previewing a themed starter page.

After you select a Starter Page (Theme), simply click Create to generate a new page. The page will open in the Document window, and you can edit and save it. When you save the page generated by a Starter Page (Theme), you will be prompted to save the image and to copy the associated CSS (formatting) files used in that page into the folder on your computer for your Web site (**Figure 19b**).

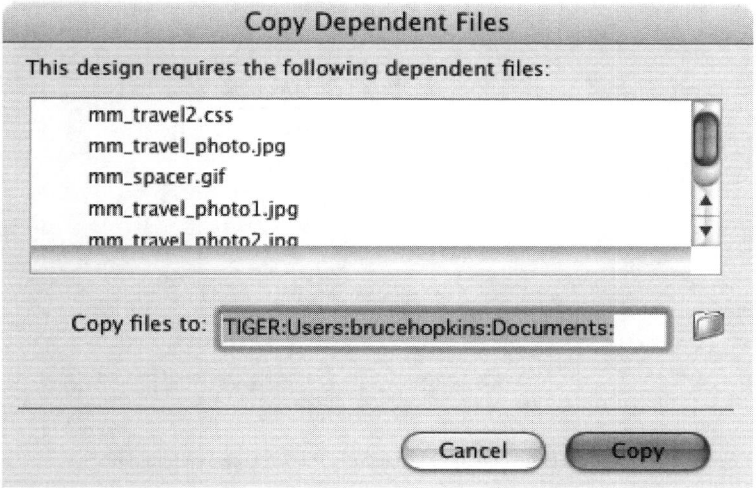

Copy Dependent Files

This design requires the following dependent files:

mm_travel2.css
mm_travel_photo.jpg
mm_spacer.gif
mm_travel_photo1.jpg
mm_travel_photo2.jpg

Copy files to: TIGER:Users:brucehopkins:Documents:

Cancel   Copy

Figure 19b Saving a page generated by a themed starter page, and copying image and CSS files with it into your Web site folder.

If you create a page from a Starter Page (Basic), you have the option of generating either a normal page or a page template. The terminology is confusing here; you are not being given the option of generating a *blank* template, but a template that can have both editable and non-editable regions. If you choose the Template option in the Create area of the New Document dialog, you will generate a standard Dreamweaver template (**Figure 19c**).

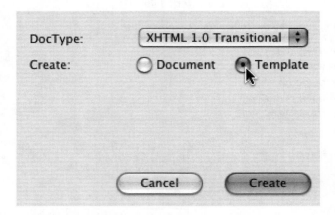

Figure 19c Saving a page generated by a basic starter page as a template.

Note
For an explanation of the difference between templates and blank templates, see the sidebar "Templates . . . and Blank *Templates," in #18, "Creating Pages from Blank Templates."*

Once you generate a page from a starter page, you edit and save it just as you would any other page.

#20 Creating Pages from Sample Style Sheets and Framesets

Dreamweaver CS3 provides a set of sample style sheets that define elements like text font, text color, link attributes, and heading styles. To be clear, these are *not* generated HTML pages—these are predesigned *style sheets.* The files that are generated from these sample style sheets have to be attached—either by linking or by importing—to an HTML page.

Note
A fuller discussion of linked and imported style sheets can be found throughout Chapter 7, "Formatting Page Elements with CSS." Here, you will learn to import a generated style sheet into an existing HTML page.

To generate a CSS file from a sample CSS style, follow these steps:

1. Choose File > New, and choose Page from Sample from the category list on the left side of the New Document dialog.

2. In the Sample Folder column, choose CSS Style Sheet.

3. Explore the available style sheets in the Sample Page column. Note that what you see in the preview area in the upper right of the New Document dialog is *only the formatting* that will be applied. The content in these previews will not be generated as part of the CSS file (**Figure 20a**).

The Full Design: Arial style sheet rewritten to use accessible measurements (ems).

Figure 20a Previewing a style sheet.

(continued on next page)

4. When you find a style you want to save as a CSS page, click Create. A CSS file will open in the document window. This file is not "previewable" as it only includes formatting code, not page content (**Figure 20b**).

Figure 20b A generated CSS page in the Document window.

5. Save the CSS file by choosing File > Save. By default, the file will have a .css (not .htm or .html) filename extension.

6. Once you have saved the sample CSS page, you can import that formatting into any open HTML page. Create, or open an existing HTML page, and view the CSS panel. Click the Attach Style Sheet icon at the bottom of the CSS panel (it looks like a link icon) (**Figure 20c**).

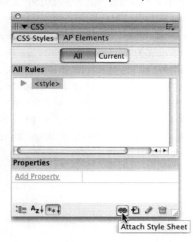

Figure 20c Clicking the Attach Style Sheet icon in the CSS panel.

7. The Attach External Style Sheet dialog opens. Use the Browse icon to locate the CSS file you saved in Step 5, and click Choose in the Select Style Sheet File dialog (**Figure 20d**).

Figure 20d Selecting a style sheet file.

(continued on next page)

#20: Creating Pages from Sample Style Sheets and Framesets

Linked vs. Imported Style Sheets

Briefly, linked style sheets are external files that define formatting for a Web page. When a linked style sheet is edited, the look of every HTML page linked to that style sheet is also changed. Imported styles, on the other hand, become part of the HTML page in which they are embedded. For more exploration of style sheets, see Chapter 7, "Formatting Page Elements with CSS."

8. Back in the Attach External Style Sheet dialog, choose Import in the Add As options area, and click OK.

You can also generate framesets from set of sample pages. Framesets appear to be a single Web page in a browser, but are actually a set of "framed" pages that work together within a single browser window. Framesets, or "frames" for short, are explained in detail in Chapter 3, "Designing Pages with Tables and Frames." You'll want to reference that chapter if you want to create pages from the set of sample frames.

To see the set of sample frames, choose File > New and choose Page from Sample in the category list on the left side of the New Document dialog. In the Sample Folder column, choose Frameset. You can preview predesigned framesets in the preview area in the upper right of the dialog (**Figure 20e**).

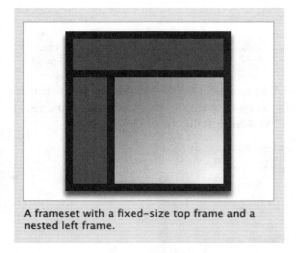

A frameset with a fixed-size top frame and a nested left frame.

Figure 20e Previewing a frameset sample.

Caution
Saving the various files involved in framesets and naming frames within framesets (two different processes) can be confusing. Before generating a frameset from the samples, review the discussions of frames in Chapter 4, "Designing Pages with Absolute Placement Objects," particularly #27, which explains in much more detail how to generate a frameset from a sample.

CHAPTER THREE

Designing Pages with Tables and Frames

Both tables and framesets have gone through a number of evolutionary transformations in their roles in Web page design. Tables originated in early HTML as a form for conveying rows and columns of data. Resourceful designers pushed the envelope, and used tables to lay out pages, using the cells created by the intersection of rows and columns to place objects on a page. Another early element in HTML, framesets, allowed designers to create "pages," in reality framesets consisting of more than one page that were packed (framed) in a browser window. These two techniques for designing page layout have in some ways been superseded by the emergence of CSS, which offers greater flexibility in design. But tables remain a highly stable and widely supported technique for page layout, as well as a uniquely appropriate tool for displaying data—their original function. And frames provide discrete, independently navigable elements in a browser window that cannot be duplicated using CSS.

In an effort to provide a designer-friendly environment for page designers, Dreamweaver's Layout mode somewhat duplicates the kind of tools you find in programs like Adobe Illustrator, InDesign, or Photoshop. In Layout mode, you actually draw boxes on the page and place text, images, or other content in those boxes. As you draw these boxes, Dreamweaver generates a table with rows and columns that provide the table framework for the boxes you draw. Since Layout mode is really another way of defining tables, I strongly recommend that readers start with #21, "Creating a Table in Standard Mode," and then move on to Layout mode. That way, after you generate a table (invisibly) in Layout mode, you'll know what it is you have created.

#21 Creating a Table in Standard Mode

A basic, useful, and safe way to design a Web page is to first define a single-cell table, and then place page content inside that cell. Constraining page content in a rectangular table—especially constraining page *width* using a table—allows you to control the width at which your page displays in a browser. Creating a one-cell table is also a useful way of familiarizing yourself with the basic concepts involved in Web page design with tables.

To create a one-cell table for page content, follow these steps:

1. Open a new page. Choose File > New and select the Basic Page category and HTML in the New Document dialog; then click Create.

   With the new page open, your cursor is in the upper-left corner of the page by default. Insert a new table at the cursor with the following steps.

2. Choose Insert > Table from the Document window menu. The Table dialog appears.

   Tip
   Alternatively, you can click the Table button in the Layout panel of the Insert toolbar. See Chapter 2, "Working in the Document Window," #14, "Using the Insert Toolbar," for an explanation of how to use the different tabs in the Insert toolbar.

3. In the Rows and Columns boxes, define the number of rows and columns in your table. It's easy to add rows and columns later, so when in doubt, simply generate a one-row, one-column table by entering 1 in both the Rows and Columns boxes.

4. In the Table width box, enter a value representing either a number of pixels or a percentage of page width. Then, choose either pixels or percent from the Table width pop-up menu (**Figure 21a**). For more on this, see #23, "Creating Fixed and Flexible Columns."

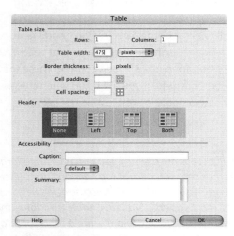

Figure 21a Defining table width in pixels.

5. The Border thickness box defines the width of the displayed border. Normally, tables used for page layout are defined with no border displayed. To display no border around a table, enter 0 (zero) in the Border thickness box. Or, to display a border, enter a value such as 1 (for 1 pixel).

Tip
Table border color is defined in the Property inspector—see #25, "Defining Table Properties."

6. The Cell padding and Cell spacing boxes define the distance between cells and the padding inside a cell. Cell padding defines the buffer between cell content (like text or images) and the cell border. Cell spacing defines the spacing between cells. To define padding, enter a value (the unit of measurement is pixels) in the Cell padding box. To define spacing (around the outside of the single-cell table), enter a value in the Cell spacing box.

(*continued on next page*)

Tip
A useful and often-used setting is to define 6 pixels of cell padding and 0 pixels of cell spacing. This prevents cell content from bumping into content in the adjoining cell, but at the same time eliminates the table "showing through" between cells, which is the point of defining cell spacing.

7. The Header and Accessibility areas of the Table dialog define features that are used by screen readers—software programs that read Web pages out loud to people who cannot read screen content. These tools are not particularly important or useful if you are using your table as a display tool. So, when defining a single-cell table for page layout, leave these areas blank.

Note
The Header and Accessibility areas are useful if you are presenting large amounts of table data. In that case, left and/or top headers "announce" the nature of the content in the associated row (in the case of left headers) or column (in the case of top headers). Similarly, table captions and summaries are not necessary or helpful if you are using a table for page layout, but they can be helpful if you are presenting data that will be read out loud by reader software.

After you define a table in the Table dialog, click OK to generate the table. You will see the table displayed in the Document window even if you defined it with no border.

Even if your Web page doesn't require intricate design, you can constrain the display width of your Web page in a table. Placing content in a table enables you to define the width of your page in a browser. Without a table to constrain width (either to a fixed number of pixels or to a percentage of the browser window width), the page content will expand horizontally to fill the browser window. In many cases, that will make the text lines too long to be readable.

Experts differ over optimum page width, but the consensus is that a 760-pixel-wide table provides a convenient, accessible, and attractive framework for presenting text and images in a browser window.

Page *height* is normally not defined in a table. This is because if table width is fixed, the content has to have a direction in which it can expand if a viewer's browsing environment enlarges the content. This happens when a visitor's screen displays a lower resolution (causing images to expand on the screen), when type font size is increased, or for other reasons.

There are two basic approaches to using a table to constrain page width—percent and pixels. Choosing a percent produces a table that is a set proportion of a browser window width. A setting of 75%, for example, will fill three quarters of a viewer's browser window with your Web page.

Defining table width in pixels allows you more control over how a page displays. Choosing a 760-pixel-wide table, for example, produces a Web page that is about 8 inches wide in typical computer monitor resolutions.

Combining fixed-width columns with a flexible-width column in some ways is the best of both worlds. Some content (like navigation bars) can be constrained to fixed widths, while other content (like large blocks of text) can stretch horizontally so that the page fills all or most of the browser window.

#22 Creating a Table in Layout Mode

After you've worked with tables for a while, you begin to "think in tables," and you can draw tables that provide boxes for content on the screen. But until you achieve that state of consciousness, and to provide a more comfortable table-drawing logic, Dreamweaver provides Layout mode.

Layout mode is a more intuitive way to draw boxes for page content, but Layout mode lacks features that define critical and basic properties of tables such as table alignment and border width. In short, you draw tables in Layout mode and then revert to Standard mode to enter content into your table and define features like table background or border color.

In Layout mode, you begin by electing to draw either a cell or a table, and then clicking and dragging the screen to create a table or cell anywhere on the page. If you elect to draw a cell and you haven't created a table yet, Dreamweaver handles that for you. If you draw a table, you can either draw cells inside that table or you can draw another (embedded) table within that table.

Note

Drawing a table inside a table increases the challenges and complexity of designing a page, and sometimes does so unnecessarily. Quite complex page designs can be achieved using a single table with many cells. There are times when a page design requires embedded tables. Techniques and challenges involved in embedding tables within tables are explained in #24, "Embedding Tables Within Tables."

To draw a table in Layout mode, follow these steps:

1. Choose View > Table Mode > Layout Mode. As soon as you select Layout mode, the Insert bar displays (if it is not already displaying) with the Layout tools.

2. To draw a table, click the Layout Table icon in the Insert bar. To draw a cell (and automatically generate a table if necessary), click the Draw Layout Cell icon in the Insert bar (**Figure 22a**).

Layout Table

Draw Layout Cell

Figure 22a The Insert bar in Layout mode.

3. Click and drag to define the table height and width. Or, a simpler, easier technique is to click the Draw Layout Cell icon in the Insert bar and draw a cell on the page. A table is generated to define the cell (**Figure 22b**).

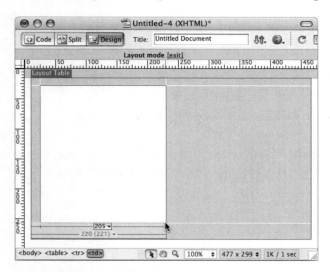

Figure 22b Drawing a cell and generating a table.

(*continued on next page*)

Define in Layout Mode, But Edit in Standard Mode

Layout mode provides access to useful tools for defining table and cell properties. But when you select a cell in Layout mode, the Property inspector does not provide easy access to tools for formatting the content of the cell. On the other hand, in Standard mode, the Property inspector allows you to format either the selected cell or the content of that cell (images or text).

4. After you define a table (by drawing either a table or a first cell), you can draw additional cells within the table. As you do, the table grid can become quite complex. You can also select a cell you already generated, and click and drag on a side or corner handle to change the height or width of that cell (**Figure 22c**).

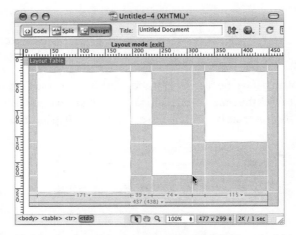

Figure 22c Generating a complex table by defining and editing many cells.

5. After you define your table structure, click the [exit] link at the top of the table to get out of Layout mode and into Standard mode.

#23 Creating Fixed and Flexible Columns

A widely used and very functional technique for page design involves creating tables that combine fixed columns with a flexible column. Very frequently, Web pages are built around tables that have a locked (fixed-width) left and right columns and a center column that expands to fill a specified percent of a browser window.

For example, a table might provide a 100-pixel-wide column on the left side of the page for navigation, a 100-pixel-wide column on the right, and a flexible column that fills all the remaining available space in a browser window (**Figure 23a**).

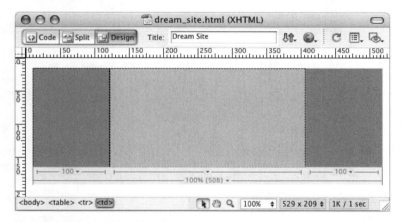

Figure 23a Fixed and flexible columns.

The steps that follow can be used to create a Web page with two fixed-width columns and one flexible-width column. To apply these steps, choose Standard mode (either by clicking the Standard icon in the Insert bar or by choosing View > Table Mode > Standard Mode).

1. Create a new three-column table by choosing Insert > Table. In the Table dialog, enter 3 in the Columns box, and enter 1 in the Rows box.

2. Set Table width to 100%.

(continued on next page)

3. Set Border thickness to 0, Cell padding to 6, and Cell spacing to 0. Click OK to generate a three-column table that will fill 100% of a browser window (**Figure 23b**).

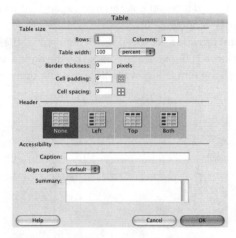

Figure 23b Defining a three-column table that fills 100% of a browser window.

4. Select the left column in the table by clicking in it or on top of it, and enter 100 in the W (Width) box in the Property inspector (**Figure 23c**).

Tip

Column width is explained in more detail in #25, "Defining Table Properties." As explained there, height and width are usually defined in pixels, which is the default setting in the Property inspector.

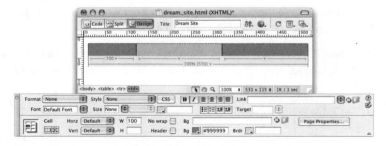

Figure 23c Setting left column width to 100 pixels.

Tip

If the Property inspector is not visible, press Ctrl-F3 (Windows) or Command-F3 (Mac).

5. Repeat Step 4, but select the right column and set the width to 100 pixels.

Tip

By default, columns that are not defined as autostretch have a fixed, or locking, width. Locking column widths only ensures that the width of the column does not get smaller than the set amount of pixels. If you place a large image in a column, the column will expand to accommodate the width of that image.

6. Switch to Layout mode by clicking the Layout Mode icon in the Insert bar, or by choosing View > Table Mode > Layout Mode. Layout mode has the advantage of allowing you to easily define a column as autostretch—a feature that is harder to access in Standard mode.

Note

When you switch to Layout mode, you will notice that column widths are calculated differently than they are in Standard table mode. In Layout mode, Dreamweaver includes cell spacing and padding in column width. So, for example, a 100-pixel-wide column with 6 pixels of spacing and 6 pixels of padding displays as a 112-pixel-wide column in Layout mode, and as a 100-pixel column width in Standard mode.

7. Click the triangle icon at the bottom of the middle column, and from the pop-up menu choose Make Column Autostretch (**Figure 23d**).

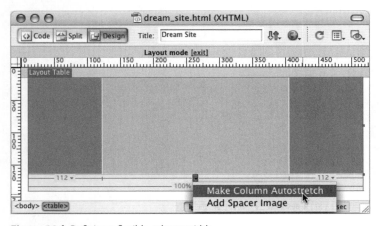

Figure 23d Defining a flexible column width.

Spacer Images

Spacer images are invisible, 1-pixel-wide images that are used by Web designers to lock column width. Browsers cannot "shrink" the display of a table column if there is an image (or a bunch of images) that fills up the column width. Understanding the "why" of this isn't really critical, but it's helpful to know that Dreamweaver locks the widths of the non-autostretch columns by inserting a repeating spacer image to prevent browsers from adjusting the width of these locked columns. Even though you don't see it, a tiny image named spacer.gif is placed repeatedly in a column to lock the width. You don't have to create this tiny image in Adobe Photoshop or another image editor program; Dreamweaver generates one by default and names it spacer. gif. The first time you lock a column width in

(continued on next page)

Spacer Images

(continued from previous page)

Dreamweaver, you will be prompted to create a spacer image file. Dreamweaver will generate and name that file. Or, if you already have a spacer file, Dreamweaver will prompt you to use it. If, in fact, you already have Dreamweaver generate a spacer.gif file, you can either use it or replace it by generating an identical one.

Note

If you have not yet generated a spacer image for your Web site, Dreamweaver will display a dialog prompting you to generate one. This spacer image is an invisible, tiny "image" that forces column width to remain at a set width.

You can now add content to the columns you defined. When the page is viewed in a browser, the middle column will expand or contract horizontally when the width of the browser window is changed.

#24 Embedding Tables Within Tables

Many page designs can be created by dividing a table into rows and columns. More complex page layouts might require embedding tables inside other tables. One reason for this is that there are properties of a table that apply to *all* cells in a table—specifically cell spacing and padding. And there may be times when you need to combine page elements enclosed in a table with no buffer (a banner on the top of a page is an example of this), with page elements that are in columns buffered with spacing between cells.

In the scenario above, a clean way to design the page would be to create one "master" table with no cell spacing or cell padding. At the top of the table, you could embed one 1-column table with no cell padding or spacing. Under that, you could embed a second table with three columns, and content separated by 6 pixels of cell spacing (**Figure 24a**).

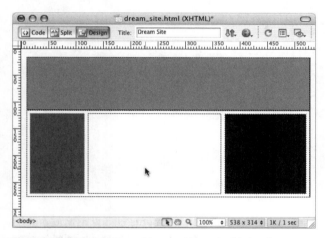

Figure 24a A page design with two tables embedded within a master table.

There are a couple tricks involved in embedding a table within a table. The following steps will walk you through the process safe and sound:

1. Create the first table with one column, one row, no border, no cell spacing, and no cell padding. See #21, "Creating a Table in Standard Mode," for details. Set the width of the table with a value in pixels or percent. This value will set the outside limits of the page width, and all tables you embed within your table will be no wider than the width you define here. Click OK to generate the table (**Figure 24b**). The table appears in the browser window.

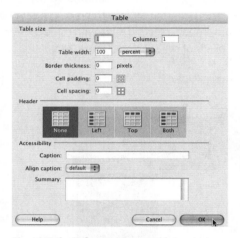

Figure 24b Defining a master table in which other tables will be embedded.

2. In order to see the table and table elements clearly as you embed tables within it, choose Expanded table view. Do this by clicking the Expanded icon in the Insert bar, or by choosing View > Table Mode > Expanded Tables Mode. A more easily visible and selectable border appears around the single-cell table.

3. As you insert tables within the table, you are actually inserting them within that table's single *cell*. Vertical alignment in tables is defined by cell. Click in the cell and choose Top in the Vert (Vertical) field in the Property inspector (**Figure 24c**).

Tip

Different cells in a table can have different vertical alignments. Oddly enough, the default vertical alignment setting for cells is middle—so content drops to the middle of the cell as you enter it. Here you want the vertical cell alignment set to Top so that content fills columns from the top.

Figure 24c Setting vertical alignment to Top.

4. With your cursor still in the single cell of the table, choose Insert > Table. Now you can define any table properties you wish—choose a number of columns and rows, define borders, and cell padding or spacing. The only trick is that if you want your embedded table to fill the table in which it is placed, you need to set the width to 100%.

5. Select the embedded table by clicking the embedded table border. Press the right arrow key on your keyboard to place the insertion point just to the right of the embedded table. Choose Insert > Table to place a new table and define table properties. Here, again, you will probably want to set the width of the second embedded table to 100% (**Figure 24d**).

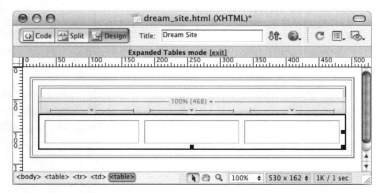

Figure 24d Two embedded tables viewed in Expanded Tables mode to make them easier to see and select.

Accessibility Issues with Using Tables as a Design Tool

Using tables as a layout device can make content confusing and inaccessible to visitors using reader software to read page content out loud. You can minimize the accessibility problems associated with tables by avoiding complex and nonlinear layouts, and instead arrange content so that it makes sense if read aloud from the top of a table to the bottom. Placing a table within a table creates serious accessibility issues, and you should consider having an alternate, table-free page for disabled visitors.

#25 Defining Table Properties

Table properties include elements like height, width, cell spacing, cell padding, border width and color, and background color or image. All these features can be defined in the Property inspector.

The trick is to select a *table* and not a cell. With the table selected, the Property inspector allows you to define table properties, and with a cell selected you can define cell properties (see #26, "Defining Cell Properties," for details) (**Figure 25a**).

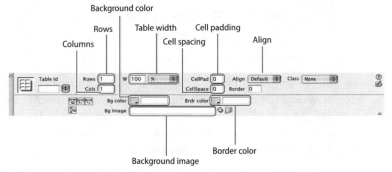

Figure 25a The Property inspector with a table selected.

Some table features are rather esoteric. Table ID is used when the table is controlled by scripts (like a JavaScript animation), and to apply style properties using CSS style sheets. The Class pop-up menu is used to apply CSS styles to the table.

Note
CSS formatting is covered in Chapter 4, "Designing Pages with Absolute Placement Objects."

Other features in the Property inspector are shortcuts for things like converting values from pixels to percent or vice versa—operations that don't normally require programmed interactivity because they really aren't that useful as design techniques.

Displaying Table Borders

Normally, tables used for design purposes are created with no border width. To ensure that browsers understand that you do not want to display borders, enter a 0 in the Border thickness box in the Table dialog; don't rely on leaving the box blank.

Even though table borders are often defined to not display in a browser, you normally *do* want to see them in the Dreamweaver Document window. Otherwise, it's difficult to know where the table is and where to enter content into the table.

By default, Dreamweaver displays table borders—even ones with no width—in the Document window. To change the setting or to toggle back to display table borders if this feature is disabled, choose View > Visual Aids > Table Borders.

These are the critical options in the Property inspector:

- The Rows and Cols boxes define (or change) how many rows or columns are in a table. Adding to the existing number adds a row below the bottom row, or a column to the right of the last existing column. Lowering the value deletes rows or columns starting from the right or bottom of the table.

- Table width (W) and height (H) can be defined in pixels or percent. Normally, table height is not defined, as it will vary depending on the amount of content in the table.

- CellPad defines space (in pixels) between the border of a cell and cell content. CellSpace defines space (in pixels) between cells.

- The Align options pull-down menu places the table on the left (default), right, or center of the page.

- Bg color defines background color; a color selection palette appears when you click the box.

- Brdr color defines the color of a border if border width is set to a value greater than zero.

- Bg image defines a tiling (repeating) image that fills the background of the table.

#26 Defining Cell Properties

When you click inside a table cell, the bottom half of the Property inspector displays properties for the selected cell. Normally, selecting a cell is easier than selecting a table and doesn't present the same confusing challenge. Unless you click the table border, when you click inside a table, you select a table cell.

Some cell properties duplicate table properties. Background color can be defined for a cell or for a table. Border color and cell background images can also be defined for both tables and cells. Other cell properties cannot be defined for a table. Vertical alignment can only be defined for cells. The Property inspector also allows you to merge selected cells or split a cell.

The Property inspector that appears for a selected cell displays formatting options for type (or other selected objects, like an image) in the top section. In the bottom section, you define cell properties (**Figure 26a**).

Tip
If you can't see the bottom section of the Property inspector, click the Expand (down-pointing) triangle in the lower-right corner of the Property inspector.

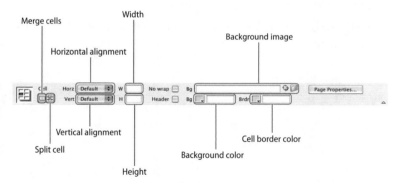

Figure 26a The Property inspector for a selected cell or cells.

To set a cell width, enter a value in the Width box. To set cell height, enter a value in the Height box. You can also adjust cell height and width by simply clicking and dragging the divider between cell rows or columns (**Figure 26b**).

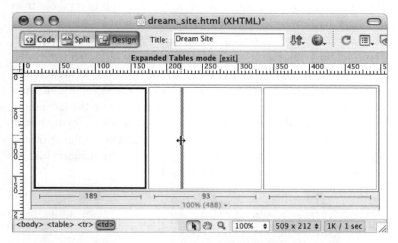

Figure 26b Changing column width by dragging the divider between columns.

To combine cells, click and drag to select contiguous (touching) cells, and click the Merge cells button in the Property inspector. To split a cell, select the cell, and click the Split cell button in the Property inspector. The Split Cell dialog appears, allowing you to define how cells are split (**Figure 26c**).

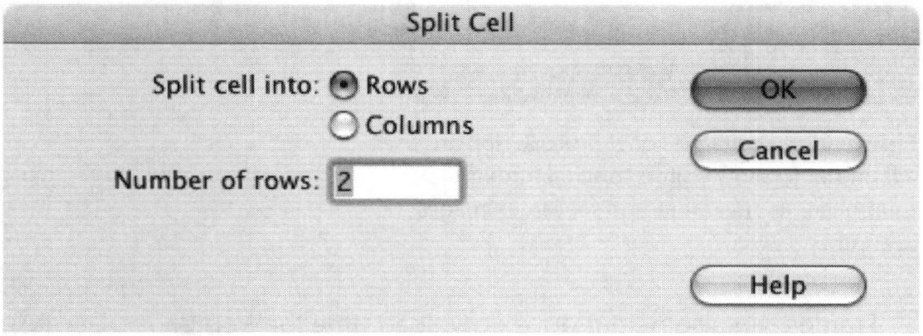

Figure 26c Splitting cells.

#27 Generating a Frameset from Samples

Frames and Search Engines

There are also significant disadvantages to designing with frames. One is that frames tend to confuse search engines, which identify content in HTML pages, not in combined frames. Visitors might end up following a search link to an HTML Web page that is intended to be displayed within a frame, and therefore see only part of the page content. Frames also pose accessibility problems for visitors with handheld browsing devices and for Web surfers who rely on reader software to read page content aloud.

However, because frames open up design possibilities that cannot be easily accomplished with other page design techniques, they remain a viable element of page design.

Frames allow you to display more than one Web page in a browser window. You can accomplish this by generating a special kind of Web page that has no content of its own, but simply serves as a container to display other Web pages that are embedded in *frames* within that container page. The whole *set* of HTML pages that work together to present more than one page in a browser is referred to as a *frameset*.

There are distinct advantages to designing with frames. Since each frame within a frameset is a separate Web page, visitors can scroll (usually vertically) within one frame, while continuing to view content undisturbed in a separate frame. Many artists and designers, for instance, use frames to display their portfolios—they use a frame on the left side of the page to allow visitors to scroll vertically down a long set of thumbnail images, and then much larger images display in a wider frame on the right side of the page. In particular, framesets are a popular form for presenting online artist portfolios (**Figure 27a**).

Figure 27a Digital designer Bruce K. Hopkins uses a frameset to allow visitors to scroll through thumbnails in one frame, and see larger images in another.

Frames can also help reduce download time for Web pages, because page content in one frame does not have to reload when new content is displayed in another frame.

One downside to designing with frames is that managing files is at least three times as confusing as working with a normal page. That's in part because each frameset includes at least three HTML pages: one to serve as the overall frameset, and at least two framed pages embedded in the frameset. The best way to manage this challenge is to generate framesets from a set of sample pages.

To see the set of sample frames, choose File > New and choose Page from Sample in the category list on the left side of the New Document dialog. In the Sample Folder column, choose Frameset. Preview predesigned framesets in the preview area in the upper right of the dialog (**Figure 27b**).

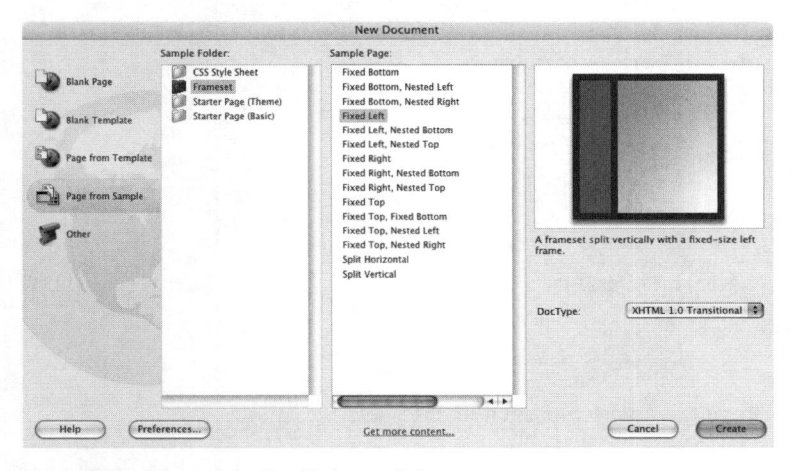

Figure 27b Selecting the Fixed Left sample frameset.

Sample Frames Won't Cramp Your Style

There are only a few widely used frameset options, and they are *all* available from the set of sample framesets in the New Document dialog. The Fixed Left option in the set of frameset page designs generates a simple, effective frameset. The narrow frame on the left serves as a navigation frame. It can contain text links, image links (often in the form of small thumbnail images), or a combination of text and image links.

Links clicked in the left frame open in the right frame. Thus, the left (navigation frame) never downloads once the whole frameset is open—it stays constant. The right side of the frameset changes as new pages open in that frame, depending on what link is clicked in the left frame.

Once you generate a frameset from a sample in the New Document window, the Frame Tag Accessibility Attributes dialog appears. Here, you assign names to all the frames in the frameset. Naming frames is *different* than naming the HTML files in a frameset. You'll be prompted to do both, so don't get confused by this. The frame name is useful in defining link targets and other frame attributes, and has to be defined separately. Normally, the default frame names in the dialog are fine (these names are not visible in browsers), so go ahead and OK each Frame Tag Accessibility Attribute dialog that appears when you generate a frameset (**Figure 27c**).

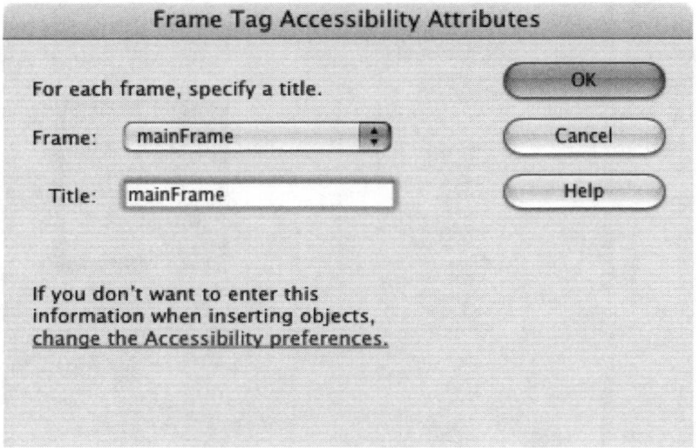

Figure 27c Assigning a frame name to frames.

To save a frameset, choose File > Save All from the main Dreamweaver window. You will be saving at least three files: the frameset file and each embedded page within the frameset.

You can edit the content of that frameset, and you can edit the formatting of the frameset itself. That process is explained in #28, "Formatting Framesets."

#28 Formatting Framesets

Frameset attributes include whether or not to display borders between pages in the frameset, as well as the width and/or height of various frames within the frameset. Both of these attributes are defined in the Property inspector. The tricky part is selecting the entire frameset to access these features.

The easiest way to select an entire frameset is to view the Frames panel (Window > Frames). Click on the border that surrounds the entire Frames panel to select the frameset. The frameset will be selected in both the Frames panel and in the Document window (**Figure 28a**).

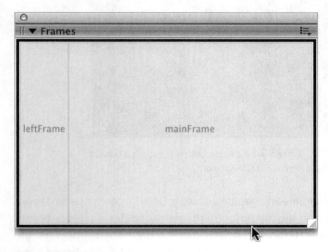

Figure 28a Selecting a frameset using the Frames panel.

Making Frames More Accessible

As noted in the introduction to this chapter, frames provide an accessibility challenge for vision-impaired visitors. This is because separating content into more than one page can be confusing when that content is read aloud.

Dreamweaver provides a way to define descriptive page titles for each embedded page. Normally, page titles are not relevant for embedded pages. The title of the container page for the frameset displays in the title bar of a browser, and for non-vision-impaired visitors, it all looks like one page.

(continued on next page)

Often, framesets are formatted so that there is no visible border between frames in a browser window. The "page" appears to be a single page in a browser, even though it is in fact at least three pages (**Figure 28b**).

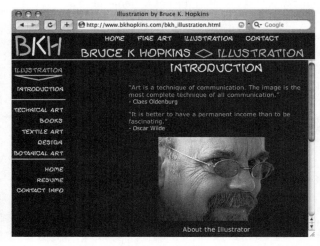

Figure 28b What appears to be a single, seamless page in a browser is actually several different HTML Web pages.

By default, framesets generated using Dreamweaver's page designs are formatted to display no border between frames. To add a border, choose Yes from the Borders pop-up menu in the Property inspector, and define the border width in pixels in the Border width field. Choose a border color from the Border color swatch (**Figure 28c**).

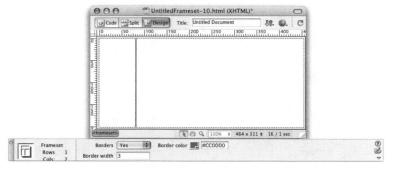

Figure 28c Defining a border between frames in a frameset.

Designing Pages with Tables and Frames

To define the widths (or heights) of frames within a frameset, use the RowCol Selection area in the Property inspector to click a row or column in your frameset. Then, choose a value for the selected column or row in the Column Value or Row Value field. Values can be either fixed (in pixels) or a percent. Or, you can make a column width Relative, which means it will fill all space left over after columns with fixed widths are displayed (**Figure 28d**).

Figure 28d Defining a frame that will fill all available space after fixed-width frames display.

You can define scroll attributes (whether or not to display scrollbars), as well as set resize permission (whether or not to allow a viewer to click and drag on the border between frames and resize them in his or her browser) for selected frames.

On the other hand, page titles for each embedded page are a navigation assistance to vision-impaired visitors. If you select the proper accessibility settings, Dreamweaver will prompt you to define page titles for each embedded page when you generate a frameset. To enable this feature, choose Edit > Preferences (Windows) or Dreamweaver > Preferences (Mac). Select the Accessibility category in the Preferences dialog, and check the Frames check box. Click OK in the dialog. After doing this, you'll be prompted to add page titles to embedded pages in framesets.

Defining Frame Attributes vs. Defining Frameset Attributes

Defining frame attributes is confusing because some attributes are defined for an entire frameset, and other attributes are defined just for a selected frame. And some attributes can be defined for both.

Define border display for your entire frameset. Define the width and/or height for each frame within a frameset as part of defining frameset properties.

Define scroll attributes (whether to display a scrollbar) for a selected frame. Also, define resize permission for a selected frame. You *can* define border parameters for a selected frame that conflict with the settings you define for the entire frameset. Don't! This will confuse browsers.

You determine whether you are defining attributes for a frame or an entire frameset by clicking to select either the entire frameset or an individual frame in the Frames panel.

First, click a specific frame in the Frames panel. The Property inspector then makes settings available for scrollbar display in the Scroll pop-up menu. You can choose Yes (always display a scrollbar), No (never display a scrollbar), Auto (display a scrollbar only as needed), or Default (whatever a browser defaults to). You can enable viewer resizing of frames by deselecting the No resize check box (**Figure 28e**).

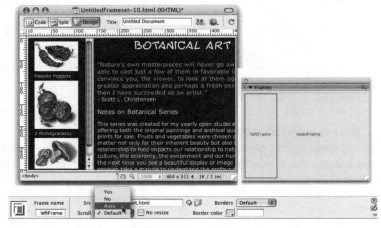

Figure 28e Enabling a scrollbar (only as needed) for a selected frame.

#29 Defining Links Between Frames

Defining links in framesets presents a special challenge. Since technically each frame in a frameset is a *different* HTML page, you need to click on a link in one page, and have the link open in a *different* HTML page. And you have to "tell" the link what page to open in. Sounds confusing, but I'll walk you through the whole process here.

For example, let's see how this works in a simple, basic, two-frame frameset with a left navigation frame and a right main frame. Links clicked in the left frame *open in the right frame*. The right side of the frameset changes, as new pages open in that frame depending on what link is clicked in the left frame.

This is done by defining a target frame for links. After you define a link for text or an image using the Property inspector (enter the linked page in the Link box), define a target for that link from the Target pop-up menu in the Property inspector.

When you generated a frameset from one of Dreamweaver's frameset page designs, you automatically assigned names to each frame within the frameset. These named frames show up in a list when you click the Target pop-up menu in the Property inspector (**Figure 29a**).

Figure 29a Choosing a target for a link in a frameset.

It can be rather disastrous if you don't define the target for a link in a frameset, as when a link doesn't open in the appropriate frame, but in the frame from which the link was launched (**Figure 29b**).

Figure 29b Ouch! A link that should have opened in the main frame opened in the left navigation frame, as well as in the main frame.

CHAPTER FOUR

Designing Pages with Absolute Placement Objects

Cascading Style Sheets (CSS) have evolved as the most flexible and powerful tool for page layout. Page layout with CSS involves writing CSS code that defines placement objects—think of them as "boxes"—that contain content like text, images, or media. The definition of these placement objects includes their location, their background color, padding within them, spacing around them, and other attributes.

Dreamweaver CS3 provides accessible designer-oriented tools for creating and editing CSS page layout in the form of what Dreamweaver calls Absolute Placement (AP) objects.

In this chapter, we will use only local CSS formatting. External style sheets, which can be used to set up styles for any or all pages in your site, are addressed in Chapter 7, "Formatting Page Elements with CSS."

Should you use tables or CSS for page design? Tables are simpler to learn, and you can feel more confident that your pages will look the way you intend in most desktop browsers.

Note
Page design with tables is covered in Chapter 3, "Designing Pages with Tables and Frames."

CSS, AP, and Compatibility

While CSS is widely supported in different browsers and devices, AP objects are less predictable because when someone viewing your site changes text size or other variables (such as screen resolution), the result sometimes is that AP objects overlap with each other, causing a big mess on the screen. One option for creating Web pages with CSS layout that do not rely on AP objects is to take advantage of a wide range of well-prepared and richly commented CSS page designs. To access those page designs, choose File > New. In the New Document dialog, select the Blank Page category, and in the Page Type column choose HTML. You will see a long list of pages that use CSS (but not AP objects) to define page layout.

On the other hand, current thought on Web site construction is that using CSS makes your content easier to distribute on different platforms and can help you make it accessible to users with disabilities. Reader software, which reads page content out loud to visitors with impaired vision, can interpret CSS layout and present page content in a more coherent way than if blocks of content are laid out in table cells. In Dreamweaver, working with Absolute Placement objects is more like designing in Adobe Illustrator, Adobe Photoshop, or Adobe InDesign; however, it is somewhat less predictable in its display in a wide range of browsing devices.

Dreamweaver provides two approaches to page design with CSS: Absolute Placement Divs (basically the elements referred to as Layers in previous versions of Dreamweaver), and Divs. AP Divs are a feature of Dreamweaver, not a part of XHTML or CSS, but they are easy to use, particularly if you've worked in a program like Photoshop. Divs are part of the XHTML spec; in Dreamweaver they are less intuitive than AP Divs to work with, but they provide more control over page design.

Note
Later in this chapter, I'll show you how to insert Divs. See #33, "Defining Div Tags."

Designing Pages with Absolute Placement Objects

#30 Defining Absolute Placement Objects

Absolute Placement (AP) Divs are containers on a Web page that hold content such as type, images, or other objects like media. AP Divs are defined both by their location on a page and their size (measured in pixels). Dreamweaver allows you to simply draw AP Divs on the page, just as if you were designing a page layout in a program like Illustrator or InDesign. As you draw, resize, or move an AP Div, Dreamweaver generates CSS code that defines or redefines the location and size of that AP Div.

To draw an AP Div in an open document, choose Insert > Layout Object > AP Div. An AP Div appears in the document. By default, this AP Div is 200 pixels by 115 pixels and is located at the top-left edge of your page (**Figure 30a**).

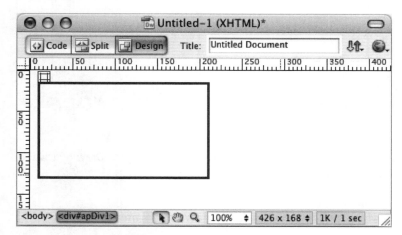

Figure 30a A default AP Div in the Document window.

When you generate an AP Div, it is selected, and you can edit it. If you deselect the AP Div by clicking elsewhere on the page, you can reselect it by clicking on the AP Div border.

You can move or relocate an AP Div in the Document window. To move an AP Div, click the AP Div handle (the icon in the upper-left corner of the selected AP Div), and simply drag it to another part of the page (**Figure 30b**).

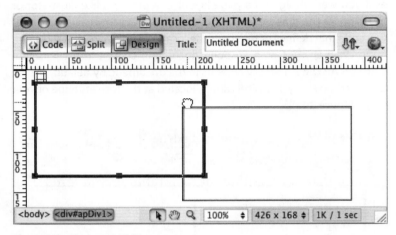

Figure 30b Moving an AP Div.

You can also draw an AP Div interactively using the Draw AP Div tool in the Layout tab of the Insert bar.

Tip
If the Insert bar is not visible, choose Window > Insert to display it.

To draw an AP Div, click the Draw AP Div tool. The cursor displays as a crosshair icon. Click and draw anywhere on the page to generate an AP Div. When you release your mouse cursor, the AP Div container is generated (**Figure 30c**).

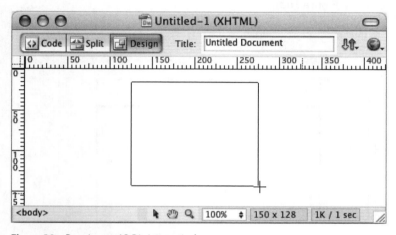

Figure 30c Drawing an AP Div interactively.

You can, of course, generate as many AP Divs on a page as you wish. For example, you might create one AP Div on the left side of your page as a placeholder for navigation elements, another AP Div on the top of your page for a banner, and a third AP Div to hold the body of your page content (**Figure 30d**).

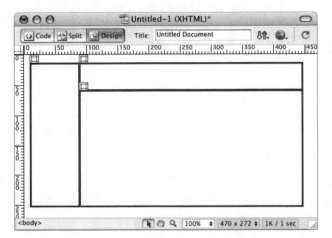

Figure 30d A typical page design with three AP Divs—one for the banner, another for a left navigation region, and the third for page content.

Dreamweaver offers tools to resize or align multiple AP Divs. This is useful, for example, if you wanted to display several thumbnail images aligned vertically (their tops aligned) on a page. To do this, first, Shift-click to select all the AP Divs you want to resize or align. Then, choose Modify > Arrange. From the submenu, you can select an alignment option (Align Left, Align Right, Align Top, or Align Bottom), or you can select Make Same Width or Make Same Height (**Figure 30e**).

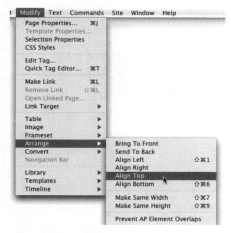

Figure 30e Aligning several AP Divs on their top edges to hold thumbnail images.

Note

If you use the Modify menu to make selected AP Divs the same height or width, the larger AP Divs will change size to match the smallest AP Div.

Finding Nonvisible AP Divs

Sometimes developers use invisible AP Divs as interactive, programmed elements that appear when some action takes place. For example, rolling over an image might cause a nonvisible AP Div to change its appearance and become visible. If you assign nonvisible attributes to an AP Div, it is often hard to select that AP Div in the Document window. AP Divs with no visibility do not display in the Document window unless they are selected.

The solution is to select a nonvisible AP Div in the AP Elements panel. View the AP Elements panel by choosing Window > AP Elements. In the AP Elements panel, you can select any AP, and the outline of the AP Div becomes visible in the Document window.

Display support for AP Divs in the Dreamweaver Document window can only be described as unpredictable. Some AP Div features can be previewed in the Document window, while others cannot. To reliably see how AP Divs will look in a particular browser, preview the page in that browser. To do this from Dreamweaver, choose File > Preview in Browser. If you have more than one installed browser, select the desired browser from the submenu. Then you will see the page (and your AP Divs) as viewers with that browser will see it (**Figure 30f**).

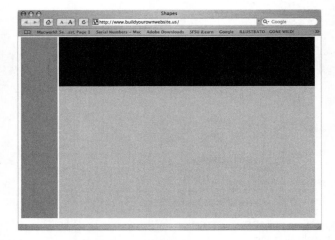

Figure 30f Previewing AP Divs in a browser.

You can also embed an AP Div within another AP Div. This is somewhat similar to embedding a table inside a table.

Note
See Chapter 3, #24, "Embedding Tables Within Tables," for a discussion of the pros and cons of that technique.

The embedded AP Div is positioned *within* the AP Div in which it is placed. To embed an AP Div within an AP Div, click inside one AP Div and then insert another AP Div. Placing an AP Div within another AP Div is technically possible, and one reason to be aware of this is that it often happens by accident. When you place an AP Div inside another AP Div, you create unnecessarily complex pages that are difficult to edit. If your CSS page designs are too complex for AP Divs, consider invoking definable Div tags.

Tip

Div tags are explored in #33, "Defining Div Tags."

AP Div Properties Are Not Universally Supported

Not all the formatting attributes that you can assign to an AP Div are supported in all browsing environments. Features like background color, background image, and overflow are particularly unpredictable.

As a general rule, if you want your site to be widely accessible in many browsing environments, use AP Divs to *place* page content, but avoid relying on AP Div formatting features.

Not all AP Div formatting features are displayed in the default Document window settings. To view AP Div backgrounds, choose View > Visual Aids > CSS AP Div Backgrounds.

#31 Formatting AP Divs in the Property Inspector

You can move and resize AP Divs using the Property inspector. Defining location and size in the Property inspector is more precise than clicking and dragging with a mouse because you can define exact location, height, and width to the pixel.

To define a location on a page in the Property inspector for a selected AP Div, enter a distance from the left edge of the page (in pixels) in the L (for Left) field, and enter a distance from the top of the page in the T (for Top) field. An AP Div with L and T values of zero will be placed in the upper-left corner of the page (**Figure 31a**).

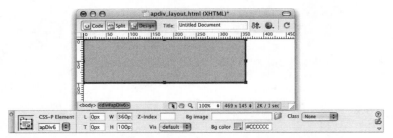

Figure 31a Placing an AP Div in the upper-left corner of a page.

Technically, you *can* create overlapping AP Divs. You might be able to produce some cutting-edge page designs this way and come close to simulating the freedom you have in programs like Illustrator, Photoshop, or InDesign to stack objects on top of each other.

If you do overlap AP Divs, you assign Z-index values to selected AP Divs in the Property inspector to define the AP Divs' "front-to-back" properties. AP Divs with higher Z-index values display *on top of* AP Divs with lower Z-index values.

Overlapping AP Divs are not universally supported in different browsing environments. They are less reliable than AP Divs in general. And, unless you are pretty expert at CSS, there are a number of pitfalls in designing with overlapping AP Divs that can sink your Web page. For instance, AP Divs often expand in size in different browsing environments in a way that can turn your page into gibberish if overlapping AP Divs are used.

The other definable elements of AP Divs are the following (**Figure 31b**):

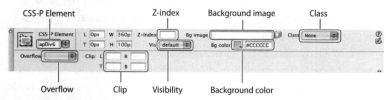

Figure 31b Defining AP Div properties in the Property inspector.

- **CSS-P Element:** Defines a name for the AP Div for use in scripts or CSS attributes. The name must contain only alphanumeric characters—no spaces—and start with a letter.

- **Overflow:** Defines how content that is larger than the AP Div will appear in a browser. By default, AP Divs stretch to fit content.

- **Clip:** Allows a specified amount of content in an AP Div to be "covered up" on the Left (L), Top (T), Right (R), or Bottom (B).

- **Z-index:** A numerical value for the bottom-to-top order of an AP Div that overlaps others. Higher-value AP Divs appear on top of lower-value AP Divs.

- **Vis:** Defines visibility. Normally AP Div content is visible, but AP Divs used in scripts are sometimes hidden, to be made visible later by actions of a visitor.

- **Bg image:** Defines the image that appears as a background in the AP Div.

- **Bg color:** Defines the background color for an AP Div. If you defined a Bg image, the image will override a background color.

- **Class:** Applies style using a CSS class. See Chapter 7, "Formatting Page Elements with CSS," for an explanation of how to define CSS classes.

Preventing AP Div Overlaps and Converting AP Divs to Tables

Because many designers find AP Divs a more intuitive way to design pages than using tables, Dreamweaver allows you to design a page in AP Divs. Then, if you choose to do so, you can convert the entire page to a table layout, which may display more predictably in various browsers than a CSS-based page. To convert AP Divs to tables in the Document window, choose Modify > Convert > AP Divs to Table.

However, if your AP Divs overlap, Dreamweaver will not convert them to a table, because tables can't handle overlapping cells. So, if you want to design in AP Divs and convert to a table, avoid overlapping AP Divs. The AP Elements panel has a Prevent Overlaps check box that will disallow you from placing one AP Div on top of another.

#32 Managing AP Divs in the AP Elements Panel

The AP Elements panel is valuable when you are designing a page with AP Divs. You can easily select AP Divs in the AP Elements panel (even if you have set the AP Divs' visibility to hidden) and make them visible in the Document window.

The AP Elements panel also provides a different and sometimes easier way to define AP Div visibility and Z-index values than using the Property inspector. For one thing, you can see the properties of many AP Divs at a time in the AP Elements panel, which comes in handy when you are designing complex interactive pages with AP Divs that are either hidden or visible, depending on the state of a script that governs their properties.

You can also rename AP Divs in the AP Elements panel, but AP Div names must be alphanumeric and cannot start with a number.

View the AP Elements panel by choosing Window > AP Elements. The panel appears with all existing AP Divs listed (**Figure 32a**).

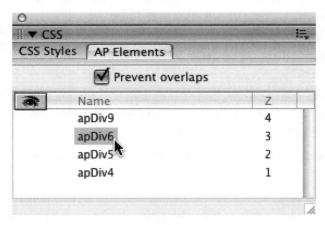

Figure 32a Selecting an AP Div in the AP Elements panel.

You select an AP Div in the Document window by clicking it in the AP Elements panel. To rename an AP Div in the AP Elements panel, double-click the AP Div name and enter a new name. You can also switch among the three visibility states in the AP Elements panel by clicking in the visibility column on the left. The closed-eye icon means the AP Div is hidden. The open-eye icon means the AP Div is visible. No icon signifies default status, which generally means the AP Div is visible unless a browser setting conflicts with it (**Figure 32b**).

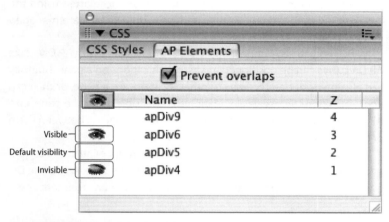

Figure 32b Defining visibility for AP Divs.

#33 Defining Div Tags

Dreamweaver AP Divs allow designers to lay out pages using familiar tools, and Dreamweaver generates CSS code to match. A somewhat less-intuitive method of generating page layout with CSS in Dreamweaver CS3 is to define Div tags. The terminology is confusing: AP Div? Div tag? The difference is that AP Divs are easier to define, but do not permit as many formatting options as Div tags. Both are generated in the Dream-weaver Document window. Neither AP Divs nor Div tags require that you learn CSS coding—in both cases Dreamweaver CS3 generates code for you. But while AP Divs can be mainly defined and formatted using the Property inspector, more complex and powerful Div tags are managed in the CSS panel.

With Divs you can define many more attributes than with AP Divs. Like AP Divs, Divs can be positioned at absolute locations on a page, but they can also be positioned *relative* to other locations on a page, or they can *float*—position themselves in relation to other objects on the page. Like AP Divs, Divs can be sized, but you can also define spacing between them or padding within them, as you can with table cells.

In fact, you can apply an almost unlimited number of attribute combi-nations to Divs, including border color, thickness, and type. And these Div attributes are more predictable in different browsing environments.

Note
For a fuller exploration of CSS formatting for objects like tables or page backgrounds, see Chapter 7, "Formatting Page Elements with CSS."

In Dreamweaver, there are almost as many ways to generate and define a Div as there are possible attributes. The following set of steps provides a digestible approach that I use to teach students how to create Divs.

To create a Div and specify its position:

1. In a new document, select Insert > Layout Objects > Div Tag. The Insert Div Tag dialog appears.

   The Insert Div Tag dialog itself does not help much with defining the positioning, size, or other attributes of the Div you want to create. But it does allow you to name it.

2. In the ID field of the Insert Div Tag dialog (**Figure 33a**), enter an alphanumeric name (start with a letter; spaces are not allowed). Pick a name that will help you remember what this object is in case you create many Divs.

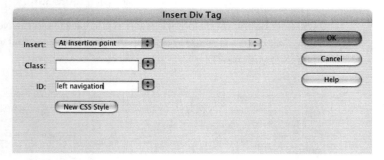

Figure 33a Naming a Div tag.

3. Do not click OK yet. All you've done so far is establish an invisible, sizeless section on your page. Instead, click the New CSS Style button in the Insert Div Tag dialog. The New CSS Rule dialog opens. In the next set of steps, you will define CSS rules that apply to the Div you created.

(*continued on next page*)

What's with the Period in the Style Name?

Classes begin with a period. You don't need to enter the period when you name the style; Dreamweaver inserts it for you. The periods in class names denote that these styles are *appended to* other styles. For example, in Chapter 7 you will learn to define styles for both heading text and body (regular) text. However, you can append (attach) a *class* style to *either* or *both* of these tags.

4. In the New CSS Rule dialog, leave the Selector Type radio button selection at Class, which is the default. Classes are highly flexible and can be applied to any element (including your Div). Select the This document only radio button. Then, in the Name field, enter a name (alphanumeric only) for the style. Then click OK (**Figure 33b**).

The CSS Rule Definition dialog opens when you click OK in the New CSS Rule dialog. Here is where you set up the class attributes that will be applied to your new Div.

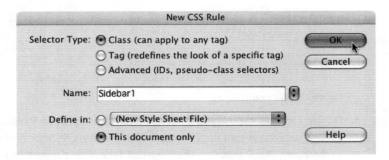

Figure 33b Naming a class with style attributes that will apply to a Div.

Note
If you select the top Define in radio button instead of the This document only button, you must create a new, external style sheet file. External style sheets are explained in Chapter 7, "Formatting Page Elements with CSS."

5. In the CSS Rule Definition dialog, click the Positioning category. Here, you will choose which type of positioning to use when specifying the location of your Div, define the Div's size, and then define its location on or relative to other parts of the page (**Figure 33c**).

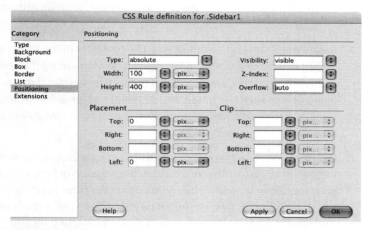

Figure 33c Defining the rules for the .Sidebar1 class, which will determine the positioning of a Div.

6. From the Type pop-up menu, first choose a positioning type.

- Choosing "absolute" places the object at specific values from the upper-left corner of the page.

- Choosing "fixed" freezes the object on a page so that when a visitor scrolls up or down, the object stays in the same place.

- Choosing "relative" places the object relative to its position in the text flow of the page. If your cursor is at the top of a Web page, absolute and relative positioning have the same effect, but if your cursor is in the middle of some text, relative positioning places the object a defined distance to the left of and below the current cursor point.

(continued on next page)

Tip
Choosing relative positioning without any offsets is often a way to give a Div a needed "hasLayout" property that Internet Explorer versions earlier than version 7 require to display some layouts properly.

- Choosing "static" places the Div container at its location in the text flow.

7. Define the width and height of your Div container in the Width and Height fields. For example, a left navigation element might have a width of 100 pixels. Choose a unit of measurement from the pop-up menu next to each box (pixels are normally used for defining dimensions in Web design, and using pixels is the most reliable way to size objects).

8. Define the position of your box in the Placement area. You can define location in pixels (or other units) either from the top or bottom of the page and either from the left or right edge of the page. For instance, a left-side navigation element might be defined as 0 (zero) pixels from the top of the page, and 0 pixels from the left edge of the page.

9. The four Clip boxes work like masking in illustration programs. Clipping hides part of the outside of the content of a CSS positioning object. Usually you will not want to clip content.

10. Visibility defines whether or not the Div is visible. By default, Divs are visible.

11. The Z-index box defines how the Div will move in front of or behind other objects. Positioning objects with higher Z-index values appear on top of objects with lower Z-index values. If your positioning objects do not overlap, Z-index values are irrelevant.

12. The Overflow pop-up menu defines how text that does not fit in the positioning object will appear in a browser. The Visible option displays all content, even if it doesn't fit in the Div. The Hidden option hides all content that does not fit in the Div. The Scroll option displays a scrollbar, so the Div looks like a miniature browser window, with its own scrollbar(s). And the Auto option leaves Div display up to the browsing environment of the user.

13. Once you have defined the options in the Positioning category, you have defined the basic location and size of your object (Div). Use the Border category to apply borders to your object. Use the Box category to define buffer spacing between content and the box (Padding) or spacing between objects (Margin). Spacing is usually unnecessary with Divs, but allowing 6 pixels of padding is often a good way to keep the content of different Divs from bumping into each other.

14. When you are finished defining options for your Div, click OK. You can enter content in your positioned Div by clicking inside it and typing, or inserting images (**Figure 33d**).

Figure 33d Inserting content into a positioned Div.

Editing the Attributes of a Div

To edit the attributes of a Div, select it, and in the Property inspector, click the Edit CSS button to open the CSS Styles panel. Double-click any attribute in the panel to reopen the CSS Rule Definition dialog, and change any attribute for the Div.

#33: Defining Div Tags

#**34** Using Rulers, Guides, and Grids

Since AP Divs and Div tags allow you to design pages in an intuitive, inter-active, graphical environment, wouldn't it be nice if you could use design features like rulers, guides, and gridlines to make it easy to align and place layout objects? Good news—you can!

Dreamweaver's rulers, guides, and gridlines display much like those in Illustrator, InDesign, and Photoshop. Combined with AP Divs and defin-able Div tags, they allow Dreamweaver's Document window to function as a graphical design workspace.

To display rulers in an open document, choose View > Rulers > Show. The View > Rulers submenu also allows you to choose between pixels, centimeters, and inches (**Figure 34a**).

Figure 34a Choosing a unit of measurement for rulers.

You can even redefine the horizontal and/or vertical zero points for the rulers. Do this by dragging the icon at the intersection of the horizontal and vertical rulers into the Document window. The point at which you release your mouse becomes the new zero point for the horizontal and vertical rulers (**Figure 34b**). To reset the ruler zero points, choose View > Rulers > Reset Origin.

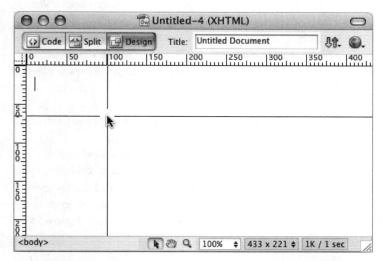

Figure 34b Setting a customized horizontal and vertical zero point for rulers.

To place a horizontal or vertical guide on the page, click and drag a ruler, and then drag it into the Document window (**Figure 34c**).

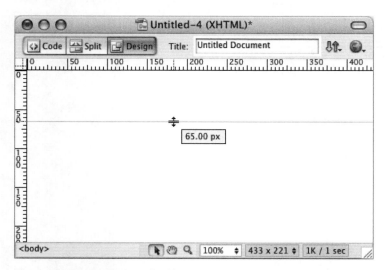

Figure 34c Placing a horizontal guide.

To edit the location of a guide, click and drag it. You can also double-click to edit the guide location or unit of measurement.

Guides can be locked to prevent accidental editing; choose View > Guides > Lock Guides. Guides can also be made "magnetic" so that they either snap to objects on the page, or objects on the page snap to them. To make a guide snap to elements on the page, choose View > Guides > Guides Snap to Elements. To make elements snap to guides, choose View > Guides > Snap to Guides. Clear guides by choosing View > Guides > Clear Guides.

Grids can be displayed by choosing View > Grid > Show Grid. Make grids magnetic by choosing View > Grid > Snap to Grid.

Define grid properties by choosing View > Grid > Grid settings. The Grid Settings dialog allows you to change the color of gridlines, spacing between grids, grid display and snap properties, and display (dots or lines). Click Apply to preview changes to the grid, or click OK to close the dialog and change grid settings in the Document window (**Figure 34d**).

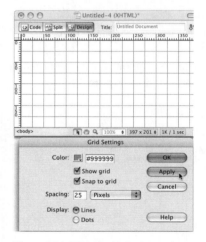

Figure 34d Editing grid display settings.

CHAPTER FIVE

Working with Text and Images

Text and images are the basic building blocks of Web sites. Text is easy to add to a Web site; you can create text right in Dreamweaver or easily copy and paste any text from a document or Web page into a Dreamweaver document.

Pictures are more of a challenge. You can't create images in Dreamweaver or copy and paste images into a Dreamweaver document.

Now for the good news. There is a wide array of image-editing programs—ranging from the one that came with your digital camera or computer operating system to Adobe Photoshop (or Photoshop Elements). Almost all of them can be used to prepare images for the Web.

Dreamweaver CS3 includes some rudimentary image-editing tools. But in general, you'll prepare images in advance (in another program) before you place them on a Web page. For that reason, #38, "Preparing Images for the Web," will explore a range of techniques available in programs other than Dreamweaver.

Once you have an image ready for your Web page, Dreamweaver makes it easy to place the image, align text to flow around the image, and assign links to either the entire image or part of the image (an image map).

Finally, one of the most underrated and valuable new features of Dreamweaver CS3 is the ability to import Photoshop (PSD) files directly into Dreamweaver. I'll explain how this works in #44, "Placing Photoshop Files in Web Pages."

#35 Formatting Text with HTML Attributes

HTML Tags—The Skeleton of Your Document

One good reason to use HTML tags that accurately reflect your document's structure is that some browsing environments either replace or don't use the CSS styles you assign to pages. For example, many sight-impaired people use customized style sheets that make text easier to read or reader software that reads the content of Web pages aloud. In both cases, HTML tags are reinterpreted to assist users with receiving the page content.

(continued on next page)

There are two kinds of text formatting in Web pages. The most basic method is assigning HTML tags to text, and then adjusting or enhancing the formatting by modifying those tags with *attributes*. HTML includes tags that define a document's structural elements, including six levels of headings (with 1 usually being the largest, and 6 usually the smallest), and the Paragraph tag. With HTML tags and attributes, you can also control text's appearance, including font color, font size, boldface, italics, and underlining.

To format text with an HTML tag as a paragraph in Dreamweaver, you don't have to select all the text in the paragraph. The tags available for this purpose are all block-level tags, which means they apply to *entire* paragraphs. This is true even if you used a line break (Shift-Enter) to create a new line within a paragraph.

With your cursor in a paragraph, choose a tag from the Format pop-up menu in the Property inspector (**Figure 35a**).

Figure 35a Assigning a Heading 1 tag to selected text.

Normal text uses the Paragraph style. There are six heading styles (Heading 1 to Heading 6).

Note
The HTML tags for headings are h1, h2, h3, h4, h5, and h6. Dreamweaver displays more intuitive options: Heading 1, Heading 2, and so on in the Property inspector.

Heading 1 is typically used for a page title. Heading 6 is often used for footnotes, legal notices, and other very small text. Other styles fit somewhere in between these extremes (**Figure 35b**).

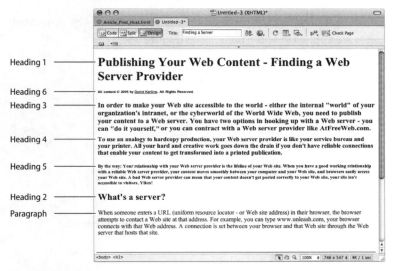

Figure 35b All six HTML heading styles applied to paragraphs.

In addition to the six heading tags and Paragraph tag, you'll use a few other basic HTML elements to format text. They are all applied via buttons in the Property inspector and include the following:

- **Bulleted List:** Automatically applies bullet icons to paragraphs
- **Numbered List:** Automatically numbers paragraphs
- **Boldface:** Formats text with boldface
- **Italics:** Formats text with italics
- **Text Indent:** Moves a paragraph away from the left margin
- **Text Outdent:** Moves a paragraph toward the left margin
- **Align Left, Align Center, Align Right, and Justify:** Define paragraph alignment

Another good reason to carefully and consciously apply HTML tags to all text is that it helps make your pages look consistent if you use an external CSS style sheet to apply styles sitewide.

Finally, structural HTML tags, like Heading 1, Heading 2, and so on, translate well if readers copy and paste content into word processors. In fact, this works in the other direction as well. For example, content created in Microsoft Word, which uses styles like Heading 1, Heading 2, and Heading 3, can be saved as an HTML page, and the styles will "translate" from print to Web.

Caution
Using the Text Indent and Text Outdent buttons inserts a blockquote HTML tag. That tag can interfere with the ability of visitors who rely on reader software to read the site content to them out loud.

Boldface and italics are applied only to selected text. The other attributes are applied to entire paragraphs (**Figure 35c**).

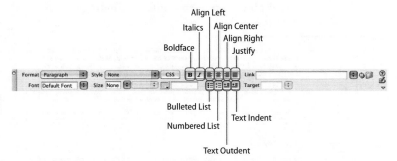

Figure 35c HTML formatting tags and attributes in the Property inspector.

#36 Applying Colors to Fonts

Font color can be assigned to selected text. With text selected in the Document window, click the Text Color icon in the Property inspector to open the Text Color palette. You can choose from the array of "Web-safe" (widely supported) colors, or use the Eyedropper tool to pick up a color on your screen (**Figure 36a**).

Figure 36a Assigning a color to selected text in the Property inspector.

Tip
Web-safe colors are especially relevant if you are primarily designing for handheld browsing devices or other browsing environments that do not support the thousands or millions of colors supported by modern computer monitors.

To choose from color schemes (sets of selected colors) or to choose from the full range of colors supported by monitors, click the Color Wheel icon that appears at the top of the Text Color palette (this is the palette that appears when you click the Text Color icon in the Property inspector). When you click the Color Wheel icon, the Colors dialog opens. The Colors dialog has five tabs: Color Wheel, Color Slider, Color Palettes, Image Palettes, and Crayons. The tab on the left is the Color Wheel. Here, you can click any color in the spectrum of monitor-supported colors. The second

Colors on the Web

Colors are generated on monitors (or other viewing devices) by combining red, green, and blue dots on the screen. The RGB color system lists percentage of intensity for red, green, and blue dots.

The range of color available by combining red, green, and blue dots is wider than the range of color available for print. Therefore, images for the Web should use the RGB color mode.

Primitive monitors and computer graphics hardware did not support large numbers of colors. Therefore, all monitors support a small set of 216 "Web-safe" colors. However, as Web-safe colors became irrelevant with the development of new hardware and monitors, a plethora of other viewing devices (especially handheld ones) that do not support a wide range of colors has given new relevance to the old set of Web-safe colors.

tab from the left is the Color Slider tab, which is the most widely used tab in the dialog. Here you can easily define RGB colors interactively, or by entering R, G, and B values from 0 to 255 (**Figure 36b**).

Figure 36b HTML formatting tags and attributes in the Color Slider tab of the Colors dialog.

There are other options in the Colors dialog as well. The Color Palettes tab allows you to access preset color schemes. The Image Palettes tab allows you to generate a set of colors from a Web image file (a GIF or JPEG file). The Crayons tab allows you to access a small set of colors represented as a box of crayons.

#37 Defining Inline Text Attributes with CSS

Building on a foundation of very few HTML formatting styles, CSS styles open the door to a range of typography that comes close to what is available in print—close, but not quite. The most important difference between Web and print typography is that when you apply fonts to Web pages, the fonts will only display correctly if they are installed on a visitor's browser. This means that when you use unusual fonts, most visitors will see a default font like Times Roman or Arial instead. However, with CSS you can define line spacing, word spacing, font size, font color, and other attributes.

To create a CSS formatting *rule* (style), click the CSS button in the Property inspector; the CSS panel appears. Here, you will create a CSS style that holds all the attributes you apply to the selected text. This style can be applied to other selections of text on the page as well. (I'll explain how to do this after I show you how to define a CSS style.)

Tip
You are defining a style with a set of formatting attributes. Later—after you define the style—you can apply that style to any text. It is not necessary to have text selected when you define the style.

122

Applying Safe CSS

Since you don't know exactly which CSS attributes are supported in your visitors' viewing environment, formatting text with CSS makes your site somewhat more likely to display improperly on a visitor's browser. For example, some older browsers, including older versions of Netscape Navigator, do not reliably support background colors. If you place white text with a black background on a white page (using CSS), a viewer using an older browser might see (or more to the point, *not*

(continued on next page)

If there is no CSS style already associated with the selected text, the CSS Styles panel appears with the Attach Style Sheet and New CSS Rule icons active, and the Edit Style and Delete CSS Property icons grayed out. You can now create a CSS Rule (style), and later you can edit it (**Figure 37a**).

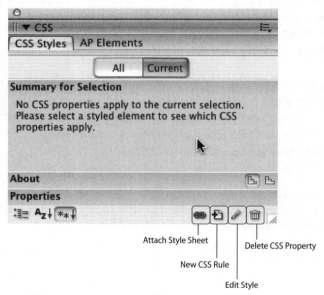

Figure 37a Defining a new style in the CSS Styles panel.

To create a new CSS style, click the New CSS Rule icon in the CSS Styles panel. The New CSS Rule dialog appears. In the Name field, enter a name for the style. In the Selector Type area, choose the Class (can apply to any tag) radio button; this defines a style that can be applied to any selected text. In the Define in area, choose the This document only radio button (**Figure 37b**).

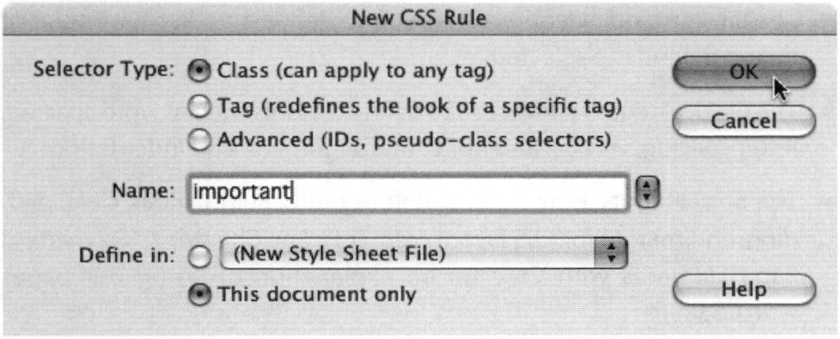

Figure 37b Creating a new style in the New CSS Rule dialog.

After you click OK in the New CSS Rule dialog, the CSS Rule definition dialog opens (**Figure 37c**).

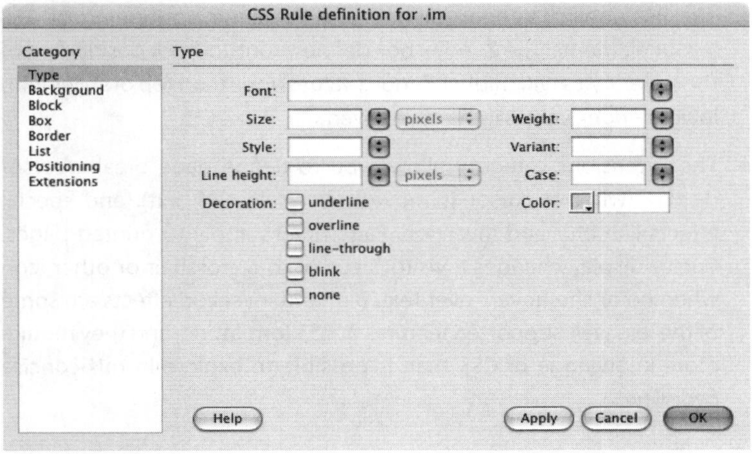

Figure 37c The CSS Rule definition dialog for a new style.

see) white type on a white page, without the black background attribute.

On the other hand, if you avoid CSS formatting in the quest for a site that will never distort in any viewing environment, your site will be too dull for most people—devoid of font sizing, spacing, and other features that make pages attractive. The solution is to use CSS, but not in a way that makes it impossible for a viewer to read your text if his or her browser does not support all the CSS features you apply.

When You Need Absolutely Formatted Text

A theme that we return to from many angles in this book is that designing for the Web is less "fixed" and more relative than designing for print. You don't know the size of a visitor's "page" when he or she views your Web page—this depends on the visitor's browsing device and browser. You also don't know what fonts he or she has installed.

When you need to design a page that displays *exactly* the same way in *every* computer-based browser, the best options are either PDF or Flash-Paper documents. Both PDF and FlashPaper retain original fonts regardless of viewing environment. The downside is that visitors require Adobe Reader or Adobe Flash Player (both free downloads) to see the documents.

The formatting options here are somewhat like those you are familiar with in your word processor:

- The Type category allows you to define font, size, weight (boldface or lightface), style (italic or roman), and line height (line spacing). Line spacing can be defined as an absolute value or as a percent, so that 150% is one and a half lines of spacing between lines.

- The Background category allows you to define a background color or image behind the selected text.

- The Block category allows you to define features such as word spacing, letter spacing, vertical and horizontal alignment, and indentation.

- The Box category allows you to define width, height, float, clear, padding, and margin for CSS layout elements. See Chapter 7, "Formatting Page Elements with CSS," for an explanation of laying out pages with CSS.

- The Border category allows you to define the style (including solid or dashed lines), thickness, and color of borders around selected text.

- The List category allows you to define the style of bullets (circle or square), and numbering (roman or arabic).

- The Positioning category allows you to define positioning of CSS layout elements. The Z-index box defines front-to-back positioning of the style. Styles with higher Z-index values appear on top of styles with lower Z-index values if the styles overlap.

- The Extensions category allows you to define page breaks, cursor display (when a cursor is moved over selected text), and special effects like blur and inversion. Page breaks apply to printed pages. Cursor display changes a visitor's cursor to a crosshair or other icon when he or she hovers over text. Blur and inversion effects are some of the less well-supported features of CSS formatting, and they require more knowledge of CSS than is possible to explore in this concise overview.

After you define a CSS style, you can apply it to selected text from the Property inspector. This is the easy part: Simply select text, and then choose a CSS style from the Style pop-up menu in the Property inspector (**Figure 37d**).

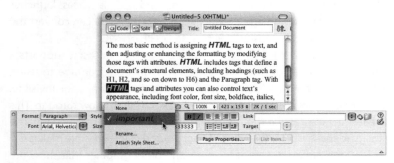

Figure 37d Applying a CSS style to selected text.

Styles Are Global

Once you define a style for a page (or once you attach an external style sheet with style definitions), the style applies to *every* tag with which it is associated. So, for example, if you define a style for h1 (Heading 1) tags or for p (paragraph) tags, that style applies to *all* text to which the respective tag is applied. However, if you apply additional formatting (like a different color or font) from the Property inspector, that attribute will override the attributes associated with the style. One way to remember this rule is, "Local trumps global." That is, formatting applied "locally" (to selected text) overrides formatting inherited from a style.

#38 Preparing Images for the Web

Web browsers recognize three types of image formats: JPEG, GIF, and PNG. The first step in preparing images for the Web is to save or export them to one of these formats.

With Dreamweaver CS3, you can now directly open or paste a Photoshop file into the Dreamweaver Document window. This process launches Dreamweaver's new Image Preview window, where you can convert the opened or pasted Photoshop file to a JPEG, GIF, or PNG.

In general, the JPEG format is much better for photos; it supports a more complex set of colors than GIF or PNG. The advantage to using GIF and PNG formats is the ability to have a *transparent*, or invisible, background that allows the Web page background to show through. This creates the impression that the image is sitting directly on the page. The ability to make a color (usually the background color) invisible makes GIF or PNG the preferred format for icons and other graphics that show the page background "through" the image (**Figure 38a**).

Figure 38a A GIF image with a transparent color allows the page background to show through.

Can you get away with simply using a JPEG image file straight from your digital camera in a Web site? Maybe, but the file probably won't work well, even though the JPEG format available as an option in your digital camera is Web-compatible. The file is likely to be too large, both in dimensions and file size. And it is likely formatted for print, not Web display.

To prepare a file for the Web, you'll want to choose appropriate color, size, and resolution settings. Web images are generally saved at 72 dpi (dots per inch). This is much *lower* than print resolution (which is normally set to at least 300 dpi) because monitor resolution is 72 dpi on Macs and 96 dpi in Windows.

When you create images for a Web page, you generally try to keep file size small. File size is not much of an issue for print documents; nobody has to sit and stare at a printed book or newspaper waiting for an illustration to download. On the other hand, several 5 MB images on a Web page will take quite some time to download over a dial-up connection.

There are two ways to reduce file size: You can make the image smaller, or you can use *compression*. Smaller images are also smaller files, and they download quickly. Many Web sites use *thumbnail* images—small preview versions of a full-sized image. Visitors who want to see a full-sized version of the image, either on the same Web page or on a separate page, can click the thumbnail.

Thumbnail images address two challenges in Web design. They reduce the time it takes to download a page (compared to downloading full-sized images), and they help solve the problem of limited space on the page. It's generally a bad idea to place images on a page that won't fit in a standard-size browser window—roughly 800 pixels (8 inches) wide and 600 pixels (6 inches) high. Providing a set of clickable thumbnails that open full-sized images is a universally applicable technique for presenting images on Web pages (**Figure 38b**).

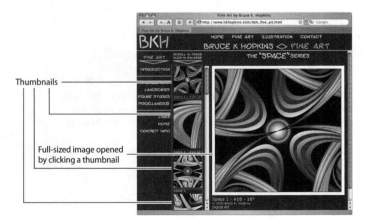

Thumbnails

Full-sized image opened by clicking a thumbnail

Figure 38b Visitors at Bruce Hopkins's Web site can click a thumbnail of an image to display the full-sized version.

Compression is a technique that reduces the number of pixels that need to be "kept track of" in an image file. This is done by defining only necessary pixels. So, for example, instead of "remembering" that there are 50 contiguous white dots in a photo, a compressed image file will define just one of these pixels and compress the file by simply noting that the other 49 pixels are identical to the defined one.

Compression can drastically reduce file size, speeding up download time. But compression also reduces quality by eliminating nuance in an image. The Save for Web window, available in Adobe products such as Photoshop, Photoshop Elements, and Illustrator, allows you to preview images with different levels of compression and compare them. The compression techniques in Adobe's Save for Web window are not crude; they offer often very high levels of compression that drastically reduce file size without significantly affecting online quality (**Figure 38c**).

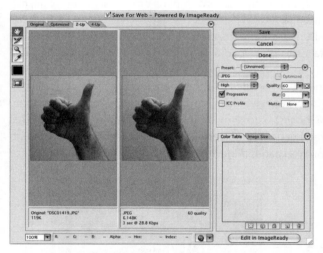

Figure 38c Comparing an uncompressed image with a highly compressed version of the same image. The photo on the right is about one-twentieth the file size of the original photo (on the left) and will download in 3 seconds over a slow dial-up modem.

#38: Preparing Images for the Web

Tip

There are many good books on how to prepare images for the Web in Photoshop and Illustrator. If you like the approach and format of this book, check out Adobe Illustrator CS3 How-Tos: 100 Essential Techniques, *by David Karlins and Bruce K. Hopkins (Adobe Press).*

The final step in the process of preparing an image for the Web is to save the image file to the folder on your computer that you use for your Dreamweaver Web site. When you do this, it will be easy to find the image as you use it on your Web page.

Tips for Preparing Images for the Web

- Save the file to JPEG, GIF, or PNG format.

- Create a thumbnail version of the image that is only about 100 pixels wide. The thumbnail will serve as a clickable link to open a larger version of the image.

- Reduce the image to a size that will fit into most browser windows. A useful guide is 760 pixels wide and 600 pixels high; keep images smaller than that.

- Experiment with compression using the Save for Web feature available in Photoshop, Photoshop Elements, or Illustrator.

#39 Embedding Images in a Web Page

Once an image is ready for the Web, you can embed it in a page in Dreamweaver. Why do I say *embed*? Because the image file remains a distinct file. To visitors to your Web site, it appears that the image is "part of the page." But in reality, a *separate* image file is displayed on your Web page using parameters you define in Dreamweaver that govern the location, size, and other elements of the image.

Start the process of embedding an image by clicking at the beginning of the paragraph of text with which the image will be associated, or in a table cell or CSS positioning element that you defined to hold the image.

Note

Defining page layout with tables is covered in Chapter 3, "Designing Pages with Tables and Frames." Creating positioning elements with CSS is explained in Chapter 4, "Designing Pages with Absolute Placement Objects."

With your cursor at the insertion point, choose Insert > Image. The Select Image Source dialog opens. Navigate to the image you want to place on the page, and click Choose (**Figure 39a**).

Figure 39a Choosing an image to embed in a Web page.

If the image file you selected is not in the folder you defined as your Dreamweaver site folder, Dreamweaver helpfully offers to save a copy of the image in your site folder. Click Yes in the dialog that appears to avail yourself of this service (**Figure 39b**).

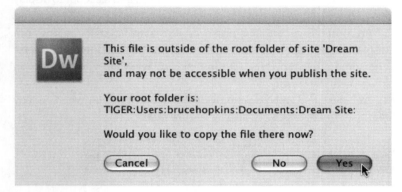

This file is outside of the root folder of site 'Dream Site',
and may not be accessible when you publish the site.

Your root folder is:
TIGER:Users:brucehopkins:Documents:Dream Site:

Would you like to copy the file there now?

Cancel   No   Yes

Figure 39b Saving a copy of an image file in your Dreamweaver site folder.

Don't Embed Images in the Middle of a Paragraph

Even if you want to display an image to the right of a line of text, embed the image at the *beginning* of the paragraph. Do this by placing the insertion cursor at the very beginning of the paragraph before choosing Insert > Image.

This might seem counter-intuitive, particularly if you're used to laying out images and text in a program like Adobe InDesign or Illustrator. But as you'll learn in #42, "Aligning Text and Images," the relationship of an image to a paragraph is a product of how the image is aligned, not of where it is inserted. Placing an image in the middle or at the end of a paragraph will make image and text alignment harder to control.

#**40** Making Images Accessible with Alt Tags

How Many People Rely on Alt Tags?

Accessibility experts estimate that as many as 30 percent of all Web visitors rely on Alt tags. Visitors with various vision limitations use Alt tags to either replace or supplement what they can (or cannot) see. For instance, many color-blind visitors rely on Alt tags to supplement what they can see in an image. Additionally, many devices such as cell phones and other handheld devices don't display images.

There are many reasons why visitors won't be able to or won't want to see images in their browser. Visitors who rely on screen reader software to read your Web site content aloud will not see your image, nor will visitors using browsers on devices that do not display images. Other visitors to your site might have low-bandwidth connections and elect not to display images.

An Alt tag is code that is displayed if its associated image does not display in a browser window. In addition, with Microsoft Internet Explorer and some other browsers, Alt tag text displays when you roll over an image with the cursor.

Well-designed Web pages provide Alt tags that display when, for any reason, an image does not display (**Figure 40a**).

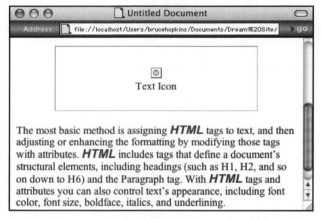

Figure 40a An Alt tag displays to identify a nondisplaying image.

Poorly designed Web pages that do not provide Alt tags simply display a tacky-looking X, question mark, or some other icon or symbol as an image placeholder when an image does not display. These sites are less accessible to visitors who are sight-impaired (**Figure 40b**).

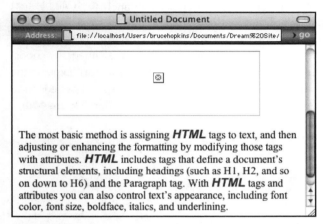

Figure 40b The image on this page doesn't have an Alt tag to identify its content.

You can define an Alt tag in the Property inspector by entering text for a selected image in the Alt field. Enter a brief description that will serve as an alternative for visitors who will not see the image (**Figure 40c**).

Figure 40c Alt tag text.

Alt tags are more useful if they are not too long; thus, the recommended maximum length is 50 characters. Sometimes that's not enough. For example, if you need to convey information depicted in a graph, map, or detailed photo, you might want to provide more information to visitors than fits in an Alt tag.

The solution is to provide a separate file that contains unlimited text. This file is accessed by the long description (longdesc) attribute. The content of a longdesc attribute is not text; it is the name of a Web page that contains a text description. The first step in providing a long description for an image is to create a separate all-text HTML file that describes the image.

Once you have created an HTML page with a long description for an image, access the longdesc attribute for a selected image by choosing the Tag inspector (choose Window > Tag Inspector). Expand the CSS/Accessibility category in the Tag panel, and use the Browse icon to navigate to the file you created with the long description (**Figure 40d**).

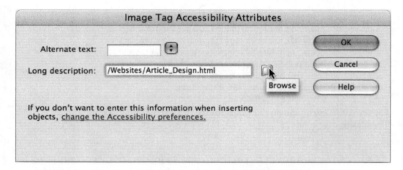

Figure 40d Attaching a long description file to a selected image in the Tag panel.

#41 Editing Images in Dreamweaver

Dreamweaver's limited set of image-editing tools allows you to crop, resample, change brightness and contrast, apply sharpening, and resize an image. When you select an image, Dreamweaver's image-editing tools will display in the Property inspector.

You can resize a selected image by clicking and dragging either the horizontal or vertical sizing handles on the image, or by clicking and dragging the corner handle. Holding down the Shift key as you resize using the corner handle maintains the original height-to-width ratio of the image. The new width and height are indicated in the W and H fields in the Property inspector. You can also enter width and height dimensions in the W and H fields. When you resize an image in Dreamweaver, the width and height display in boldface type in the Property inspector, and you can use the Reset Image to Original Size icon to revert to the original size (**Figure 41a**).

Reset Image to Original Size icon

Figure 41a Size indicated in the Property inspector.

Caution
There are significant drawbacks to both enlarging and shrinking image dimensions in Dreamweaver. If you make an image larger, you will significantly degrade the quality of the image because there is not enough data saved in the image file to display more pixels. As a result, the image will appear grainy, blurry, or raggedy. You will not lose quality in the same way if you make an image smaller. The image file will have enough data to display a smaller version of the image. However, the image quality will often still degrade because Dreamweaver's resizing tools are not sophisticated enough to figure out how to properly eliminate some of the image data. Programs like Photoshop and Photoshop Elements have resampling features that intelligently add or remove pixels as you resize an image. In short, it's best if you can size your image before you bring it into Dreamweaver.

The first two tools in the set, the Edit tool and the Optimize tool, launch a specified image editor, or launch Fireworks—an image editor that was part of the old Macromedia suite and was packaged with Dreamweaver before the Adobe acquisition.

Note

If you placed a Photoshop (PSD) file in Dreamweaver, that image will be converted into a Web-accessible format for display. However, if you edit that image using the Edit tool in the Property inspector, the Photoshop file will reopen for editing in Photoshop. For more exploration of placing Photoshop files in Dreamweaver, see #44, "Placing Photoshop Files in Web Pages."

The Crop tool, which works like a crop tool in programs like Photoshop, can be used to trim an image. The Resample tool reduces file size after you make an image smaller in Dreamweaver. Until you resample, the image displays in smaller dimensions on the Web page, but the file is not smaller. This means that the resized image will take the same amount of time to download that it did before it was resized. You can reduce file size and eliminate unnecessary pixels by clicking the Resample icon in the Property inspector. The Brightness and Contrast tool and the Sharpen tool will open dialogs with very simple sliders that adjust how an image looks (**Figure 41b**).

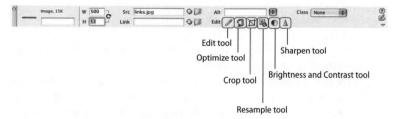

Figure 41b Image-editing tools in the Property inspector.

To open the Brightness/Contrast dialog for a selected image, click the Brightness and Contrast icon in the Property inspector. Select the Preview Edit check box to see the effect of the changes you made to the brightness and/or contrast (**Figure 41c**).

Figure 41c Previewing changes in brightness and contrast.

Similarly, the Sharpen dialog has a Preview check box so you can see the effect of the changes you made to the sharpness (**Figure 41d**).

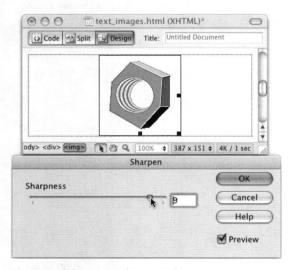

Figure 41d Previewing changes in sharpness.

Generating and Using Thumbnails

Thumbnails are valuable tools in presenting images on a Web page. They take very little space and download quickly, allowing visitors to preview a full-sized image by clicking the thumbnail. Dreamweaver CS3's utility for generating thumbnails requires Fireworks (a trial version can be downloaded from Adobe). The utility that generates thumbnails is actually designed to create a Web photo album (a slide show), but you can use this tool to create thumbnail images from a folder of images. To create thumbnails, follow these steps:

1. In the Document window, choose Commands > Create Web Photo Album (it is not necessary to have a particular page open to do this). The Create Web Photo Album dialog will appear. Unless you are generating a Web photo album, you can skip the first three fields in the dialog. In the Source images folder field, navigate to and select the folder that contains copies of all your full-sized images.

2. In the Destination folder field, navigate to and select the folder in which the generated thumbnails will be saved.

3. In the Thumbnail size field, choose a size (100 x 100 pixels is standard).

4. In the Photo format pop-up menu, choose a quality for the thumbnails. There are two usable options here: JPEG—smaller file creates fast-loading but poor-quality images; and JPEG—better quality creates thumbnails with more accurate color, but somewhat larger files and longer download time. If high-quality thumbnails are important to conveying your content, choose JPEG—better quality.

5. The other two options in this dialog (GIF webSnap 128 and GIF webSnap 256) are only relevant if you are creating a Web photo album. You can click OK, kick back, and relax while Dreamweaver (and Fireworks) create a set of thumbnails.

#42 Aligning Text and Images

A flexible, reliable technique for combining images and text is to align an image either right or left. Aligning an image will flow text to the right (for a left-aligned image) or to the left (for a right-aligned image) of the image (**Figure 42a**).

Figure 42a Left-aligned *(top)* and right-aligned *(bottom)* images.

You can also define a horizontal and vertical buffer space between images and the text that flows around them.

Aligned images are associated with a paragraph of text. They are not locked in place on the page, but instead move up or down on the page with the paragraph, depending on the size of the visitor's browser window.

To align a selected image, click the Align field in the Property inspector and choose Left or Right from the pop-up menu (**Figure 42b**).

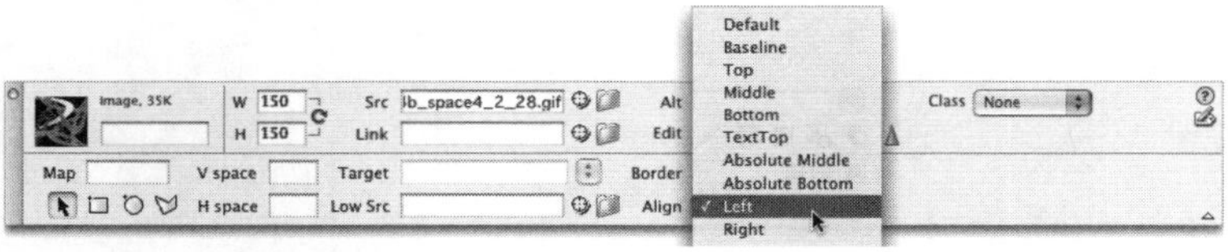

Figure 42b Left-aligning an image in the Property inspector.

When you align images in relation to paragraph text, you almost always want to define horizontal and vertical spacing to separate the edge of the image from the text. If you don't define horizontal and vertical spacing around the image, the image will bump into the text characters (**Figure 42c**).

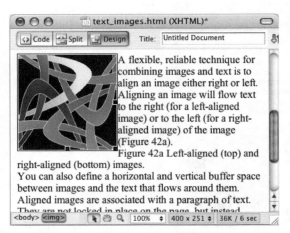

Figure 42c An image with no horizontal spacing bumps into the paragraph text.

You can assign vertical spacing to a selected image in the Property inspector by entering a value (in pixels) in the V space field. Assign horizontal spacing by entering a value (in pixels) in the H space field (**Figure 42d**).

Tip

A good standard setting for keeping images from bumping into text is 2 or 3 pixels of vertical spacing and 5 pixels of horizontal spacing.

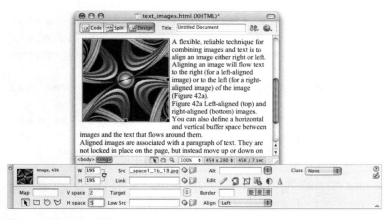

Figure 42d Assigning 2 pixels of vertical spacing and 5 pixels of horizontal spacing around an image.

Spacing around selected images appears as a blue line in the Document window. The blue line will disappear when you deselect the image.

Other Alignment Options

You might notice other alignment options in the Align pop-up menu aside from Left and Right. These options are used to align tiny images that are supposed to appear in a line of text. The ability to do this is, in large part, a holdover from an era when operating systems did not support much in the way of symbols, and it was necessary to provide a way to embed and align tiny images within lines of text. Although these evolutionary relics are still available, they are not widely used and cannot be used to flow text around an image.

#43 Defining Image Maps

In Chapter 2, "Working in the Document Window," you will find instructions on how to define links. Links can be launched from either text or images. A single image, however, can contain more than one link. Breaking an image into sections, each with its own link definition, is called *creating an image map*. Image maps are used in a variety of Web graphics. One obvious example is an actual map, where a visitor can click a location (such as a state, city, or restaurant) and launch a link that opens a new page to display the area of the map where he or she clicked.

Image maps are often used to create navigation bars from a single image. A wide, thin graphic that stretches across the width of a page, for instance, can be divided into many links by creating multiple image maps on the same graphic.

Image map sections can be rectangles (including squares), ovals (including circles), or polygons (multisided shapes).

To create an image map from an image already embedded in your page, follow these steps:

1. Select the image to which the image map will be applied.

2. Click the Rectangular, Oval, or Polygonal Hotspot tool in the lower-left corner of the Property inspector (**Figure 43a**).

Polygonal Hotspot tool
Oval Hotspot tool
Rectangular Hotspot tool
Pointer Hotspot tool (used to select already created hotspots)

Figure 43a Hotspot tools in the Property inspector.

3. Draw a rectangle or oval by simply clicking and dragging the image with the appropriate hotspot tool selected. Polygonal hotspots are a bit trickier. To define a polygonal hotspot, choose the Polygonal Hotspot tool, and click (*do not click and drag*) spots on the image. The hotspot is defined as you create additional points (**Figure 43b**).

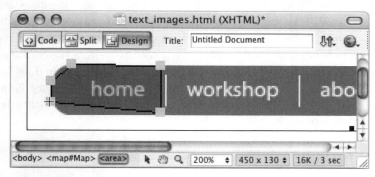

Figure 43b Defining a polygonal hotspot.

4. You can move a defined hotspot by selecting it with the Pointer Hotspot tool and dragging the whole hotspot. To delete a hotspot, select it with the Pointer Hotspot tool and press the Delete key. To resize a hotspot, select a single handle and drag it (**Figure 43c**).

Figure 43c Editing the shape of a polygonal hotspot.

(continued on next page)

5. As soon as you finish drawing a hotspot, or if you select a hotspot with the Pointer Hotspot tool, the Property inspector adapts and displays properties just for the selected hotspot, not for the entire selected image (**Figure 43d**). In the Map field, you can name your map (or just accept the default name). In the Link field, click the blue Browse for File (folder) icon to navigate to a file in your Web site, or enter a URL in the field. In the Target field, choose _blank if you want the link to open in a new browser window. If you don't want to open the link in a new browser window, don't enter anything in the Target field. You can define a separate Alt tag for the hotspot by selecting a tag from the Alt menu. Or, you can enter alternate text in the Alt field in the Property inspector. (For an explanation of Alt tags, see #40, "Making Images Accessible with Alt Tags.")

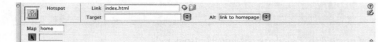

Figure 43d Defining a hotspot.

Hotspots are widely supported in browsers, but they appear differently in different browsers. Like everything involved in your Web pages, you should try to test your hotspots in several viewing environments.

#44 Placing Photoshop Files in Web Pages

Web browsers do not support the native Photoshop (PSD) format. Until the advent of Dreamweaver CS3, this meant that Web designers had to convert those Photoshop files into Web-compatible JPEG, GIF, or PNG formats *in Photoshop* before placing them in Dreamweaver Web pages. Saving Photoshop files to JPEG, GIF, or PNG format is easily done in Photoshop itself, which shares with Adobe Illustrator the Save for Web utility—a powerful, interactive environment for fine-tuning the conversion of non-Web-compatible formats to Web-compatible formats. One obvious limitation to this system is that Web designers without access to Photoshop can't handle Photoshop files. Or, for those designers with access to Photoshop, this required launching a separate program to convert the Photoshop file to a JPEG, GIF or PNG format.

Dreamweaver CS3 uses a different module to convert Photoshop files to Web graphics. The new Image Preview dialog in Dreamweaver is pulled out of Fireworks. Designers who are familiar with the Save to Web features in Illustrator and Photoshop will find the interface familiar, and Web designers who are used to Fireworks will find the Image Preview dialog very similar to that in Fireworks. With the Image Preview dialog now part of Dreamweaver, you can place a Photoshop file directly in a Web page in Dreamweaver. Or, you can copy and paste selected content directly from Photoshop to Dreamweaver.

Note
Unfortunately, the ability to copy and paste from Adobe Photoshop is not yet (in CS3) implemented for Adobe Illustrator vector images.

Dreamweaver converts that file to a JPEG, GIF, or PNG format, and retains the original Photoshop file. Dreamweaver's Image Preview window is similar to the Save for Web window in Photoshop and Illustrator, and provides a comprehensive set of options for converting Photoshop files to Web-compatible formats.

Tip
For a discussion of the pros and cons of different Web-compatible image formats, see #38, "Preparing Images for the Web."

Which Format Is Best?

The Image Preview dialog allows you to convert Photoshop images to JPEG, GIF, Animated GIF, or one of three levels of PNG format. Photoshop images are generally best for photos as they manage color better than GIF, and better than most PNG formats. If you convert your image to a JPEG, use the Quality box to select image quality. Higher-quality image files are larger and take longer to download, but they maintain color and fidelity better than lower-quality images. Selecting the Progressive check box enables images to "fade in" as they download into a browser, instead of appearing line by line, starting at the top of the image.

GIF images are small and efficient, but of low quality. Animated GIFs can be used to display multiple images as animation, but

(continued on next page)

GIF images allow you to make one color transparent. This feature is usually used to make the image background transparent, and can be applied by choosing Index Transparency from the Transparency pop-up menu (**Figure 44a**).

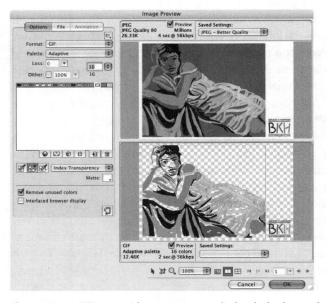

Figure 44a A GIF image with transparency applied to the background.

Progressive downloading (for JPEG images) and interlacing downloading (for GIFs) allows images to "fade in" when they download into a browser, instead of appearing line by line. These options are available in the preview window for selected GIF or JPEG conversions, and are generally a more pleasant way to display large images as they download into a viewing environment.

Photoshop files that are converted to Web-compatible file formats in Dreamweaver display a small PS (Photoshop) icon in the Edit area of the Property inspector when the image is selected. Click the Photoshop icon to edit the Photoshop source file.

To place a Photoshop file in a Dreamweaver Web page, follow these steps:

1. Click in the Web page at the point at which the image will be inserted.

2. Select Insert > Image. The Select Image Source dialog appears. Navigate to a Photoshop (PSD) file, and click the Choose button. *Or*, you can copy an image from Photoshop into your operating system clipboard, and then paste that image into the Dreamweaver document window.

3. After you place a Photoshop (PSD) file, *or* copy and paste selected content from Photoshop into Dreamweaver, the Photoshop image appears in the Image Preview dialog. An easy way to compare file formats and settings is to switch to the "4-Up" view, where you can see and compare different options. To view four options at once, click the 4-Up icon to display four different preview windows (**Figure 44b**).

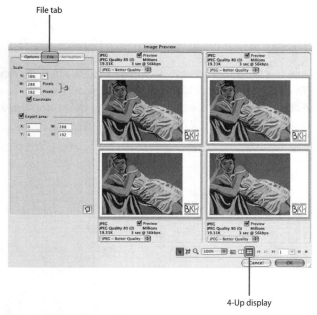

Figure 44b Displaying four preview windows.

(continued on next page)

are not a likely option for converted Photoshop images.

PNG format allows you to constrain file size by using either the 8 or 24 options, or you can maximize quality with PNG 32. The PNG 8 option generates a smaller image, with a limited palette of colors. The PNG 24 format provides a virtually unlimited range of colors, and the PNG 32 format, which produces even larger sized files, allows for more control over brightness. The Image Preview dialog relieves you of a need to understand the technical aspects of these different PNG formats. Simply preview your image in various formats, and choose a conversion format based on how it looks in the preview section of the dialog and the download time associated with a conversion.

For more discussion of Web-compatible image file formats, see #38, "Preparing Images for the Web."

A Good Feature...
with a Missing Link

The ability to import
Photoshop files or to
copy and paste from
Photoshop into Dream-
weaver is a new feature
introduced by Adobe
into Dreamweaver CS3.
One might expect that
when you click the Pho-
toshop icon in the Prop-
erty inspector and open
that image in Photoshop,
upon resaving the Pho-
toshop file, the image
in the Web page would
automatically update.
However, that does not
happen. Instead, the
file has to be resaved,
and then reinserted into
Dreamweaver. Or, you
can copy and paste

(continued on next page)

4. Select one of the four preview windows using the Pointer tool. With a preview window selected, you can experiment with cropping or with different settings (**Figure 44c**).

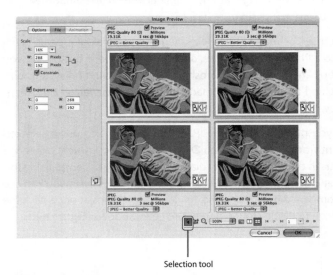

Selection tool

Figure 44c Selecting a preview window.

5. You can use the Crop tool to crop an image in a selected preview window. To crop an image, click the Crop tool, and click and drag on any of the corner or side anchors to crop the image before conversion (**Figure 44d**).

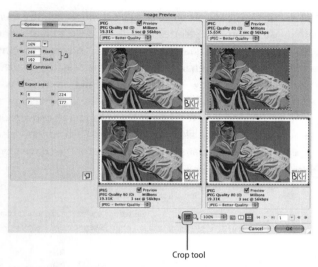

Crop tool

Figure 44d Cropping a Photoshop image before converting it to a Web-compatible format.

Note

The Export area check box must be selected in the File tab before you can convert.

(continued on next page)

the edited image from Photoshop back into Dreamweaver, replacing the edited image. You *can* automatically apply editing changes to images that you edit in Fireworks, where clicking the Done button not only saves the Fireworks file, but updates the image in Dreamweaver.

To update a Photoshop image in your Web page, you can open it in Photoshop by clicking on the PS icon in the Property inspector, but then you still have to copy and paste the image from Photoshop into Dreamweaver to update that image in the Web site.

6. In the Options tab, select one of your four preview windows, and experiment with different formats, palettes (for GIF and PNG formats), and settings. As you adjust image quality, color palettes, and other options, you'll see a preview of the generated image in the selected preview window. Each preview window has a pop-up menu from which you can select from seven presets. These presets provide a good range of options, and are a good way to experiment with image conversion if you are not fluent in image file format features. Each window also displays the file size and estimated download time for the conversion. **Figure 44e**).

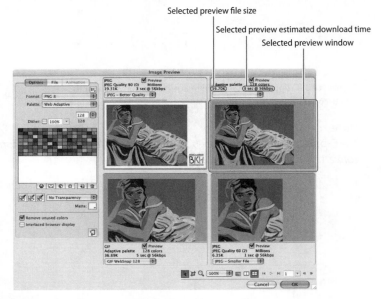

Selected preview file size

Selected preview estimated download time

Selected preview window

Figure 44e Previewing four different image conversion options for high-quality JPEG, smaller-file JPEG, 8-color PNG, and GIF.

7. After you define the image format and settings for the converted image, click OK. The Save Web Image dialog opens. Assign a filename in the Save As box, and click Save. If the Image Tag Accessibility Attributes dialog opens, enter a short description of the image in the Alternate text box and click OK.

CHAPTER SIX

Planning and Embedding Site Elements

If your Web site is just a handful of pages, you can manage the content on each page more or less independently. That is, you can open each page, one at a time, and edit content.

However, when your site is more complex than just a few pages (and most are), you'll find Dreamweaver's features for managing embedded site content essential.

Dreamweaver allows you to create page elements, such as navigation bars, page banners, icons, and bits of text (for example, a copyright notice), and then embed these elements in any of your site's pages. These elements can be text, images, or a combination of text and images. There are two different kinds of site elements in Dreamweaver:

- Template pages provide a common design for all pages to which they are attached.

- Library items are objects that are embedded in any number of pages.

Both template pages and library items are *updatable sitewide*. This means that if you embed a logo, copyright notice, text, or image (or a combination of text and images) in your pages and you edit the template or library item that defines that object, *all pages* that are created from the template or that have the library item embedded in them will update automatically.

This chapter explains how to create template pages, how to generate new pages from a template, how to define library items, and how to embed library items in pages.

#45 Creating Template Pages

The central concept in creating and using template pages is that they include *editable* and *noneditable* regions. Noneditable template page regions are parts of the page that are defined in the template; they can only be edited in the template file. Once they are edited, they apply to all pages with which the template is associated.

Let's explore a typical template page. The page might have a banner across the top, a navigation bar on the left, and a copyright/navigation bar at the bottom. The template defines these elements. A region in the middle of the page could function as an editable region—and would have different content on every page on the site (**Figure 45a**).

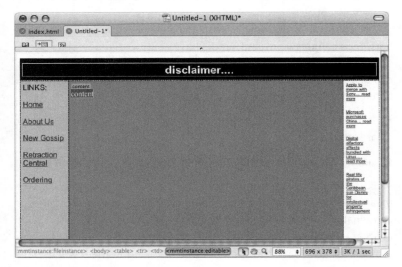

Figure 45a A page that uses a template.

To create a template page, choose File > New to open the New Document dialog. Select Blank Page in the category (left side) column of the dialog, and click the HTML Template in the Page Type page column. If you wish, you can use one of the available layouts in the Layout column as a basis for your template, but normally you will want to select <none> in the Layout column in order to design your template from scratch. Click the Create button (**Figure 45b**). The template page will open.

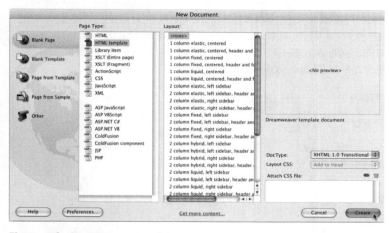

Figure 45b Creating a new template.

The Document window for a template page looks just like the Document window for a regular page, except that <<Template>> appears in the title bar of the window.

Tip
Just to review where we are in the process: At this stage, you are defining the template page. This page will then be used to generate an unlimited number of actual site pages, based on the template you are defining.

There are two steps to creating a template page. First, create all the *noneditable* elements that will appear on *every* page. Then, create the editable regions.

Two (Too) Many Meanings for "Template"

The term "template" in Dreamweaver refers to two different things:

1. Dreamweaver provides "Blank Template" pages. You can see these in the Blank Template category of the New Document dialog. These are pages designed by Dreamweaver that you can put content into.

2. Dreamweaver *templates* are pages you design that have both editable and noneditable regions. It is these templates that are being discussed here.

When you define template pages, you don't draw editable regions; you take existing page elements (such as a table, table cell, or CSS layer), and you make these elements editable when you use the template to generate new pages. Therefore, the standard strategy for creating a template page is to first create a page layout using either CSS layers or tables. You can then place noneditable content in tables or table cells (if you are designing with tables) or in a CSS layer.

To make an element on the page—like a table, table cell, or AP object—into an editable region, click inside the element, and then choose Insert > Template Objects > Editable Region (**Figure 45c**). The New Editable Region dialog will open. Enter a name for the region in the Name field, and then click the OK button to define the region.

Figure 45c Defining an editable region on a template page.

In addition to editable regions, template pages can (but do not have to) include noneditable content. Any text, image, or media that you place on a template page that is *not in an editable region* becomes part of every page generated by that template.

You might, for example, have copyright information that appears at the bottom of every page generated by the template, or you might have contact information or a navigation bar on every page. You can include on a template page anything you can put on a regular Web page. Just keep in mind that any content that is not in an editable region will appear on *every* page generated using the template you are defining.

Template pages can be rather complex. Optional editable regions can or cannot be on a page. This is at the discretion of the designer of the individual page. For example, you might make it possible for content authors to include an image on a page, but you might not want to display an empty image box if no image is available. In this case, you could include an optional editable region where the image would appear—if there was one.

Repeating regions are used for highly complex commercial data-driven sites. They allow data to pour into a template page, and for editable regions like tables to expand to accommodate the data. Again, this kind of site development is complex and beyond the scope of this book. However, if you were embedding a table to display the results of a search query that might have any number of results (between 1 and 10, for instance), you could design a repeating region that would display anywhere from 1 to 10 search results. You can even embed editable regions inside other editable regions.

Once you have defined a template page with a noneditable region (if you wish to make it part of the template) and at least one editable region, you're ready to save the page and use it to generate an unlimited number of pages. Save the page by choosing File > Save. The Save As Template dialog will open. Enter a short description in the Description field, and enter a filename in the Save as field (**Figure 45d**).

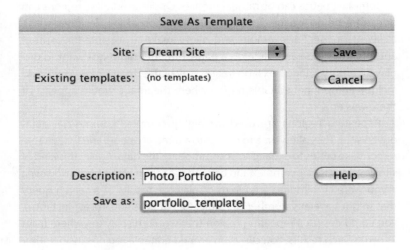

Figure 45d Saving a template.

Note

By default, Dreamweaver will automatically create a Templates folder on your site and will save all template pages in that folder. Dreamweaver templates are saved with a .dwt file extension.

#46 Generating New Pages from Templates

To create a new page from a template, choose File > New to open the New Document dialog. In the New Document dialog, click the Page from Template category on the left side of the dialog. In the Site column, click the site on which you are working (if you have more than one). In the Templates for Site column, click (don't double-click) one of the templates. You can preview any available template page by clicking it to see a thumbnail image of the template in the Preview area of the dialog (**Figure 46a**).

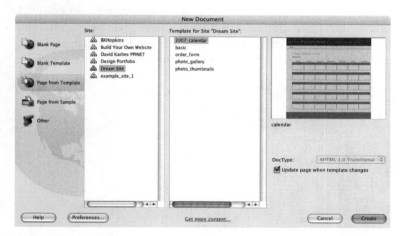

Figure 46a Viewing templates for a Web site.

Templates as a Web Design Tool for the Masses

In addition to saving time, page templates allow designers who don't know much about Dreamweaver to edit or create Web pages. In a typical setup, a design guru (like you!) will design the templates. Page formatting and many page elements are noneditable elements of the template. A single table cell, table, or CSS layer is set aside as an editable region, and novice designers can copy and paste text and/ or place images in this editable region.

Adobe distributes a special program called Contribute that can be used *only to add or change content* in editable regions of Dreamweaver templates. Contribute is used in environments where many people are contributing content to a site that was designed by someone using Dreamweaver.

Tip

The Update page when template changes check box is selected by default. Most of the point of designing with templates is that when you edit the template, all pages generated by that template will update to reflect the changes to the template file. So, normally you will leave this check box selected.

After you select a template, click the Create button in the dialog to generate a new page. The new page will include all noneditable content (images, text, or media) that is part of the template. To enter unique content for the generated page, click in the editable region for the template, and enter text, images, or other content. If there are multiple editable regions, click in every region and enter content (**Figure 46b**).

Figure 46b Entering an image and text in an editable region.

After editing the editable region on a template page, save the page by choosing File > Save. Assign a filename, and save the page as you would any Web page.

#**47** Updating Templates

Your Web site consists of 2,304,451 pages. Okay, let's say it consists of 230 pages. In any case, consider this scenario: You need to change an element that appears on every page. That might be a newly designed company logo, an updated news notice, or a drastic personnel change.

In any case, you can easily update all the affected pages on your site in minutes by editing the template on which your site pages are based.

Then comes the slow part: After you update a template, you still need to upload all changed pages to your server. Because this is confusing to many people, I included a separate How-To at the end of this chapter on managing template updates at a remote server (see #51, "Uploading Templates and Library Items").

You can easily open and edit a template either from the File menu or from an open page that is associated with the template. If you have a page open that was generated from the template you want to edit, choose Modify > Templates > Open Attached Template (**Figure 47a**).

Figure 47a Opening a template page.

If a page associated with your template is not open, choose File > Open, and navigate to the template file in the Open dialog.

Updating Templates Takes Time

In this technique's scenario, I posed the hypothetical and exaggerated example of a Web site with millions of pages. However, even if your site has only hundreds of pages, Dreamweaver takes some time to update pages when a template is changed.

With the template page open, edit the noneditable regions (that is, any region that is not defined as an editable region). After you edit the page content, choose File > Save. The Update Template Files dialog will open. The dialog lists all files generated from the template you are saving. If you only want to update some of the pages generated from the template, select the files to update. Then click the Update button to apply the changes in the template to all (or selected) pages (**Figure 47b**).

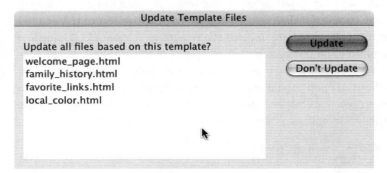

Figure 47b Saving a template page and updating files.

The Update Pages dialog will then appear. Here, you can select the Show log check box to generate a list of affected pages (**Figure 47c**). When the update process is completed, click the Close button to close the Update Pages dialog.

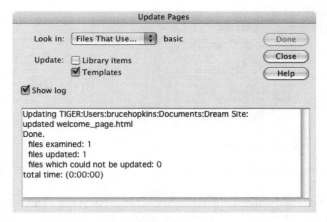

Figure 47c Viewing a log of updated pages.

#**48** Creating and Placing Library Items

Library items are like templates in that they are associated with pages and they update sitewide. They are different in that library items are *embedded in a page*, and they can be placed in pages generated by templates, in template pages themselves, or in just a regular Web page. Another way to think of it is that templates are entire pages, while library items are just individual elements that can be inserted into any page.

Library items can be text, images, or even media plug-ins (like a Flash animation), or they can be a combination of these. For example, if you want to place an article on every page or on several pages, you could embed the article as a library item. When the time comes to update or change the article, you can edit the library item and update the article on every Web page in which it is embedded.

You can define a library item two ways. You can drag content from an existing page into the Library window, or you can define library content from scratch in the Library window.

Library items and templates often provide alternative ways of accomplishing similar tasks. Both can be updated. For example, you could create all pages on a Web site using a template that has company contact information on the page as noneditable content. If the company moves, you can update the address on every page generated from a template by making a change to the noneditable content in the template.

Another approach would be to embed company contact information as a library item. When the contact information changes, you can update the library item and the change will be reflected in the content of every page in which the item is embedded.

I personally tend to avoid using *both* templates and library items. When you mix and mesh the two, it becomes confusing to keep track of where the content is coming from. If the main object is to create consistent-looking pages, templates are often the best option for updating content. If you're embedding updatable content for an existing site or for a site where consistent page layout is not critical, library items are often an easy way to embed updatable content in your site.

To drag existing content into the Library window, follow these steps:

1. Choose Window > Assets to view the Assets panel.

2. In the column on the left side of the Assets panel, click the Library icon (the last icon in the column). Any existing library items will display (**Figure 48a**).

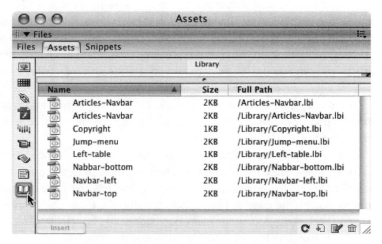

Figure 48a Viewing the Library category of the Assets panel.

3. Click and drag to select the content on your page that will become a library item. Drag the content to the top window in the Library category of the Assets panel (**Figure 48b**).

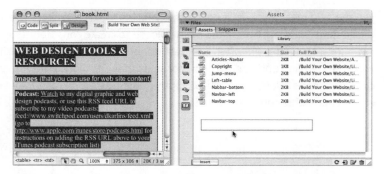

Figure 48b Dragging content to the Library category of the Assets panel.

Planning and Embedding Site Elements

Note

When you drag content to the Library category, a warning dialog alerts you that the content may not appear the same when it is embedded in a page. See the accompanying sidebar for an explanation of this occurrence.

4. Enter a name for the new library item by clicking the item in the Names list at the bottom of the Library category of the Assets panel and entering a new name.

You can also create a library item from scratch. There are four icons at the bottom of the Library category of the Assets panel (**Figure 48c**):

- The Refresh Site List icon generates an updated list of library items associated with the open Web site.

- The New Library Item icon creates a new library item.

- The Edit icon opens a window to edit the selected library item.

- The Delete icon deletes the selected library item.

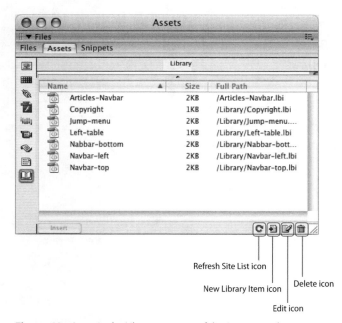

Figure 48c Icons in the Library category of the Assets panel.

Library Items Adopt the CSS Style of the Page in Which They Are Embedded

Library items may look different on different pages because they adopt the CSS styles of the page in which they are embedded. Normally, this is no big deal. If all the pages on your Web site use the same CSS styles for formatting, then the embedded library item will look the same on every page.

But there's another wrinkle in the process: If you edit a CSS style, it will change how the embedded library items with that style attached to them will appear on Web pages. This is not a bad thing; it just means that library items are governed by an external style sheet applied to a page the same way other page objects are.

See Chapter 7, "Formatting Page Elements with CSS," for an explanation of how to manage sitewide formatting with CSS.

To create a new library item, follow these steps:

1. To generate a new library item, first create any kind of content (including text or images) in the Document window. Select that content and drag it into the top half of the Library category of the Assets panel. As you do, a new library item named Untitled appears in the bottom half of the Library category of the Assets panel.

2. Create a new name for the library item by clicking Untitled in the bottom half of the Library category of the Assets panel, and entering a new name for the new library item.

3. To create additional library items, click the New Library Item icon at the bottom of the Library category in the Assets panel.

Once you create a library item, you can drag it from the Library category of the Assets panel to any page on your Web site. Do this by simply dragging the library item to an open page in the Document window (**Figure 48d**).

Figure 48d Dragging a library item to a page.

#49 Updating Library Items

When you edit a library item, the item will update on every page in which it is embedded. To edit a library item, click the item in the Library category of the Assets panel, and click the Edit icon at the bottom of the panel. The library item will then open in the Library Item window, which looks like the Document window, except that the title bar includes <<Library Item>> (**Figure 49a**).

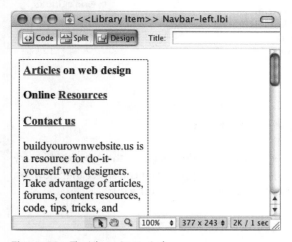

Figure 49a The Library Item window.

The Library Item window is just like the Document window, except that it is used to edit library items. You can edit in the Library Item window just as you would in the Document window. After you edit the library item in the Library Item window, choose File > Save to save your changes. The Update Library Items dialog will then appear with a list of all pages in which the library item is embedded.

Library Items Can Include Anything

Library items are really HTML snippets (blocks of HTML code) that are embedded in other HTML pages. Therefore, you can include text, images, and even media plug-ins in a library item.

Library items are saved with an .lbi file extension. They are proprietary objects in Dreamweaver—you can't edit a library item if you open a site with Adobe GoLive or another Web editing tool.

You can select some of the pages in the list to update, or simply click the Update button to update the entire list (**Figure 49b**).

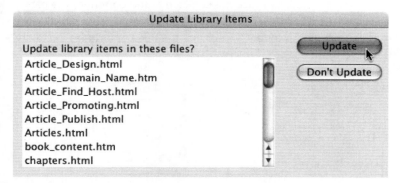

Figure 49b Updating pages with a library item embedded in them.

After Dreamweaver finishes updating pages with embedded library items, the Update Pages dialog will appear. You can select the Show log check box to see a list of all updated pages (**Figure 49c**).

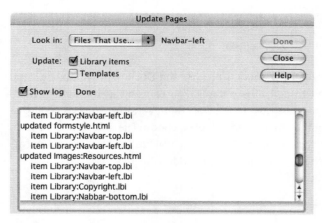

Figure 49c Viewing a list of updated pages with an embedded library item.

#50 Including Navigation in Templates and Library Items

It's often useful to create templates with navigation bars in them, or with navigation bars that are library items, which can be embedded in any page. Whether you place navigation bars (or just regular links) in templates or library items, Dreamweaver will make sure they link when you generate pages from a template with links, or when you pop a navigation bar onto a page by dragging a library item to that page.

Including navigation links in a template or library item works because when you create new pages from templates or embed library items in pages, any links in those templates or library items automatically get updated to reflect the location within your site's directory structure.

To appreciate the handiness of this, image a scenario where you have created dozens of Web pages from a template that included a link bar. You save those pages to different folders (directories) in your Web site. If Dreamweaver didn't update links for each saved page, the links would all be corrupted since the paths between pages are different, depending on the folder in which a page is saved.

Here's how Dreamweaver updates links in template pages and library items: When you save a page generated from a template that has links, for example, a blank dialog appears and Dreamweaver prompts you to "update links" (**Figure 50a**).

Figure 50a Updating links when a page generated from a template is saved.

Dreamweaver Manages Files, Folders, and Links

When Dreamweaver inserts a library item on a page in *any* subfolder (directory) on a site, it updates any links in that library item relative to the location where the file is saved. And, when a page made from a template is saved in any subfolder, the links are updated relative to the saved location.

You'll notice that the Template folder and the Library Item folder don't even get uploaded to the server. They are used to *generate* pages only. Library items and templates are not actually Web pages, and don't get uploaded to your server. Management of links sitewide is one of the biggest reasons to use Dreamweaver and one of the things it's really good at doing.

Note

A navigation bar *refers simply to a set of links (sometimes in a one-row, multiple-column table) or sometimes just a set of links separated by spacing or vertical bars ("|"). The essential point is that you can create this navigation bar and use it in library items or template pages.*

As long as the links are defined correctly for a template or library item, you can use embedded library-item navigation bars or template-page navigation bars to easily create global uniform navigation bars on your pages. And these navigation objects can be easily updated, either by editing a template or by editing a library item.

#51 Uploading Templates and Library Items

One of the things my clients and students (and fellow developers) find most confusing in Dreamweaver is managing changes to templates and library items on a remote server. Here's why: When you edit a library item (or template), all pages associated with that library item or template are automatically updated *on your local site*. These pages are *not* automatically updated *at the remote server*. Because this can be confusing and frustrating, I'll walk you through the process.

When you save changes to an edited template, you are prompted to update all pages generated by the template. When you edit and save changes to a library item, you are prompted to save all changes to pages in which the library item is embedded.

This changes the pages on your local site. You *cannot* update the pages on your remote server by simply uploading the revised template or library page. It is not possible to update pages on a remote server by uploading a library item or template page. You update the pages on your local server, and then you have to *upload all changed pages* to the remote server.

How do you keep track of which pages need to be uploaded to the remote server after you edit them by changing a template or library item? One way is to actually pay attention to the logs generated by Dreamweaver that list the changed pages. These logs can be copied and pasted into a word processor for easier management.

I usually use this trick: After I update files by editing a template or library item, I sort my files in the expanded Files panel by modified date. Do this by clicking the Modified column title in the Files panel (**Figure 51a**).

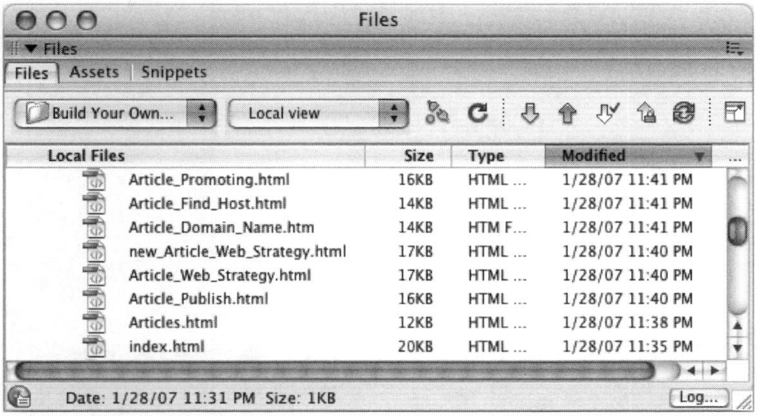

Figure 51a Files sorted by the date on which they were modified.

Managing Local-to-Remote Transfers

Dreamweaver provides some sophisticated tools for uploading files to the remote server that match various criteria, including uploading all files that are newer on the local site than they are on the remote server.

These tools are explored in Chapter 1, "Creating a Web Site," #8, "Transferring Files Between Local and Remote Sites," and #9, "Synchronizing Remote and Local Content."

With the files sorted by modified date, Shift-click to select all the files modified on the current date. Click the Put File(s) icon in the Files panel to upload the files to the remote server (**Figure 51b**).

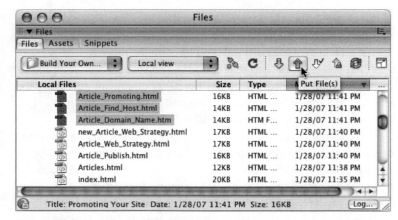

Figure 51b Uploading selected (recently changed) files.

CHAPTER SEVEN

Formatting Page Elements with CSS

In Chapter 4, "Designing Pages with Absolute Placement Objects," and in Chapter 5, "Working with Text and Images," I explained how to use CSS (Cascading Style Sheets) for page design and text formatting. Beyond controlling page positioning and text format, you can use CSS to format almost any element on a page.

You can use CSS to format:

- Body tags that define pagewide formatting, such as page background, margins, and default font color, type, and size

- HTML tags ranging from images to tables

- Links with special attributes

- Special printable page formatting

Before you dive into formatting with CSS, a note of caution: Don't *rely* on CSS styles to make your page readable in a browser. You should apply styles for formatting in such a way that even if the style is *not* supported in a browser, the page still works. In other words, don't rely on styles to convey essential information. For example, do not create white text on a black background; if your visitors' browser does not support the black background, they will only see (or more to the point, *not* see) white text on a white page. On the other hand, if you place red text on a yellow background, visitors will see that red text on a white page, even if the yellow background is not supported by their browser. If for some reason your style sheet link is broken or corrupted at your remote server, visitors will see the default style.

#52 Formatting Page Elements with Style Sheets

Large, professional Web sites are formatted with *external style sheets*. External style sheets are files that define formatting for an unlimited number of Web pages. These files provide several levels of control over a Web site that cannot be achieved any other way:

- They ensure consistent formatting and a consistent look and feel throughout your Web site.

- They are a powerful productivity tool. They allow you to instantly attach a complex set of formatting rules to a new or existing Web page.

- They allow you to *update* or edit the look of an entire site almost instantly.

External style sheets are separate files, with a .css file extension. You generate them automatically in Dreamweaver using the CSS Styles panel. You can open a CSS file in its own Document window and examine the CSS code if you choose. In any case, Dreamweaver takes care of creating and editing the CSS file as you define the CSS attributes.

The concept works like this: A single style-sheet file (or sometimes a few files) stores all the information needed to format every Web page to which that style sheet is attached. When a visitor opens the HTML page to which a CSS file is attached, the browser automatically looks to the CSS file to find out how to display the page. This process does not take any noticeable time. Visitors to your Web site simply see a page with formatting, even though the formatting rules are stored in a separate (CSS) file.

The easiest way to generate a CSS (style sheet) file in Dreamweaver is to create a new style. As you do, you'll have the option of including that style in a new CSS file. In the following steps, you'll define a style and save it in a new style sheet. These steps can be adapted to generate a CSS file using any tag as the initiating style.

1. In the Document window, click the New CSS Rule icon at the bottom of the CSS Styles panel (**Figure 52a**). The New CSS Rule dialog will appear.

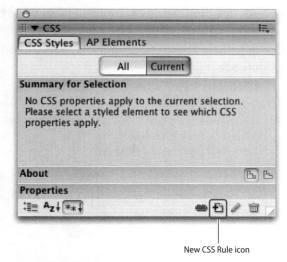

New CSS Rule icon

Figure 52a The New CSS Rule icon in the CSS Styles panel.

2. In the Selector Type area of the dialog, click a radio button to choose the type of style you wish to define.

- Choose Class to apply formatting rules, which are independent of tags, to any selected text. If you are creating a Class style, enter a name for your style in the Name box.

(continued on next page)

Updating CSS Throughout a Site

If you have created a huge Web site with hundreds or even thousands of pages and have *not* attached a style sheet or multiple style sheets to the pages, Dreamweaver does not offer a quick one-step process for this. So, attach style sheets *as you create pages*. Once you have attached a style sheet to multiple pages on your Web site (even thousands of pages), you can instantly update the appearance of the pages by editing your style sheet. Simply follow these steps:

1. Open any page that has the style sheet attached.

2. In the CSS Styles panel, click the triangle next to the attached CSS file to toggle to expand it. A list of files will display.

(continued on next page)

- Choose Tag to define formatting for HTML elements, such as headings, paragraphs, images, tables, or pages. When the Tag radio button is selected, every HTML tag appears in a pull-down menu next to the Tag field.

- Choose Advanced (IDs, pseudo-class selectors) to define links, among other things.

Note

Heading tags that are listed in the Property inspector as Heading 1, Heading 2, etc., are listed by their HTML tag names here (e.g., h1 equals the Heading 1 tag).

3. Click the Define in radio button, and choose (New Style Sheet File) from the menu (**Figure 52b**).

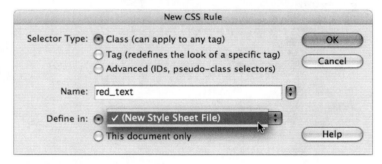

Figure 52b Generating a new style sheet.

4. Click OK in the New CSS Rule dialog. The Save Style Sheet File As dialog will appear. This is a typical Save As dialog, except that it automatically generates a CSS file with a .css file extension and translates any formatting you define into CSS coding. Navigate to the folder in which you want to save the style sheet, and enter a filename in the Save As field. Then click Save to generate the new CSS file.

5. After you click Save, the CSS Rule Definition dialog for the style you are defining will open. Different categories in the Category list offer formatting options for different kinds of page elements. Now, simply note that there is a wide array of formatting options available, and that whatever formatting options you define will be encoded into the CSS file you named and saved in Step 4 (**Figure 52c**).

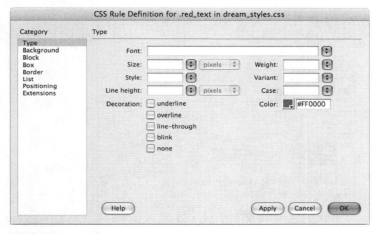

Figure 52c The CSS Rule Definition dialog.

Note
See Chapter 5, "Working with Text and Images," and especially #37, "Defining Inline Text Attributes with CSS," for an explanation of available text format options. Creating CSS rules for other page elements is explored in several techniques in this chapter.

6. After you create a style sheet file, the file is visible in the CSS Styles panel. When you expand the CSS file (click the triangle next to it to

(*continued on next page*)

3. There are several ways to edit style attributes. In the bottom half of the CSS Styles panel, the Properties area displays formatting for selected styles. You might find it intuitive to simply double-click any of the formatting attributes to edit the style. Or, you can double-click the style itself in the All Rule area in the top half of the panel to open the CSS Rule Definition dialog, and edit the style in that dialog. (This familiar dialog looks just like the one you used to define the style.)

4. When you click OK in the CSS Rule Definition dialog (or make changes in the bottom half of the CSS Styles panel), the changes are automatically applied to all pages to which the edited style sheet file is attached.

Should You Apply CSS to Table and Image Tags?

Maybe. Keep in mind that if you apply a style to the Table tag—for example, a yellow background color—that style applies to *all* tables on your site (assuming you are using an external style sheet). I find this a bit heavy-handed. I like to apply different background colors to tables within my site, so I usually don't define a table style. When I manage very large sites, I usually define a CSS style for the Table tag because I don't want or need to custom-define background colors for every table.

On the other hand, I normally define a style for images. I'll use a style to define the border thickness and color that appears around the images. I like to keep this style standard throughout my site. For more information, see #55, "Formatting Image and Page Styles."

toggle to expand), all styles within the style will display. Formatting attributes display at the bottom of the CSS Styles panel (**Figure 52d**).

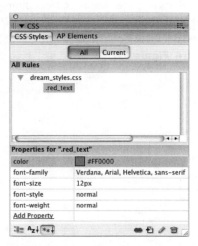

Figure 52d Viewing a CSS style in an attached style sheet in the CSS Styles panel.

After you create a CSS file, you add styles to the file *without* creating a new style sheet. So, after you have created your first style and generated a CSS file, the *next* time you create a new style, click the New CSS Rule icon in the CSS Styles panel, but this time simply accept your existing CSS file in the New CSS Rule dialog (**Figure 52e**).

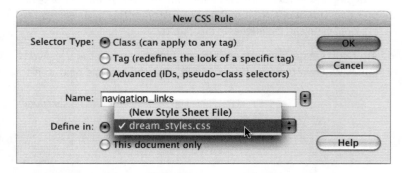

Figure 52e Defining additional styles for an existing CSS file.

As soon as you define a style in an external style sheet, that style is available to be attached to any new or existing page. To attach a style sheet to a page, open the page, and click the Attach Style Sheet (link) icon in the CSS Styles panel. The Attach External Style Sheet dialog will open (**Figure 52f**).

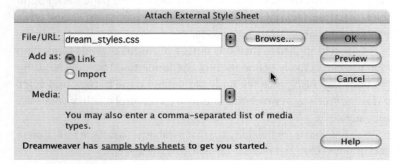

Figure 52f Attaching a style sheet to an open page.

Navigate to your CSS file in the File/URL field, choose the Add as Link option, and click OK to attach the style sheet.

As you add and edit styles to the CSS file, all pages to which the CSS file is attached will update to reflect the new formatting.

#**53** Defining Page Style Using the Body Tag

The Body tag is a special tag. It underlies all other tags on a page. Think of the Body tag as the tag you will use to define page layout options such as margins and background color. The Body tag defines page background color (or pattern file), page margins, default font characteristics, and other attributes that apply to an entire page.

A CSS style applied to the Body tag is a powerful, sitewide formatting tool. You can actually define most of the formatting for your site using the Body tag. Also, since the Body tag defines page background color, this is another way in which this one style can control much of your site's appearance.

To define a style for the Body tag that establishes a default font, a page background color, and margin specs, follow these steps:

1. Click the New CSS Rule icon in the CSS Styles panel. The New CSS Rule dialog will open.

2. In the Selector Type area of the dialog, click the Tag radio button. From the Tag pop-up menu, choose body (**Figure 53a**).

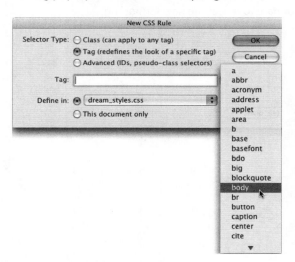

Figure 53a Defining a Body tag.

Don't Define Too Much

Normally, when you define a Body tag, you won't define font size or attributes such as italics or boldface. Remember, a Body tag provides the *basic* default formatting for text. You'll want different tag styles to look different, and normally you'll define font size as you define the Paragraph tag (p) and heading tags (h1, h2, and so on). Any attributes you define for these tags will override the Body tag definition.

For example, if you defined the Body tag to display default text in dark-gray Arial font, then *all* styles included in the style sheet would by default appear in dark-gray Arial font. Heading 1 (h1) text would be larger than Paragraph (p) text. All text would be dark-gray Arial font by default.

3. In the Define in area of the dialog, either choose an existing or new CSS file from the pop-up menu (both options are available), or click the This document only radio button to define a Body tag that will format only the currently open page.

4. Click OK in the New CSS Rule dialog to open the CSS Rule Definition dialog for your Body tag. In the Type category, choose a font from the Font pop-up menu.

5. In the Background category of the CSS Rule Definition dialog, choose a swatch from the Background color area to select a background color for your page(s) if you want something other than the default white color (**Figure 53b**).

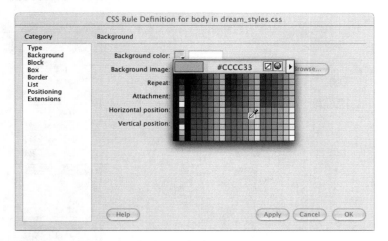

Figure 53b Defining page background color.

6. If you wish, you can define a tiling background image instead of a background color. Do this in the Background category by clicking the Browse button to locate and choose an image file.

(continued on next page)

Page Formatting Overrides External Styles

All CSS formatting can be either embedded in a single page or attached to that page via an external style sheet. In fact, the "Cascading" in Cascading Style Sheets refers in part to the fact that different levels of styles defer to each other. CSS applied to a page overrides CSS applied through an external style sheet.

This fact may set off an alarm for astute readers: If page formatting over-rides formatting from external style sheets, the page formatting will "trump" the style rule applied via the attached style sheet. In other words, if you have *local* styles defined in a page, they override formatting applied by an attached external style sheet.

180

Tip

*By default, background images tile horizontally (on the Y-axis) and verti-
cally (on the X-axis). In other words, they fill the entire page background
when you attach them to a Body tag style. You can use the Repeat pop-
up menu in the Background category of the CSS Rule Definition dialog to
change the default settings. Options include Repeat-Y, which repeats the
image only along the Y-axis (vertically), or Repeat-X, which repeats
the image horizontally. Or, you can choose No-Repeat to not repeat the
background image at all.*

7. Different browsers display different default page margins. To define a
set margin, select the Box category in the CSS Rule Definition dialog,
and enter values for top, left, bottom, and right margins (**Figure 53c**).

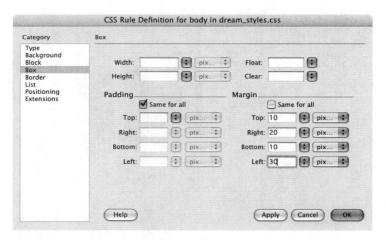

Figure 53c Defining page margins.

#54 Formatting HTML Text Tags with CSS

There are six HTML heading styles: h1 (Heading 1) to h6 (Heading 6). Defining custom styles for these heading styles and the Paragraph tag is at the heart of designing a look and feel for your Web site. If you have formatted print documents with programs like Adobe InDesign, QuarkXPress, or even Microsoft Word, you probably understand the basic concept of defined styles. This concept applies to Web design as well.

Defined styles provide uniform text formatting, either on a page or, when the styles are defined in an external style sheet, throughout your site. For example, every major heading on your site might be 14-point Arial and purple. All paragraph text might be 10-point Arial, dark gray, and double-spaced.

The following are some of the more useful formatting options available in the CSS Rule Definition dialog:

- The Type category defines font, size, weight, style (italic or roman), and line height.

- The Background category defines a background color or image behind type.

- The Block category defines features such as word spacing, letter spacing, vertical and horizontal alignment, and indentation.

- The Box category defines width, height, padding, and margins for CSS layout elements.

- The Border category defines the style, thickness, and color of borders around text.

- The List category defines the type of bullet or numbering.

- The Positioning category defines positioning of CSS layout elements.

- The Extensions category defines page breaks, cursor display (when a cursor is moved over selected text), and special effects like blur or inversion.

Before walking through the process of defining CSS styles for HTML tags, it might be helpful to quickly review the difference between styles for HTML tags and *class* styles that are independent of HTML tags. When you assign formatting to selected text using the Property inspector, you often generate what is called a *custom* or *class* style to apply a set of formatting rules to any selected text. What happens is that behind the scenes, Dreamweaver CS3 automatically generates custom class styles whenever you apply formatting like font, size, or color to selected text using the Property inspector. These custom class styles can be applied to any selected text. The drawback, in contrast to HTML tag styles, is that custom class styles do not apply automatically to any text, while HTML tag styles automatically attach themselves to any text with that tag. All text you enter will normally have the Paragraph tag, so when you define a style for the Paragraph tag, the tag is automatically applied to much of the text on your page or Web site.

To prepare your site for CSS formatting applied to paragraph and heading text, the first step is to go through your Web page(s) and assign HTML tags to text if you have not done so already. This is covered in Chapter 5, #35, "Formatting Text with HTML Attributes."

With HTML tags applied to text on your page(s), you're ready to define CSS styles that will apply to these tags. To do this, follow these steps:

1. Click the New CSS Rule icon in the CSS Styles panel (**Figure 54a**). The New CSS Rule dialog will open.

Figure 54a Creating a new style by clicking the New CSS Rule icon in the CSS Styles panel.

2. Here, you will first choose an HTML tag for which you will define a style. In the Selector Type area of the dialog, click the Tag radio button. From the Tag pop-up menu, choose the tag for which you are defining a style (**Figure 54b**).

Figure 54b Defining a new Heading 1 (h1) style in the New CSS Rule dialog.

3. In the Define in area of the dialog, either choose a style sheet from the menu, or click the This document only radio button.

Note

See #52, "Formatting Page Elements with Style Sheets," for an explanation of defining styles in external style sheets.

4. Click OK in the New CSS Rule dialog to open the CSS Rule Definition dialog. The formatting options here may be familiar if you have been working with formatting in Dreamweaver. If not, a summary of available formatting options is in the "CSS Formatting Options" sidebar.

5. After you define a CSS style, you can click the Apply button in the CSS Rule Definition dialog and see how the style looks when applied to the page. When you finish defining a CSS style for a tag, click OK. The style definition is automatically added to an external style sheet, or to your page (depending on the selection you made in the Define in section of the New CSS Rule dialog when you began defining the style).

Why Would You Want to Create Styles for "This Document Only"?

One of the big advantages of external style sheets is that they apply a uniform set of formatting attributes to all Web pages to which they are attached. That provides a consistent look and feel for your Web site. And external style sheets can be quickly and easily edited, with the effect of reformatting an entire Web site.

But what if you have a page that you do *not* want to have the same look and feel as the rest of your site? This might be a Web page with content not integrally related to the site content. Or, it might be a page that you want to have its own unique look. In that case, you could define styles and choose the This document only radio button.

#55 Formatting Image and Page Styles

In addition to defining CSS styles for HTML text tags (like paragraph or heading text), you can also use CSS styles to define the appearance of *any* HTML tag. This can get somewhat complex and can involve CSS formatting that is beyond the scope of this book. But you can also define CSS styles for commonly applied tags, like images or tables.

It often makes sense to define styles for the Image tag and the Table tag. You can define border thickness, color, background color, and other features of tables or images.

To define a style for the Image or Table tag, follow these steps:

1. Click the New CSS Rule icon in the CSS Styles panel. The New CSS Rule dialog will open.

2. In the Selector Type area of the dialog, click the Tag radio button. From the Tag pop-up menu, choose the tag for which you are defining a style. The Image tag is img. The Table tag, intuitively enough, is table (not shown) (**Figure 55a**).

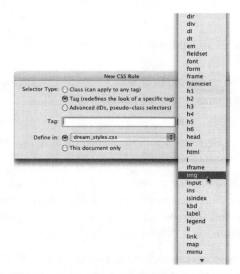

Figure 55a Defining a new style for all images in the New CSS Rule dialog.

3. In the Define in area of the dialog, either choose a style sheet from the menu, or click the This document only radio button.

Note

See #52, "Formatting Page Elements with Style Sheets," for an explanation of defining styles in external style sheets.

4. Click OK in the New CSS Rule dialog to open the CSS Rule Definition dialog. Most likely you will not be applying any options from the Type category in the CSS Rule Definition dialog. Most formatting options applying to text are not relevant for defining image or table properties. However, you can define attributes in the Background (background color or image), Box (borders), or Border (styled borders) categories to customize images or tables throughout your site.

5. After you define a CSS style, you can click the Apply button in the CSS Rule Definition dialog and see how the style looks when applied to the page. When you finish defining a CSS style for a tag, click OK. The style definition is automatically applied to an external style sheet, or to your page (depending on the selection you made in the Define in section of the New CSS Rule dialog when you began defining the style).

#56 Applying CSS to Links

By default, links are displayed in blue type (or blue borders for images). Visited links are purple. And active links (ones in the process of being opened) are red. And, by default, all links display with underlining. You can customize the appearance and behavior of links using CSS. CSS formatting is applied to links so ubiquitously that sophisticated Web browsers expect to find features like rollover display or nonunderlined links on sites.

CSS formatting allows you to define four link states. In addition to the three HTML states (regular, visited, and active links), CSS can define a fourth state—hover. Hover state displays when a visitor hovers his or her mouse cursor over the link.

There are many style approaches used for hover link formatting. Sometimes designers turn off underlining for all other link states but will have it appear when a visitor hovers over a link (**Figure 56a**). Other times, designers define a color or background-display change when a link is hovered over.

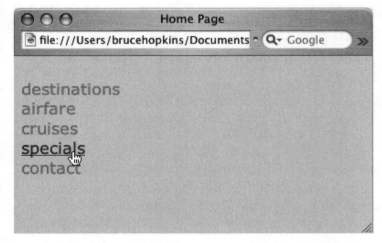

Figure 56a An underscore appears under the hovered-over link, but is not visible in links that are not hovered over.

Normally, you will *not* define font or font size to link style definitions. That's because links inherit the font and font size of the HTML formatting tag assigned to the text. For example, Heading 1 (h1) text might include text that is a link. Or, paragraph text might include some text that functions as a link. In either case, the font and font size will not change for the link text.

There are two schools of thought on whether or not links should always appear with underlining.

The "accessibility" school argues that displaying underlined links in default colors (blue for unvisited links, purple for visited, and red for active) is universally understood, and makes links as unambiguous and accessible as possible for a wide range of visitors in the largest set of viewing environments.

The "aesthetic" school argues that such default-colored, underlined links are boring, traditional, and unnecessary—that today's sophisticated Web visitors can distinguish links as long as consistent formatting (usually a unique font color that is used only on links) is applied.

Between the two extremes, you have the option of having links that, for example, display underlining when rolled over or that use the traditional blue color, but do not display underlining.

Formatting Page Elements with CSS

What normally *will* change is font color and maybe font attributes like underlining or background. So, when you define CSS styles for links, you will normally avoid defining font or font size and instead define font color and special attributes (like underlining or background).

To create a CSS formatting *rule* (style) for links on a page (or in a Web site, via an external CSS file), follow these steps:

1. With a page open, click the New CSS Rule icon in the CSS Styles panel. The New CSS Rule dialog will open.

2. In the Selector Type area of the dialog, click the Advanced (IDs, pseudo-class selectors) radio button. From the Selector pop-up menu, choose one of the four link states: link, visited, hover, or active.

Note
You will define each of the four link states separately. Link (unvisited link), visited, hover, and active are each a unique style. And, in order for these link styles to be interpreted correctly in browsers, you need to create them in the order listed above. If you need to reorder styles, you can click on any style in the CSS Styles panel and drag it up or down in the panel to reorder.

3. In the Define in area of the dialog, either choose a style sheet from the menu, or click the This document only radio button to define styles that will be applied only to the open page (**Figure 56b**).

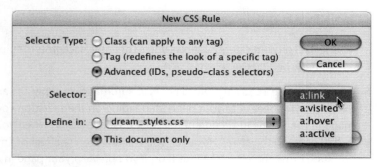

Figure 56b Defining an unvisited link style.

(*continued on next page*)

4. Click OK in the New CSS Rule dialog to open the CSS Rule Definition dialog for the link state you are defining. The formatting options you are likely to use for a link state are as follows:

- The Type category allows you to define a color for the selected link state using the Color box. The check boxes in the Decoration area allow you to turn underlining on or off. By default, links are underlined, so select the None check box to turn underlining *off*. Simply deselecting the Underline check box will not turn underlining off (**Figure 56c**).

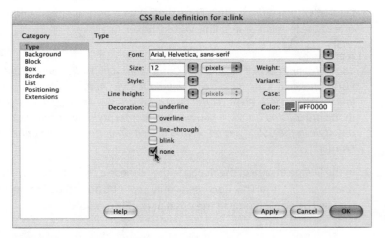

Figure 56c Turning underlining off for a link state.

- The Background category allows you to define a background color or image behind the selected text.

5. After you define a CSS link style, click OK to automatically apply it to an external style sheet or to your page (depending on the selection you made in the Define in section of the New CSS Rule dialog when you began defining the style). However, you will not see the effect of any link state other than link (unvisited) until you preview your page in a browser. To do this, choose File > Preview in Browser, and if more than one browser is available, choose a browser from the submenu.

#**57** Defining CSS for Printable Pages

Many times, you will want to define different styles for printed pages than you use for monitor display. For example, you might change a light-colored font to black for printing or remove page or table background images.

You do this by creating and attaching a separate CSS file—a separate external style sheet—that holds print formatting rules. You can also preview how a page will look when printed in the Document window.

To define a new style sheet for printer output, you can create an external style sheet with CSS tag styles, link styles, or even class styles. Then you name the external style sheet that contains the print styles print.css (**Figure 57a**).

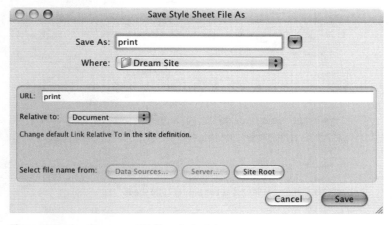

Figure 57a Creating a new CSS file called print.css.

Tip
Review the other techniques in this chapter for all the information you need to create an external style sheet.

Useful Print Formatting

Useful special formatting features for printed versions of pages include the following:

- No colored print: Many people print documents on laser printers that print only in black.

- No backgrounds: They interfere with readability.

- Different margins: They accommodate standard 8½-inch-wide paper.

- Page breaks: They break content into discrete sections.

After you define a distinct set of printable styles in the print.css style sheet file, attach the print.css file as the printer style sheet:

1. Open the Web page to which the printer CSS styles will be attached.

2. In the CSS Styles panel, click the Attach Style Sheet (link) icon.

3. In the File/URL field of the Attach External Style Sheet dialog, click Browse and navigate to the print.css file. In the Add as area, leave the Link radio button selected.

4. From the Media pop-up menu, choose print (**Figure 57b**).

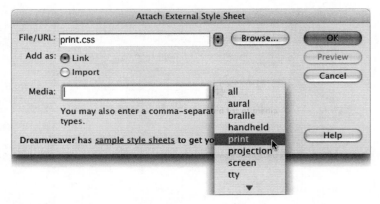

Figure 57b Defining print.css as the printer style sheet.

You can attach multiple style sheets to a page and define different CSS files to different media using the same process. To preview your printer styles, click the Render Print Media Type icon in the Style Rendering toolbar (**Figure 57c**). If the Style Rendering toolbar is not visible, choose View > Toolbars > Style Rendering.

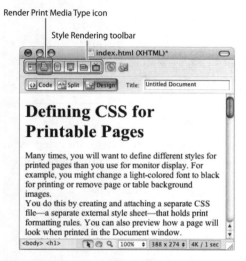

Render Print Media Type icon

Style Rendering toolbar

Figure 57c Previewing the applied print style sheet.

One class style attribute that is only relevant to print style sheets is the page break attribute. To define a page break in the printed version of a Web page, follow these steps:

1. Open the Web page to which the printer CSS styles will be attached.

2. Click to place your insertion point where the page break should occur on the printed version of the Web page.

3. Click the New CSS Rule icon in the CSS Styles panel. The New CSS Rule dialog will open.

4. In the Selector Type area of the dialog, click the Class (can apply to any tag) radio button. From the Name pop-up menu, choose a style name, such as page_break.

5. In the Define in area of the dialog, choose your print.css external style sheet from the pop-up menu.

(*continued on next page*)

#57: Defining CSS for Printable Pages

6. Click OK in the New CSS Rule dialog to open the CSS Rule Definition dialog (**Figure 57d**).

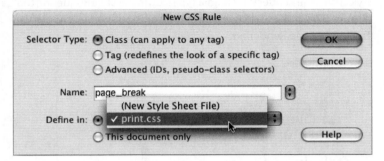

Figure 57d Creating a page break style.

7. In the CSS Rule Definition dialog, choose the Extensions category. In the After field, choose always from the pop-up menu (**Figure 57e**).

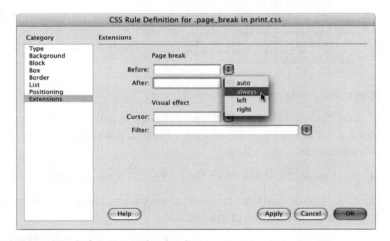

Figure 57e Defining a page break style.

After you define a page break style, you can apply it anywhere by inserting the style from the Property inspector (**Figure 57f**).

Figure 57f Inserting a page break style.

CHAPTER EIGHT

Collecting Data in Forms

Forms provide a uniquely interactive element in a Web site. Through a form, you not only *convey* content, you also *collect* content. This content can range from orders for products, feedback on site content, service requests, and subscription list sign-ups, to surveys, forum discussions, and opinion polls.

Some form content is managed using scripts that run in the visitor's browser. Such scripts are referred to as *client-side* data handling. A jump menu, for example, collects data (the page a visitor to your Web site wants to go to, for example), and acts on that input (by opening a new Web page). And the client-side script does that *without* sending any data to a server. Other forms collect data and send it to a server, where scripts on the server manage the data. These are called *server-side* forms. Most form data is managed by server-side scripts. One example of a server-side script is a mailing list form. Visitors enter information (at least an e-mail address, and maybe more) into a form. That data is then stored in a database on a remote server. It can be accessed to send out mailings.

In short, this chapter explains how to design two kinds of forms:

- Forms that manage data in the browser (client-side)

- Forms that connect to scripts at a server (server-side)

In this chapter, you will learn how to connect a form to an existing server script (but not how to program the scripts), and I'll throw in some tips on where you can find already-packaged server scripts to handle things like search forms, sign-up mailing lists, and discussion forums.

Adobe has implanted several Spry tools in Dreamweaver CS3 that make it easy to define forms with attached validation scripts. These scripts test form content before it is submitted to make sure certain rules are met; specifically in the case of the new Spry form fields, they require that a visitor fill in a form field before submitting the form. So, for example, if you want to require that visitors fill in the E-mail Address field in a form before they submit it, you can place a Spry Validation Text Field in your form. The last four How-Tos in this chapter explain how to use these Spry validation widgets.

#58 Creating Jump Menus

One great example of a client-side form is a jump menu—where a visitor selects a page in your Web site from a pop-up menu. A jump menu works because script (in this case, using JavaScript) acts on a form and effects an action (in this case, opening a new Web page) based on data the visitor entered into the form (the page he or she chose from the jump menu). Dreamweaver creates jump menu forms and automatically generates the required JavaScript.

Jump menus are an efficient and attractive way to allow visitors to navigate your site. You can provide a long list of target links in a jump menu without using much valuable space on your Web page (**Figure 58a**).

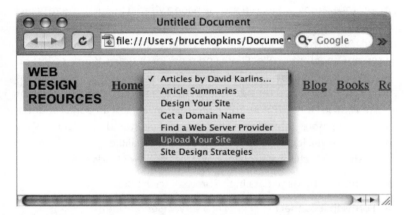

Figure 58a Providing a long list of navigation options in a jump menu.

Jump menus use JavaScript to handle form input. In other words, when a visitor chooses a Web page (or other link, like an image file) from the jump menu, a script generated by Dreamweaver opens the selected page in a browser window. You don't need to worry about this JavaScript. But you can look at it in Code view in the Document window if you're interested in seeing what the JavaScript looks like (or, if you know how to, you can edit the generated JavaScript in Code view of the Document window).

To create a jump menu, follow these steps:

1. With a page open in the Document window, choose Insert > Form > Jump Menu. The Insert Jump Menu dialog will open.

2. In the Text field of the Insert Jump Menu dialog, enter the text that will appear in the jump menu.

Note
The text you enter in the Text field defines the name of the menu item. You don't have to enter anything in the Menu Item field; that information is automatically generated by what you type in the Text field.

3. In the When selected, go to URL field, either enter a URL for a link, or use the Browse button to navigate to and select a file on your site (**Figure 58b**).

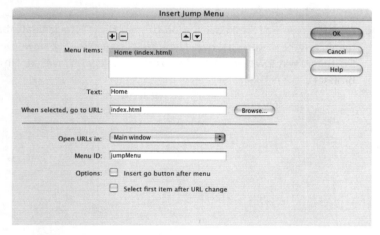

Figure 58b Defining a jump menu link.

4. Define additional jump menu options by clicking the "+" button in the dialog, and entering new text and URL. Repeat to enter as many jump menu options as you need. Delete an item from the jump menu by selecting it and clicking the "−" button.

(continued on next page)

5. To change the order of an item in the jump menu list, select the item and use the Up and Down arrow buttons in the dialog to move the selected item up or down in the list (**Figure 58c**).

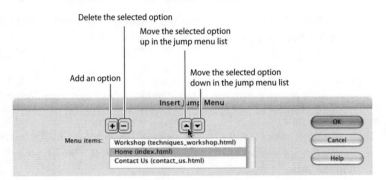

Figure 58c Moving a jump menu link up in the list of options.

6. After you define all the links in the jump menu, click OK to generate the menu. Test the menu in a browser (you can't test it in the Dreamweaver Document window because the jump menu works with JavaScript in a browser).

To edit an existing jump menu, you need to open the behavior that Dreamweaver created to control the jump menu. View the Behaviors panel (choose Window > Behaviors). Click the jump menu to select it. As you do, you will see Jump Menu listed in the second column of the Behaviors panel. Double-click it to reopen the Jump Menu dialog and edit the jump menu (**Figure 58d**).

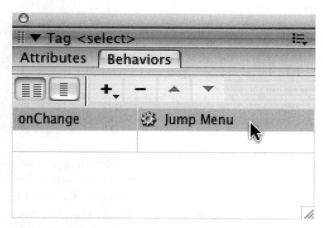

Figure 58d Opening the Jump Menu dialog by double-clicking Jump Menu in the Behaviors panel.

The Jump Menu dialog looks just like the Insert Jump Menu dialog, and you can add, remove, or move menu items or change menu options in this dialog.

#59 Embedding Forms Linked to Server Databases

Helpful CGI Scripts, Forms, and Hosting Services

In addition to the FreeFind search service, there are a few other useful sources for scripts and hosting to manage form data. These sites provide various sets of available forms and scripts that collect Web statistics, collect feedback, manage message boards, generate survey polls, allow guestbook listings, and store and manage e-mail lists.

- www.thefreecountry.com
- www.cgispy.com
- www.sitegadgets.com
- http://cgi.resourceindex.com

You can find online database and script services by searching for "CGI scripts." CGI stands for Common Gateway Interface, and is the protocol (system) that is used (with options for various programming languages) to manage form input.

There are many online services that provide you with server-side databases and scripts, and these services often host online databases and scripts as well (or else they tell you how to copy them to your server). For example, there are services that allow you to host a mailing list at their server. They provide you with HTML that you copy into your Web page. That HTML contains the coding for the form, as well as a connection to a script at a server that manages the data put into the form.

One of the most popular, easy-to-use, reliable, and professional online form-and-script services is the FreeFind search engine service (www. freefind.com). FreeFind will index your site (compile a list of all words in your site in a database), and provide you with a form that visitors can enter search criteria into.

Follow these steps to place a FreeFind search field on an open Dreamweaver Web page. You can also use them as a model for using similar services.

1. Go to www.freefind.com, and enter your e-mail address and your site's URL. Click the Instant Signup button. FreeFind will e-mail you a password and login and a link to the FreeFind control center. Follow the link, log in, and click the link for a free search field (or you can choose one of the more elaborate, ad-free pay options).

2. Click the Build Index tab in the FreeFind control center, and then click the Index Now link. FreeFind will build a database, at the FreeFind server, of all the words in your Web site.

3. Click the HTML tab and choose one of the four available types of search field forms you can use (the options are Site Search Only, Site and Web Search, Web Search Only, or Text Links).

4. Select all the HTML for the search field you selected, and choose Edit > Copy from your browser menu.

5. Back in Dreamweaver, click in the Document window to set the place where the search field will be inserted. Then choose View > Code to switch to Code view. Don't worry about any of the code you see—your cursor is in the spot you clicked in Design view. Choose Edit > Paste to place the HTML code, and switch back to Design view to see the search field (**Figure 59a**).

Note

The form copied from FreeFind includes hidden fields, indicated by icons in the form. These fields have information that directs search queries to the index FreeFind prepares for your particular site.

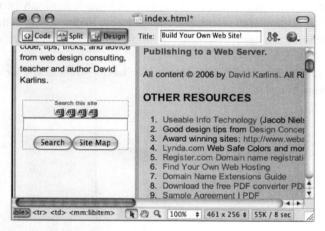

Figure 59a Placing a search field from FreeFind.

Test your search field in a browser. The search field form has fields and buttons. You can reformat the fields and buttons using the techniques for defining form and form field attributes covered in the rest of this chapter. In other words, you can customize the way this form looks—you just can't delete any of the form fields. Further techniques in this chapter will cover how customization works, so you can customize forms you get from CGI hosts.

Sending Form Content via E-mail —Pro and Con

The easiest way to collect form content is to have the content sent to an e-mail address. This is the model used in this technique. The advantage is that it requires no scripting on your part. The downside is that it requires the person submitting the form to have an installed e-mail client on his or her system. Although many users who have Internet access on their system have an e-mail client as well, people using public computers at schools or libraries will not have access to e-mail clients. For some applications, this is a problem.

#60 Defining a Form in Dreamweaver

Form data is collected using different kinds of form fields. Text is entered into text boxes or text areas. Options can be selected from sets of radio buttons. Data can be uploaded using file fields. And forms are submitted (or cleared) using Submit (or Reset) buttons.

None of these form *fields*, however, works without a *form*. It's important to be conscious of this. Many of my students get frustrated trying to figure out why their sets of form fields aren't doing anything when the problem is that those form fields are not nested inside a form.

Further, a page can have more than one form. That's often not a good idea from a design standpoint, but you can imagine situations when you might give visitors a choice of different forms to fill out.

To create a form in an open Web page in Dreamweaver, simply click to place the location of the form, and choose Insert > Form > Form. The form will display as a dashed red box. The Property inspector displays the form name.

Make sure you have clicked *inside the form* before you add any form fields (**Figure 60a**)!

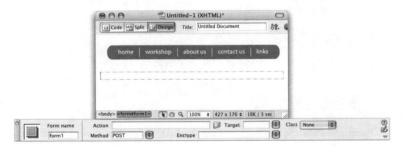

Figure 60a A form placed on a page in Dreamweaver.

Forms can be a big hassle for visitors with disabilities. Form accessibility issues include making it easy for disabled visitors (who, for example, cannot use a mouse) to move from field to field in a form, and to easily select form fields. Dreamweaver CS3 promotes accessibility in many ways, including form design. If you enable accessibility preferences for form design, Dreamweaver will prompt you to enter accessibility features for each form field as you place it in the form.

To activate prompts for accessibility options in forms, choose Edit > Preferences (Windows) or Dreamweaver > Preferences (Mac), and select the Accessibility category. Select the Form objects check box if it is not already selected (**Figure 60b**).

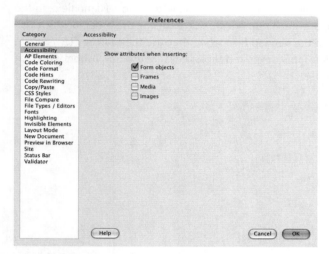

Figure 60b Activating prompts for accessibility options when designing forms.

With form accessibility options activated, Dreamweaver will prompt you with the Input Tag Accessibility Attributes dialog when you insert a form field into a form. The accessibility options allow for visitors to fill out the form without using a mouse, or if they are relying on reader software, to have an identifying label read to them.

Server-Side Script Developer Resource

Setting up a server database and generating scripts on it to manage data is beyond the scope of this book, but is covered in detail in *Macromedia Dreamweaver 8 Advanced for Windows and Macintosh: Visual QuickPro Guide,* by Lucinda Dykes (Peachpit Press).

You can enter a label in the Label field in the Input Tag Accessibility Attributes dialog, and use the radio buttons in the Style and Position areas to format and position the tag (**Figure 60c**). In the Access key field, you can enter a key (normally a letter) that visitors can use to select that field. For example, you might assign the letter N to a Name field. In the Tab index field, enter a numerical value to define the order in which visitors will tab to the defined field when they use their Tab key to navigate between fields. Tab indexes and access keys are used by visitors who cannot use a mouse.

Figure 60c Defining access features for a form field.

Caution
Support for access keys is not standardized in all browsers, and so designers are divided on the usefulness of access keys to make forms more accessible.

#61 Defining a Form Fieldset

A fieldset is a design tool used to draw boxes around sections of a form. Fieldsets are particularly useful if you have a long form. Long forms tend to be intimidating or confusing, and by breaking groups of fields into boxed fieldsets, you can make your form more inviting and less overwhelming.

You can also use fieldsets to emphasize a set of fields in a form. For example, if there is some information that is required or that you particularly want to collect, you can enclose that group of fields in a fieldset (**Figure 61a**).

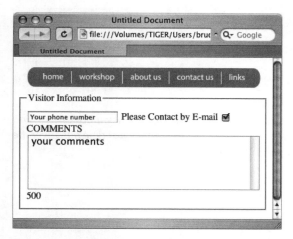

Figure 61a A group of fields set off in a form by a fieldset.

To place a fieldset in a form, first make sure your cursor is inside the form. You don't need to worry, initially, about the placement of the form *fields* you want to enclose in the fieldset. You can copy and paste them into the fieldset after you create it. Or, you can click and drag to select the fields you want to include in the fieldset, and then create the fieldset—that way, the fields are automatically enclosed in the fieldset.

Fieldsets Are for Design Purposes

Don't get overly confused about the role of fieldsets. They do not affect how a form collects and processes input. And they are not the same as creating a new form. Each form collects a set of data and sends it somewhere—usually to a server database where it is processed. Separate forms can send data to separate databases. Fieldsets, on the other hand, simply draw boxes around sections of a single form to help organize form content to make it more accessible to users.

With your cursor inside a form, choose Insert > Form > Fieldset. The Fieldset dialog appears. In the Legend box, type a name that will appear at the top-left corner of the fieldset. This is the label that visitors will read when they see the form in their browsers (**Figure 61b**).

Figure 61b Assigning a legend to a fieldset.

Tip

You can edit a fieldset legend right in the Document window. There is no need (and no way) to reopen the Fieldset dialog; just type right over the existing fieldset label to change it.

#62 Placing Text Fields and Text Areas

Text fields are used to collect all kinds of information in a form. E-mail addresses, phone numbers, purchase prices, zip codes, names, and a wide variety of other data can be entered into text fields.

Text *fields* collect a single line of text. Text *areas* can collect multiple lines of text. Text areas are used to collect comments, descriptions (like descriptions of problems for online service forms), guestbook entries, and other text that requires more than one line.

To place a text field or a text area in a form, follow these steps:

1. With your cursor inside an existing form, choose Insert > Form > Text Field.

   Tip
   If you have enabled accessibility options, you'll be prompted to enter them before defining the field itself. See #60, "Defining a Form in Dreamweaver," for an explanation of these accessibility features.

2. After you place the text field, you can define the field attributes in the Property inspector (**Figure 62a**). In the TextField field, enter a name that will help you remember the content of the field. In the Char width field, enter the number of characters that will display on a single line in a browser as a visitor enters data.

Figure 62a Defining a one-line text field, with input formatted using a CSS Class style.

3. In the Max chars field, you can enter the maximum number of characters that can be entered into the field.

4. In the Init val field, enter text that will appear in the field in a browser before any user interaction. Sometimes (but not always) form designers will include text like "your e-mail goes here" in a field. Visitors then replace that content with their own entry.

(continued on next page)

5. In the Type options, choose Single line for a text field, and Multi line for a text area. If you choose Multi line, the Num Lines field appears in the Property inspector. Enter the number of lines that will display in the form (you cannot define a limit for the number of characters that are entered). In the Wrap pop-up menu, choose default, so text wraps in the browser window.

6. Enable the Password option to display content entered into the field as asterisks.

7. You can use the Class pop-up menu to attach a CSS Class style to the field.

Tip
See Chapter 5, "Working with Text and Images," and in particular #37, "Defining Inline Text Attributes with CSS," for a discussion of how to create and apply custom class styles.

As you define text field or text area attributes in the Property inspector, they display in the Document window.

#63 Placing Check Boxes

You can place any number of check boxes in a form. Check boxes provide two options for visitors: checked or unchecked. And you can define a default state for a check box as either checked or unchecked.

To place a check box in a form, follow these steps:

1. With your cursor inside an existing form, choose Insert > Form > Checkbox.

Tip
If you have enabled accessibility options, you'll be prompted to enter them—including a label—before defining the field itself. See #60, "Defining a Form in Dreamweaver," for an explanation of these accessibility features. Do enter a label (check boxes need text to tell visitors what they are checking, and generated labels do this well); the label will display to the left or right of the check box.

2. After you place the check box, if you did not generate a label, you need to enter some text in the form (normally to the right of the check box) that identifies what is being selected when a visitor selects the check box.

3. In the Property inspector, enter a name for the check box in the check box field. In the Checked value field, enter a value to go with the check box name. For example, if the check box is asking if a user wants to be contacted, the check box name might be "contact," and the checked value might be "yes."

Tip
There are different styles and systems for identifying and collecting data in check boxes, and if you are designing a form in conjunction with a database programmer, check with him or her on how to manage this.

4. Select one of the Initial state option buttons to define whether the default state of the check box is checked or unchecked (**Figure 63a**).

Figure 63a Defining a check box.

Tip
You can use the Class pop-up menu to attach a CSS Class style to the field. See Chapter 5, #37, "Defining Inline Text Attributes with CSS," for a discussion of how to create and apply custom class styles.

Radio Buttons vs. Check Boxes

Radio buttons (aka option buttons) and check boxes represent two different ways to allow visitors to make selections from a set of options in a form. Radio buttons force a visitor to choose *just one* from a set of options.

One frequently encountered situation in which radio buttons are the best way to collect information is when you are collecting credit card information from a purchaser. In that case, you want him or her to select one, and just one, type of card from a list of cards you accept.

On the other hand, check boxes (aka option boxes) allow visitors to choose, or not choose, any number of options. For instance, you might ask a person filling out a form if they want to be contacted by e-mail, phone, snail mail, or text messaging. If you want to allow them to choose any combination of these options (including all or none of them), use check boxes.

#64 Placing Radio Buttons

Radio buttons differ from check boxes in that they always are organized in groups. You never have a single radio button—if you are asking a question for which a user can supply no, one, or several answers, use check boxes. The purpose of radio buttons is to compel a user to choose *one* from a *group* of options.

To create a radio button group, follow these steps:

1. With your cursor inside an existing form, choose Insert > Form > Radio Group. The Radio Group dialog appears (**Figure 64a**).

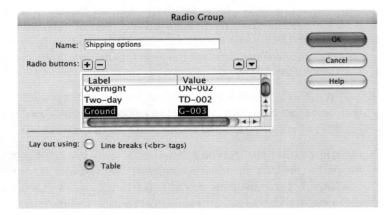

Figure 64a Defining a group of radio buttons.

2. In the Name field, enter a name that indicates *to you* the nature of the group of options. For example, if you are inquiring as to a type of shipping (Overnight, Two-day, Ground, etc.), you might call your group "Shipping_options."

3. In the Radio buttons area of the dialog, click the Label column. In the first row enter a label that will appear for visitors. Next to that label, in the Value column, enter the data that will be sent with the form. For example, a label might read "Two-day shipping" to make clear to a user what he or she is selecting. But the value sent to your shipping department might be "TD-002"—an internal code that tells them how to handle and bill shipping.

Radio Buttons Get Generated with Labels

Among the advantages of using Dreamweaver's Label dialog is that accessible labels are generated along with the radio button group and individual radio button values. There is no need for a distinct process of defining accessibility options for radio button groups if you use Dreamweaver's radio button group feature.

Collecting Data in Forms

4. In the second row, enter another label and value. Use the "+" button to add more rows of labels and values, and the "–" button to delete a selected row. Use the Up and Down arrow buttons to move selected rows up or down in the list of radio buttons.

5. In the Lay out using area, choose either Line breaks radio button (for separated rows) or Table radio button (for rows designed in a table).

6. After you define the radio button options, click OK in the dialog to generate the radio button group.

After you generate a radio button group, you can edit (or delete) radio buttons individually. If you want to add a radio button, you can copy and paste an existing one from the group and, in the Property inspector, change the Checked value (but not the Radio Button) content (**Figure 64b**).

Figure 64b Editing a single radio button.

Radio Button Group Names

Why don't you change the Radio Button information when you edit radio buttons? Because the Radio Button value defines the *group*. The values of individual radio buttons within a group can change, but the group name must be the same for all buttons in the group. You can test your radio button group in a browser; if you choose one option from within the group, all other options should become deselected. If that doesn't happen, you haven't assigned the exact same group name (in the Radio Button field in the Property inspector) to each radio button.

Because radio buttons are organized into groups, they are a little more complicated to define than other form fields. And because Dreamweaver is the ultimate Web design program, it includes a dialog (Radio Group) that manages the whole process of defining a radio button group easily.

#65 Placing Lists/Menus and File Fields

Menus and file fields are two different types of fields that can be placed in forms. Menus allow visitors to choose from a list of items. File fields allow users to upload files when they submit a form. In this How-To, we'll explore both these types of fields. (Consider this two How-Tos for the price of one—I had to sneak them both into the same How-To to keep the book at an even 100 How-Tos!)

Menus (sometimes called pop-up menus) allow visitors to choose one option from a pop-up menu.

The main difference between menus and list menus is that list menus allow users to select more than one choice from a list, while regular menus restrict users to choosing just one item. List menus are usually a confusing way to collect data and are rarely used.

File field forms allow visitors to attach files from their own computers to the form and send them along with the form.

To create a menu, follow these steps:

1. With your cursor inside an existing form, choose Insert > Form > List/Menu. You use this menu option to create *either* a menu or a list menu. Later, you will decide whether to make your menu a list menu or a regular menu.

Tip
If you have enabled accessibility options, you'll be prompted to enter them before defining the field itself. See #60, "Defining a Form in Dreamweaver," for an explanation of these accessibility features.

2. To create a list for the menu, click the List Values button in the Property inspector. The List Values dialog will appear. In the Item Label column, enter the text that will display in the menu (for example, "Alaska"). In the Value column, enter the value that will be collected and sent in the form (such as "AK"). Use the "+" button to add new items to the list and the "–" button to delete selected items. After you define the list, click OK (**Figure 65a**).

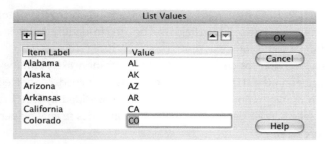

Figure 65a Defining a list/menu.

3. After you generate a menu (or list), use the Property inspector to define additional features. If you click the List option button in the Type area of the Property inspector, you can convert the menu into a list menu. And if you choose the List option, you can click the Allow Multiple check box in the Options area of the Property inspector to allow users to choose more than one option from the menu. List menus can also display more than one option at a time in the drop-down menu.

4. You can add, delete, or edit actual menu (or list) items by clicking the List Values button in the Property inspector. This will open the List Values dialog where you can edit or change the order of menu (or list) options. You can change the initially selected option in the Property inspector by clicking an option in the Initially selected area (**Figure 65b**). You can assign a CSS style using the Class pop-up menu.

Figure 65b Choosing an initially selected option for a pop-up menu.

You can allow visitors to attach files to the form submission by inserting a file field in a form. Choose Insert > Form > File Field. You can define character width in the Property inspector. A Browse button appears next to the field that the user can use to navigate to and select a file to upload.

Tip
Don't constrain the number of characters that visitors can use to define an uploaded file by entering a value in the Max chars field in the Property inspector. There is no point to setting a limit on number of characters in an uploaded file's name.

#66 Using Hidden Fields

Don't Mess with Hidden Fields in Imported Forms

If a CGI script provider gives you HTML to create a form to send data to a server, the provider will likely include hidden fields. These hidden fields define how the data is processed at the server. It's best if you don't edit or delete them.

Hidden fields send information to a server that is not entered by the visitor filling out the online form. Hidden fields can be used to identify things like the page from which a form was sent.

Normally, you won't be creating hidden fields. It's more likely that they will be included in the HTML for a form that you download, connected to an existing server script. For instance, the form provided by FreeFind to link to a search index database at their server includes several hidden fields (**Figure 66a**).

```
	<td width="136"> <form action="http://search.freefind.com/
find.html"
method="GET" target="_self">
	  <center>
	    <font size=1 face="arial,helvetica" > <a href="http://
search.freefind.com/find.html?id=43349981">
	    Search this site</a><br>
	    <input type="HIDDEN" name="id" value="43349981">
	    <input type="HIDDEN" name="pid" value="r">
	    <input type="HIDDEN" name="mode" value="ALL">
	    <input type="HIDDEN" name="n" value="0">
	    <input type="TEXT" name="query" size="20">
	    <br>
	    <input name="SUBMIT" type="SUBMIT"
value="Search">
	    <input type="SUBMIT"
name="sitemap" value="Site Map">
	    </font>
	  </center>
	</form></td>
```

Figure 66a Examining hidden field values in Code view.

If you do need to create a hidden field in a form, choose Insert > Form > Hidden Field. The field, of course, does not display in the form; it appears only as an icon in the Document window. Enter a name for the field in the HiddenField field in the Property inspector, and enter a value in the Value field.

#67 Placing Form Buttons

In order for form content to be sent to a server, there must be a Submit button in the form. Submit buttons are usually matched with a Reset button. The Reset button clears any data entered into the form, and allows the user to start fresh.

To place a button in a form, choose Insert > Form > Button. Use the Property inspector to define the button as a Submit or Reset button. In the Action area of the Property inspector, choose the Submit form or Reset form radio button (**Figure 67a**). No other settings are usually applied to Submit or Reset buttons, but a Submit button is essential if the form content is to be sent to a server.

Figure 67a Defining a Reset button.

You can define custom labels for either the Submit or Reset button by entering text in the Value field for either button. Don't get too fancy; visitors are used to seeing buttons that say something like "Submit" or "Reset." But if you enter different text in the Value field, that text will display in browsers and can be previewed in the Document window (**Figure 67b**).

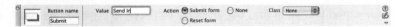

Figure 67b Creating a custom label for a Submit button.

What Are Image Fields?

Image fields are images in a form. They are sometimes used to create customized Submit or Reset buttons, but doing that takes scripting that is not available directly in Dreamweaver.

If you want to place an image field, choose Insert > Form > Image Field. When you do that, the Select Image Source dialog opens, and you navigate to and choose an image to insert into the form.

As noted, Dreamweaver CS3 does not provide any preset attributes for an image field, so when you drop an image into a form using the Image Field menu option, all that happens is that an image appears in your form. If you want that image to act as a button, you have to define a script for that button using JavaScript, or generate a JavaScript action using the Behaviors panel. This is not an intuitive process.

#68 Defining Form Actions

Form actions define how the data in a form is sent to a database on a server. Form actions are defined in the Property inspector with the *form*—not any specific form field—selected.

Tip
To select a form, click the dashed red line defining the form border. Or, click the <form> tag in the tag selector area on the bottom of the Document window.

The three important fields in the Property inspector for a form are the Action, Method, and Enctype fields. What you enter into these fields is determined by how the programmer (who set up the script and database to which the form data is being sent) configured the database and scripts at the server. Normally, Method is usually set to POST but can sometimes be set to GET; this again depends on how data is transferred to the server, and is defined by how the server is configured. The Action field contains the URL of the Web page at the server that has the script that will manage the data.

Enctype, short for "encryption type," is sometimes used to define how characters are interpreted and formatted. Your server administrator will tell you what, if any, enctype coding is required for forms to be processed by your server.

Since form actions are determined by the settings at your server, the information you enter into the Property inspector is provided by your server administrator. In the case of forms designed to match server scripts, those forms normally come with Action settings defined (**Figure 68a**).

Figure 68a Inspecting form action settings provided by a server administrator—in this case the FreeFind search engine.

If you want to collect data in a form and have it sent to an e-mail address, you can do this easily without having to work with additional server configuration or scripts. In the Action field, type mailto:(your e-mail address). From the Method pop-up menu, choose POST. In the Enctype field, type "text/plain" (**Figure 68b**).

Figure 68b Defining an action that will send form content to an e-mail address—in this case, mine!

#69 Defining a Spry Validation Text Field Widget

Many times, you will want to test content entered into a text field before you allow a visitor to submit the form. For example, you might require a visitor to enter his or her name before submitting a form. In that case, the validation test would be that a visitor could not leave the Name field blank before submitting it. The Spry Validation Text Field widget can detect a blank field and alert the person filling out the form that a name is required before the form can be submitted.

Or, you might want to test content entered into a text field even beyond determining whether or not the field was left blank. If, for example, you are collecting a zip code from the visitor, you can test to see if the data entered into the zip code field actually is a five- (or nine-) digit zip code. You can use the Spry Validation Text Field widget to verify that the data submitted in the form field conforms to the criteria you define, and again, force people to provide data that at least looks like a zip code before the form can be submitted.

To place a Spry Validation Text Field widget in a form, follow these steps:

1. *Within a form,* select Insert > Spry > Spry Validation Text Field.

   Note
   If you have accessibility prompts turned on, you will be prompted to enter accessibility attributes for the text field. Form field accessibility attributes are explained in #60, "Defining a Form in Dreamweaver." You can enter accessibility attributes, or not. Click OK to insert the form field.

2. A text field appears in your form. With the new text field selected, the Spry text field options are displayed in the Property inspector.

3. In the Spry TextField box in the Property inspector, enter a field name with no spaces or special characters (use alphanumeric characters). The field name is used to process data, and is not displayed in a browser.

4. By default, the Required check box is selected in the Property inspector. Leave this check box selected to make the text field a required field.

(continued on next page)

Spry Validation Text Field Widgets Don't Verify Actual Data

To be clear: None of the Spry Validation Text Field widgets actually looks up data and verifies that it is accurate. But they do verify that at least the correct form of data has been submitted, eliminating forms that are sent to your server that don't have required information fields filled in.

5. If you want to test data entered into the text field to meet validation criteria (for instance, the data must be in the form of an e-mail address, a zip code, a URL, or a phone number), select one of those options from the Type pop-up menu in the Property inspector (**Figure 69a**).

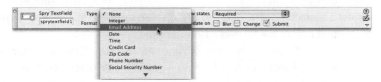

Figure 69a Choosing Email Address as the validation type.

6. Many of the preset validation types include additional options. For example, if you chose to test input for zip codes, you can test for five-digit ("US-5"), nine-digit ("US-9"), British ("UK"), or Canadian ("Canada") format. The Format pop-up menu displays these options (**Figure 69b**).

Figure 69b Selecting from zip code–testing options.

7. The Enforce Pattern check box makes it impossible for users to enter characters that do not conform to the validation rule. For example, if you define validation rules for a U.S. zip code, and a user tries to enter a letter (like A), that character will not appear in the field.

8. Use the Hint box in the Property inspector to provide initial content in the text field (for instance, you might use "youremail@email.com" to suggest to users that they need to enter a complete e-mail address), you can enter that initial text in the Hint box in the Property inspector.

9. Choose when to validate the field entry from the set of Validate on check boxes. Use Blur to validate when a user clicks outside the text field. Select Change to validate as the user changes text inside the text field. Choosing Submit validates when the user clicks the Submit button in the form.

10. Many of the preset validation types include rules of how many characters will be allowed and/or maximum and minimum values. For example, the five-digit zip code validation type will only accept five numbers. However, you can also create your own custom validation rules by choosing Integer (number) from the Type pop-up menu in the Property inspector, and then defining a maximum (Max chars) and/or minimum (Min chars) number of characters, and a maximum (Max value) and/or minimum (Min value) value for numbers entered into the field.

11. The Preview States pop-up menu in the Property inspector just defines what state is displayed in the Document window in Dreamweaver. The state that displays in a browser will depend on whether or not the user conforms to or breaks the validation rules.

12. You can edit Spry validation rules at any time by selecting the turquoise Spry Textfield label and changing values in the Property inspector.

Inside Spry Validation Widgets

Spry validation widgets were introduced into Dreamweaver CS3 by Adobe, and basically involve three elements: HTML code that defines the basic page element, JavaScript that controls interactivity (how something on the page responds to user input), and finally CSS files that define how the Spry validation widget *looks*.

All Spry validation widgets generate JavaScript to allow a form field to test input before processing the form. They also generate new CSS files that contain the formatting that defines the color, background color, text format, and so on for the form field and for form field input. These generated CSS files can be edited. For an exploration of how to edit external CSS files, see Chapter 7, "Formatting Page Elements with CSS."

#70 Defining a Spry Validation Textarea Widget

How Many Characters Are Too Many for a Form?

Some thought needs to go into how many characters you elect to allow in a comment field. My friendly HMO, for instance, allows me something like 25 characters or fewer to describe my medical condition, providing a nice way to raise my frustration level when I need to communicate with them and can't get through by phone! Hopefully, other constraints are set more reasonably. There is a point to preventing someone from sending you his or her upcoming screenplay in a comment box.

Text area fields are used almost exclusively for comments. And comments, in our digital age, are one of the more available ways that customers, clients, students, patients, and people in general communicate with organizations and businesses.

If you place a text area field in a form, you might well want to use the Spry Validation Textarea widget to define a few rules for how much content can be entered into the field.

The Spry Validation Textarea widget can be used to make a text area field required. For example, if customers are asked to describe what kind of service their laptops need, you might want to insist that they describe their problem before submitting a request for service.

To place a Spry Validation Textarea widget in a form, follow these steps:

1. *Within a form,* select Insert > Spry > Spry Validation Textarea.

   Note
   If you have accessibility prompts turned on, you will be prompted to enter accessibility attributes for the text field. Form field accessibility attributes are explained in #60, "Defining a Form in Dreamweaver." You can enter accessibility attributes, or not. Click OK to insert the form field.

2. A text area appears in your form. With the new text field selected, the Spry text field options are displayed in the Property inspector.

3. In the Spry Textarea box in the Property inspector, enter a field name with no spaces or special characters (use alphanumeric characters). The field name is used to process data and is not displayed in a browser.

4. By default, the Required check box is selected in the Property inspector. Leave this check box selected if you want to make the text area a required field.

5. Use the Hint box in the Property inspector to provide "hint" content in the text field (for instance, you might have text like "your comment here" or "comment required"). You can enter that initial text in the Hint box in the Property inspector (**Figure 70a**).

Figure 70a Defining hint content for a comment field.

6. Choose when to validate the field entry from the set of Validate on check boxes. Use Blur to validate when a user clicks outside the text field. Select Change to validate as the user changes text inside the text field. Choosing Submit validates when the user clicks the Submit button in the form.

7. Enter values in the Max chars and/or Min chars boxes in the Property inspector to constrain the number of characters that can be entered into the field (**Figure 70b**).

Figure 70b Constraining the number of characters in a text area field to no more than 500.

(*continued on next page*)

8. If you define a maximum number of characters in the text area field, you can use the Counter options to define whether to display a count of used or remaining characters (**Figure 70c**).

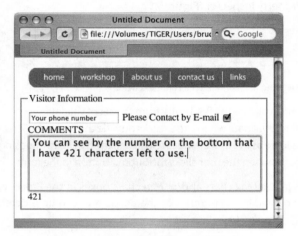

Figure 70c Viewing remaining characters in a browser.

9. The Preview States pop-up menu in the Property inspector just defines what state is displayed in the Document window in Dreamweaver. The state that displays in a browser will depend on whether or not the user conforms to or breaks the validation rules.

You can edit Spry validation rules at any time by selecting the turquoise Spry Textarea label and changing values in the Property inspector.

#71 Defining a Spry Validation Checkbox Widget

Sometimes a check box provides an option that a user can either choose or not. Do you want to receive unsolicited e-mail? Do you have a discount code? Did you hear about this Web site from a friend? In all these cases, a form designer will likely allow the user to select, or not, any or all of the check boxes.

In other cases, clicking a check box is mandatory to submit a form. Required check boxes are used to verify that a visitor had read a license agreement before downloading software or that a visitor agrees to set terms before reading site content. In situations like these, you can use a Spry Validation Checkbox widget to require that a visitor select a check box before submitting a form.

To insert a Spry Validation Checkbox *in an existing form*, follow these steps:

1. With your cursor in a form, select Insert > Spry > Spry Validation Checkbox.

   Note
   If you have accessibility prompts turned on, you will be prompted to enter accessibility attributes for the text field. Form field accessibility attributes are explained in #60, "Defining a Form in Dreamweaver." You can enter accessibility attributes, or not. Click OK to insert the form field.

2. The Required option is selected in the Property inspector. This is the main point of using this widget, and it is likely you will need to define no other options. However, you can define when to validate the field entry using the set of three different Validate on check boxes. Use Blur to validate when a user clicks outside the text field. Select Change to validate as the user changes text inside the text field. Submit is always selected, and validates when the user clicks the Submit button in the form (**Figure 71a**).

Figure 71a Defining validation for a check box triggered by a user clicking the Submit button.

(continued on next page)

3. The Preview States pop-up menu in the Property inspector just defines what state is displayed in the Document window in Dreamweaver. The state that displays in a browser will depend on whether or not the user conforms to or breaks the validation rules.

4. You can edit Spry validation rules at any time by selecting the turquoise Spry Checkbox label and changing settings in the Property inspector.

You will notice that the Property inspector for a Spry check box includes an Enforce Range (Multiple) option. This allows you to define a minimum number of check boxes that must be selected before the form can be submitted.

Defining a validation rule for a group of check boxes is technically possible in Dreamweaver but requires some hand-coded HTML, and is not a particularly accessible feature of Dreamweaver CS3.

Is this something you would want to research and apply to your forms? Maybe, maybe not. There is controversy among form designers as to whether it is appropriate to use check boxes in groups. Some schools of form design teach that radio buttons are always used when a visitor has to choose from a set of options, and check boxes are always used to provide a set of independent choices. For example, if a customer has to choose a type of credit card, the set of radio button options might include Visa, MasterCard, American Express, and Discover Card. Every customer who makes an online purchase has to choose one—and just one—of these options. On the other hand, check boxes can be used to allow visitors to get e-mail discount coupons or to subscribe to a newsletter. Customers can select neither of these options, either of them, or both. I tend to favor this approach to form design, but other form design folks like the ability to group check boxes and require people filling in an online form to choose one—and just one—check box from a group.

#72 Defining a Spry Validation Select Widget

Spry Validation Select widgets are used to create validation rules for pop-up menus. (The formal name for what most folks refer to as pop-up menus is "select menus.") In the main, Spry Validation Select widgets are used to force users to make a selection from a pop-up menu. For example, if the pop-up menu lists a set of geographical regions and you need to know what geographical region a client is located in, you might make it a requirement that before submitting a form, the client provides his or her location.

Creating a Spry Validation Select widget is a two-part process. Unlike the other Spry validation widgets surveyed in this chapter, the Spry Validation Select widget does not generate a working form field; it only generates the validation script. So, you need to both generate the validation widget *and* create a pop-up menu with options.

Defining labels and values for (pop-up) menus is covered in #65, "Placing Lists/Menus and File Fields," earlier in this chapter. Here, I'll walk you through generating a Spry Validation Select widget that provides a validation script for a menu.

To generate a Spry Validation Select widget, click in a form, and choose Insert > Spry > Spry Validation Select. An empty menu is generated. You can populate the menu after you define the validation rules in the Property inspector.

The unique validation option for a menu is that you can elect to force visitors to choose an option from the menu. And, you can constrain the selected option to a menu option with a value. Let's start with the basic option: By default, Spry Validation Select scripts create a required form. If a user doesn't select an option from the menu, he or she will not be able to submit the form (**Figure 72a**).

Figure 72a The Property inspector displays the default validation rule for Spry Validation Select widgets—blank values are not allowed.

Menu Labels and Values

Labels are what display in a pop-up menu. *Values* are assigned to labels, and are submitted to a server when a visitor chooses from the list of labels in a menu. You can assign the same value to a number of labels. So, for example, if you want several menu options to trigger a validation script, you can assign the same value to those labels, and then make that value the invalid value in the Property inspector for a selected Spry Validation Select widget.

In addition to screening for blank value submissions, you can also define a value (besides blank) that you assign to menu options that are not accepted. For instance, if you are collecting data in the menu about where someone bought your product before you provide support for their purchase, you might define a form that would not accept menu selections like "I don't know" or "I stole it!" In that case, you would define a value (like "1," for instance) for all menu options that you will not accept, and enter that value in the Invalid value field, along with checking the Invalid value check box (**Figure 72b**).

Figure 72b Defining an invalid value of 1.

After you attach a validation script to a menu, click the *menu field* (as opposed to the turquoise validation script label) in the Dreamweaver Document window. In the List/Menu Property inspector, click the List Values button to open the List Values dialog. Here, you enter labels and values for your menu.

CHAPTER NINE

Embedding Media

Media—audio and video files—has always been a dynamic, entertaining, attention-grabbing, and fun element of Web content. Media content has also, historically, been some of the least *accessible* Web content due to long download times and uneven implementation of the plug-ins (software) required to see and hear online media.

As Bob Dylan has said, "the times, they are a-changin'." The steady increase in the availability of high-speed Internet connections (along with improvements in streaming techniques that allow media to begin playing more quickly) means more and more people browsing the Web will enjoy video clips without having to endure an inordinate wait. Surveys and estimates indicate that the vast majority of visitors have appropriate software to watch and hear media in the most widely used formats—Windows Media, Flash, QuickTime, and RealMedia.

Another factor in the widespread acceptance of online video is the increasing number of people who have high-quality sound systems and larger screens and/or screens that display millions of colors.

You can add digital media to your site quickly and easily. This book cannot explore the whole fascinating and wide-ranging scope of software tools and techniques involved in generating video or audio files. But almost every computer shipped these days comes with at least a basic program for editing and producing digital audio and video files you create with your digital video camera, audio recording device, or whatever level of media production tools is available to you.

#73 Creating Flash Text in Dreamweaver

Flash Text looks like type, but technically it is media in the sense that it is a graphical media file that requires a media player (the Flash Player).

You generate Flash Text right in Dreamweaver, and the object you create is saved as a Flash movie in the Flash SWF file format. Since Flash Text is, essentially, an embedded Flash movie, Dreamweaver has to generate HTML code that embeds a Flash file. In order for the link to work and not get corrupted, Dreamweaver has to know the filename of the HTML document you are working on. Therefore (and here's the point), save your page before generating and embedding a Flash Text object.

Once you've saved the page into which the Flash Text will be embedded, follow these steps to generate and embed Flash Text:

1. With your cursor at the point where you want to insert the Flash Text, choose Insert > Media > Flash Text. The Insert Flash Text dialog will open. Select the Show font check box to activate the preview feature that displays the actual font you select in the Text field of the dialog.

2. In the Text field, enter the text you want to appear on your page as Flash Text (**Figure 73a**).

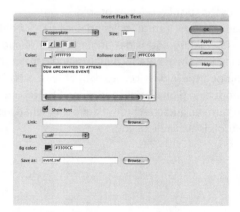

Figure 73a Previewing Flash Text as you generate it in the Insert Flash Text dialog.

3. From the Font pop-up menu, choose a font. In the Size field, enter text size in points.

4. Use the Bold, Italic, and the Left-, Center-, or Right-align icons under the Font pop-up menu to assign style and alignment to the text.

5. From the Color pop-up menu, choose a color or enter a hexadecimal color value in the Color field. If you want the text color to change when a visitor rolls his or her cursor over it, enter a rollover color by using the Rollover color pop-up menu or entering a hexadecimal color value in the Rollover color field.

6. If your Flash Text is linked to another page or file, enter the link in the Link field. With the Target pop-up menu, you can change the target browser window for the link from the default (opens in the same browser window) to _blank (opens in a new browser window).

7. Choose an optional background color from the Bg color pop-up menu, or enter a hexadecimal color value in the Bg color field.

8. In the Save as field, Dreamweaver automatically generates a filename with a SWF file extension. You can accept that filename, or enter a new one.

Tip
The filename you assign must be unique—that is, there must not be any other file with that name.

9. After you have defined your Flash Text, you can click the Apply button to see how it looks on the page. When the text looks the way you want it to, click OK.

You can edit the appearance of Flash Text objects by selecting them and choosing formatting features from the Property inspector, or you can edit the content of Flash Text objects by clicking the Edit button in the Property inspector.

The Property inspector has a couple formatting options that are not available in the Insert Flash Text dialog. Use the V Space field to define vertical spacing between the Flash Text and objects above or below it. Use the H Space field to set horizontal spacing. The Quality pop-up menu allows you to convert the Flash file to a lower-quality, faster-loading file.

Remember to Keep Flash Text Accessible

Depending on your accessibility settings—defined in the Accessibility category of the Preferences dialog, accessed by choosing Edit > Preferences (Windows) or Dreamweaver > Preferences (Mac)—you might get prompted to add accessibility options for Flash Text after you OK the Insert Flash Text dialog. Assigning a title to the Flash Text object allows reader software to read that content out loud.

#74 Creating Flash Buttons in Dreamweaver

Each Flash button is a unique Flash (SWF) file (**Figure 74a**). In order for Dreamweaver to generate a file in the correct folder, with appropriate links to appear in the page, you have to first save the Dreamweaver Web page *before* inserting Flash buttons. Once you do this, follow these steps to generate and embed Flash buttons:

Figure 74a A set of Flash buttons on a Web page.

1. With your cursor at the point where you want to insert the Flash button, choose Insert > Media > Flash Button. The Insert Flash Button dialog will open. As you design the button, a preview of it will appear in the Sample field at the top of the dialog (**Figure 74b**).

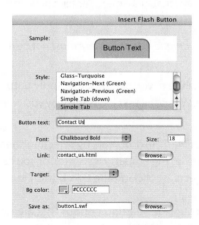

Figure 74b Previewing Flash button text as you generate it in the Insert Flash Button dialog.

2. In the Style field, choose a design for your button from the list.

3. In the Button text field, type the text you want to appear in your Flash button.

Flash Text vs. Flash Buttons

Like Flash Text, Flash buttons are small Flash objects generated in Dreamweaver, and saved to the Flash Player format (SWF). And, like Flash Text, Flash buttons display any font and font size, regardless of browser or system settings (provided the viewer has the Flash Player installed on his or her system).

There are more important similarities between Flash Text and Flash buttons. A Flash button (like Flash Text) can be defined as a link, can have a defined link target, and can have a defined background color.

The difference between Dreamweaver's Flash Text and Flash buttons is that Flash buttons include graphic designs available through dozens of included Flash button styles and more styles that can be downloaded from the Adobe Dreamweaver Exchange.

4. From the Font pop-up menu, choose a font. In the Size field, type the text size in points.

5. Normally Flash buttons function as navigation buttons. Use the Link field or the Browse button to define a link.

Tip
See Chapter 2, "Working in the Document Window," #17, "Defining Links," for a full explanation of links and how to define them.

6. Use the Target pop-up menu if you want to change the target browser window for the defined link from the default (opens in the same browser window) to _blank (opens in a new browser window).

7. Choose an optional background color from the Bg color pop-up menu, or enter a hexadecimal color value in the Bg color field.

8. In the Save as field, Dreamweaver automatically generates a filename with a SWF file extension. You can accept that filename or enter a new one. There's no good reason to change the default button filename.

9. After you have defined your Flash button, click the Apply button to see how it looks on the page. When the text looks the way you want it to, click OK.

Flash Buttons Made Accessible

Depending on your accessibility settings—defined in the Accessibility category of the Preferences dialog, accessed by choosing Edit > Preferences (Windows) or Dreamweaver > Preferences (Mac)—Dreamweaver might display the Flash Accessibility Attributes dialog each time you create a Flash button. Assigning a title to a Flash button allows reader software to read that content aloud.

Editing Flash Buttons

You can edit the appearance of Flash button objects by selecting them and choosing formatting features from the Property inspector, or you can edit the content of a Flash button by clicking the Edit button in the Property inspector.

Use the V Space field to define vertical spacing between the Flash buttons and objects above or below them. Use the H Space field to set horizontal spacing. The Quality pop-up menu allows you to convert the Flash file to a lower-quality, faster-loading file.

#**75** Embedding Flash and Flash Video Files

When you embed a Flash file or a Flash Video file in a Web page in Dreamweaver, you can adjust the size of the movie, define the size and color of a background behind the movie, and even adjust features like whether or not the movie plays automatically when the page in which it is inserted opens, or if a visitor has to click a Play button to watch the movie.

Despite the similar-sounding names, Flash movies (SWF files) and Flash Video (FLV files) are different things. Flash movies, often referred to as SWFs (often pronounced "swiffs"), present animated and interactive content online, created with Adobe's Flash authoring tool. The SWF format is also sometimes used to display digital artwork online.

Flash *Video* is a format for sharing movies online, similar to QuickTime, Windows Media, or RealMedia movies. The Flash movie format (SWF files) is a long-established format for presenting animation and interactivity online. Flash movies are often used for animated ads or interactive forms. The SWF format is the only Web-friendly format that supports vector graphics—graphics that can be enlarged in a browser without distorting the artwork. Complex Flash files can be as engaging and sophisticated as video games. The SWF format is actually the file formatted for the Flash Player, while editable Flash files are saved to FLA format.

Flash Video (FLV) files are different. Adobe is promoting the FLV format as a kind of "universal" video format that transcends other competing media formats. Flash CS3 includes a utility that converts files from Windows Media, QuickTime, and other formats to Flash Video (FLV). The Flash Video (FLV) format is used, for example, as the video format central to the popularity of YouTube (www.youtube.com).In this How-To, I'll show you how to embed both SWF files (Flash movies) and Flash Video in a Web page.

When you embed a Flash movie (a SWF file) in a Web page, the movie appears as a gray box. When selected, the Property inspector for the movie is active (**Figure 75a**).

Figure 75a The Property inspector for a Flash movie.

Use the Loop and AutoPlay check boxes to enable (or disable) looping (repeating) or autoplay (the animation plays when a page is loaded).

The V Space and H Space fields allow you to define vertical (V) or horizontal (H) spacing between the Flash movie and other objects on the page.

The Quality pop-up menu allows you to compress the Flash file (choose Low) for faster downloading and lower quality.

In the Scale pop-up menu, the Default setting maintains the original height-to-width ratio of the original animation (that is, it prevents the animation from being distorted) when the Flash object is resized. The Exact Fit option in the Scale pop-up menu, on the other hand, allows you to stretch the animation horizontally or vertically if you change the original height and/or width.

The Align pop-up menu can be used to align the Flash object left or right, so text flows around the animation.

The Bg pop-up menu can be used to define a background color. The background color is active if you resize the Flash object and maintain the height-to-width aspect ratio by choosing the Default setting in the Scale field.

The Reset size button restores the Flash object to its original size. The Edit button opens Flash (if you have it installed) to edit the Flash object.

The Play button displays the Flash object in the Document window. Toggling to Stop displays the editable gray box.

Dreamweaver CS3 allows you to embed movies that have been saved to the Flash Video format (FLV), and then choose from a nice little set of player controls that display in a browser window to make it easy for visitors to control the movie.

How Accessible Are Flash Movies?

Flash files require the Adobe Flash Player, which is installed on a large percentage of computers, and is also available as a free download (via www.adobe.com).

To embed a Flash Video file, follow these steps:

1. Choose Insert > Media > Flash Video. The Insert Flash Video dialog will open (**Figure 75b**). Use the Browse button to navigate to a Flash Video (FLV) file (or enter the URL of a file on the Internet) in the URL field. Unless you are working with a special streaming server (and your server administrator will know this information), choose Progressive Download Video from the Video type pop-up menu.

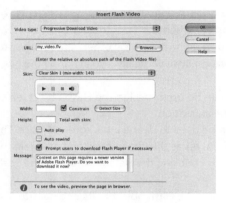

Figure 75b Embedding a Flash Video file.

2. Click the Detect Size button in the dialog to detect the size of the video. Keep the Constrain check box selected since it is unlikely that you will want to distort the height-to-width ratio of the video. You can enter a new value in either the Width or Height field to resize the video (if you selected the Constrain check box, the nonedited dimension will automatically adjust to keep the height-to-width ratio of the video the same as the original).

3. After detecting the video size, you can use the Skin pop-up menu to select a player control set. Note that player controls require various sizes of videos (that's why you detected the video size in Step 2 first).

4. You can enable the Auto play, Auto rewind, or Prompt users to download Flash Player features if necessary using the check boxes in the dialog. If you elect to prompt users to download the Flash Player, you can accept or edit the text message that displays.

Many Flash Video parameters you set when you embed the video can be edited in the Property inspector.

#76 Embedding QuickTime Media

QuickTime movies can be easily embedded in Dreamweaver pages. And you can easily reset the size at which QuickTime movies will display. However, Dreamweaver does not provide easy-to-use sets of controllers for QuickTime movies like it does for Flash Video. Features like background color, autoplay, and scale (enlargement of a video by displaying it at a lower resolution) are all defined with parameters that have to be entered manually.

To embed a QuickTime movie, choose Insert > Media > Plugin. The all-purpose Select File dialog (that is used for all types of plug-ins, not just QuickTime files) will open. Navigate to the QuickTime (MOV) file you wish to insert, and click Choose (Mac) or OK (Windows).

The embedded QuickTime movie appears as a very minimalist 32-pixel square box, regardless of the size of the actual movie. To display the movie at an appropriate size, enter a height and width in the Property inspector. You can also enter vertical (V) or horizontal (H) spacing in the Property inspector. The Align pop-up menu can be used to align the movie on the left or right side of the page (**Figure 76a**).

Figure 76a Defining dimension parameters for an embedded QuickTime movie.

You have to manually enter display parameters into the Parameters section of the Property inspector. Click the Parameters button in the Property inspector to display the Parameters dialog. You can add parameters by clicking the "+" symbol in the dialog. Enter a parameter by entering it in the left column, and enter a value in the right column.

Useful QuickTime Parameters

Following are a few useful parameters for controlling the display of QuickTime movies:

- The BGCOLOR parameter defines the background color. Enter standard colors (like red, blue, green, black) or hexadecimal color values.

- The SCALE parameter enlarges a video by making the resolution more grainy. Setting scale value to 2, for example, doubles the size of the video display without affecting the number of pixels.

- The AUTOPLAY parameter can be set to true (the video plays when the page opens) or false.

- The VOLUME parameter defines the default volume for the video when it plays on a scale of 1 (quiet) to 10 (loud).

234

Downloading the QuickTime Player for Windows

QuickTime audio and video files require the Apple QuickTime Player (a free download, available at www.apple.com/ quicktime). The Quick-Time Player *is* installed on all Macs. However, by default, QuickTime Player is not installed on many Windows computers.

Find More QuickTime Parameters

Parameters for embedding QuickTime movies can be found at www. apple.com/ quicktime/ tutorials/embed.html.

After you set parameters, click OK to close the Parameters dialog (**Figure 76b**).

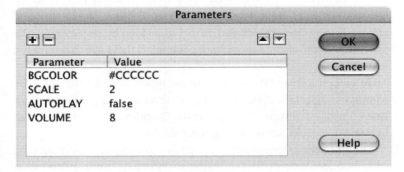

Figure 76b Defining background color, scale, autoplay, and volume preset for a QuickTime movie.

You can preview your QuickTime movie in the Dreamweaver Document window by clicking the Play button in the Property inspector, but you'll have more reliable preview results if you preview the page with the movie in a Web browser (choose File > Preview in Browser, and select a browser from the available list if you have more than one).

#77 Embedding Windows Media

Like QuickTime movies, Windows Media files (which can be WMV, AVI, and other file types) can be easily embedded in Dreamweaver. And you can easily reset the size at which Windows Media movies will display. As with QuickTime movies, Dreamweaver does not provide easy-to-use sets of controllers for Windows Media movies. And, as with QuickTime movies, you need to manually define parameters to control features like autoplay, initial volume, and whether or not a player control displays in the browser with the video.

To embed a Windows Media movie, choose Insert > Media > Plugin. The Select File dialog (used for all types of plug-ins) opens. Navigate to the Windows Media file you wish to insert, and click Choose (Mac) or OK (Windows).

The embedded Windows Media movie is placed on the page in a 32-pixel square box, regardless of the size of the actual movie. To display the movie at an appropriate size, enter a width and height in the Property inspector. You can also enter vertical (V) or horizontal (H) spacing in the Property inspector. The Align pop-up menu can be used to align the movie on the left or right side of the page (**Figure 77a**).

Figure 77a Embedding a Windows Media file.

The best way to see how your Windows Media file will look in a browser is to preview the movie in a browser (choose File > Preview in Browser, and select a browser from the available list if you have more than one).

To define how the Windows Media file displays and plays in a browser, you enter parameters into the Parameters area of the Property inspector. Click the Parameters button in the Property inspector to display the Parameters dialog. You can add parameters by clicking the "+" symbol in the dialog. Enter a parameter in the left column, and enter a value in the right column.

Where Do You Find Windows Media Parameters?

There are many versions of Windows Media Player, and they use different parameters. While QuickTime parameters are standardized and managed by Apple, the world of Windows Media is less defined. You can Google for Windows Media parameters, but you'll have to sort through competing and conflicting sets of parameters. The bottom line is that Windows Media video will display in a visitor's browser window in unpredictable ways. While Windows Media is almost universally supported, developers who need tight control over the display of embedded video turn to Flash Video, Real video, or QuickTime.

Following are a few useful parameters for controlling the display of Windows Media movies:

- The AUTOSTART parameter with the Value set to true plays a movie automatically when the page opens. When the value is set to false, it does not, and requires the visitor to start the movie using a control.

- The displaybackcolor parameter can have the Value set to false (no background color) or a color (like red, blue, green, or black) or a hexadecimal value.

- The ShowAudioControls can have the Value set to true (a volume control displays) or false (no control).

After you set parameters, click OK to close the Parameters dialog (**Figure 77b**).

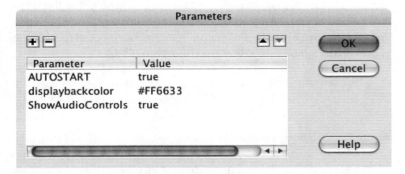

Figure 77b Parameters for a Windows Media movie.

CHAPTER TEN

Adding Effects and Interactivity with Spry

New to Dreamweaver CS3, Spry widgets provide access to dynamic and interactive elements that until now had to be created in other programs. Spry widgets include Menu Bars, tabbed panels, accordion effects, and collapsible panels.

In this chapter, I'll first walk you through the process of creating tabbed panels in some detail, and then show you how to apply the techniques I explain there to other Spry widgets.

The Spry widgets in this chapter can be edited in the Property inspector. For example, if you create a Menu Bar, you can assign text and links to menu options in the Property inspector. But, in general, you cannot do much, if any, formatting for Spry widgets in the Property inspector. Instead, you format Spry widgets by editing style sheets that get generated by Dreamweaver whenever you create a Spry widget. This chapter assumes that you have a basic familiarity with CSS styles, and custom class styles in particular. It will be helpful to keep Chapter 7, "Formatting Page Elements with CSS," bookmarked as you use this chapter to define and format Spry widgets.

There are a few things to be aware of when you create Spry widgets:

- Documents must be saved before you insert Spry widgets.

- Spry widgets generate lots of CSS styles and JavaScript files, and these files are saved every time you save a page with a Spry widget.

- You control basic features of the Spry widget, like text and links, in the Property inspector. But you format Spry widgets (elements like font, text color, background color, and so on) in the CSS Styles panel by editing the CSS style for the Spry widget.

Later in this chapter, I'll show you how to apply effects to objects on your page. Effects animate your page and make page elements react to visitor actions by changing location or size or appearance. Editing effects requires some ability to work in the Behaviors panel, so for these features, you might find yourself jumping over to Chapter 11, "Adding Interactivity with Behaviors," for background.

#78 Inserting Tabbed Panels

Tabbed panels transform a single Web page into a series of tabbed panels that look like distinct Web pages to a visitor. Tabbed panels are one way to create an easily navigable Web site.

To enter content in a tabbed panel, click a tab. The selected tab displays a blue outline. Click in the Content area below the tab, and enter content for that tab. Tab content can be anything you would place on a regular Web page, including text and images (**Figure 78a**).

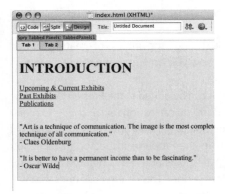

Figure 78a Entering content into a tabbed panel.

You can add (or delete) tabbed panels for a selected tabbed panel in the Property inspector. To select an *entire tabbed panel* as opposed to a single tab, click the border of the entire tabbed panel. When you do this, the Tabbed Panels Property inspector allows you to add panels by clicking on the "+" icon in the Panels section of the Property inspector (**Figure 78b**).

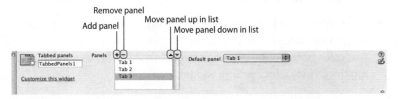

Figure 78b Adding a tabbed panel.

Chances are, you will not want your tabbed panels named Tab 1, Tab 2, and so on. Instead, you'll want tab names that reflect the content of the actual tab, like "Home," "Contact Info," "About Us," or whatever label makes sense for your content. To change the name of a tabbed panel, double-click the current label (for example, Tab 1), and type a new label.

Tip

When you hover over a tabbed panel, you will see an eye icon. Clicking the eye icon makes the tabbed panel invisible. This is a technique that can be used with JavaScript to make tabs appear and disappear. That level of JavaScripting is beyond the scope of this book, but be aware that if you do click the eye icon, the selected tab will not be visible.

To format elements of the tab like background and text color, select the CSS Styles panel (choose Window > CSS Styles), and view the styles for the SpryTabbedPanels.css. When you expand this CSS file in the CSS Styles panel, a set of class styles appears in the CSS Styles panel. In the lower part of the CSS Styles panel, you can change the properties of any style you select in the top part of the panel. I'll show you how to edit a few frequently changed elements of a panel style, and then you can experiment with other properties.

To change background color for nonselected tabs, click the .Tabbed PanelsTab style in the CSS Styles panel, and choose a background color from the background-color property (**Figure 78c**).

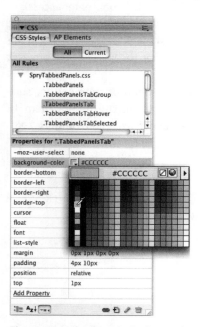

Figure 78c Changing the background color for nonselected tabs.

Use the CSS Styles Panel to Format Tabbed Panels

You can change the background color of tabbed panel elements in the CSS Styles panel:

- To change the background color for a hovered-over tab, choose the .Tabbed PanelsTabHover style in the CSS Styles panel, and choose a background color from the background-color property.

- To change the background color for a selected tab, choose the .TabbedPanels Tab-Selected style in the CSS Styles panel, and choose a background color from the background-color property.

- To change the background color for a tabbed content area, select that tab in the Document window, choose the .Tabbed PanelsContentGroup style in the CSS Styles panel, and choose a background color from the background-color property.

Format the content of tabbed panels the same way as formatting text or images.

#79 Inserting a Spry Menu Bar Widget

Menu Bars, which display submenus when they are hovered over, are a very useful and appealing page element. Menu Bars allow a lot of menu options to be accessed from a clean, uncluttered main menu. And the interactivity they provide when a visitor hovers over a menu option adds energy and dynamism to your page.

The Spry widget for inserting Menu Bar widgets allows you to generate Menu Bars with two levels of submenus. That means a user can click on a menu option, see a submenu new set of options, choose one of those options…and pick from yet a second submenu.

To generate a Menu Bar widget, you must first save the page into which the Menu Bar widget will be inserted. Then, choose Insert > Spry > Spry Menu Bar. The Spry Menu Bar dialog appears, and you can choose between a horizontal or vertical Menu Bar.

After you generate a Menu Bar widget, you can define some basic Menu Bar properties in the Property inspector. Select menu items or submenu items on the left side of the Property inspector. In the Text box, enter the text that will appear in the menu. In the Link box, enter the link that will open when the item is clicked. In the Title box, enter accessibility text (this text will appear in a browser window when a user hovers over the menu option). Leave the Target box blank to open the link in the same browser window, or enter _blank to open the link in a new browser window.

Use the "+" and "−" symbols above the menu or submenu (or sub-submenu) columns to add or delete new menu items. Use the Move Item Up or Move Item Down icons to change the order of menu items (**Figure 79a**).

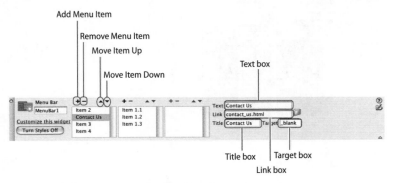

Figure 79a The Property inspector for Menu Bars.

#80 Formatting Spry Menu Bar Widgets

When you select a Menu Bar widget (or as you create one), you will notice a Turn Styles Off button in the Property inspector. Turning styles off pretty does not affect how the style is rendered in a browser but it turns off formatting in the Document window. You can adjust the formatting of different Menu Bar properties of a selected Menu Bar in the CSS Styles panel.

Every Menu Bar generates at least a dozen CSS styles. You edit the formatting of the Menu Bar by adjusting these styles. Some of the CSS Style options control relatively inconspicuous elements of the Menu Bar, but all of them can be edited in the CSS Styles panel.

To edit the styles associated with a Menu Bar widget, expand the SpryMenuBarHorizontal.css (or SpryMenuBarVertical.css if you created a vertical Menu Bar). When you do this, you will see a list of class styles associated with this style sheet. Selecting one of these class styles in the top part of the CSS Styles panel allows you to edit properties for that style in the bottom half of the CSS Styles panel.

To change the background or text color for the Menu Bar, select the style ul.MenuBarHorizontal a (or for a vertical menu bar, select the style ul.MenuBarVertical a). With the style selected in the CSS Styles panel, use the background-color swatch box in the bottom half of the CSS Styles panel to choose a new background color, and use the Color swatch to change font color.

Change the background and text color of a hovered-over horizontal menu option using the ul.MenuBarHorizontal a.MenuBarItemHover, ul.MenuBarHorizontal a.MenuBarItemSubmenuHover, ul.MenuBarHorizontal a.MenuBarSubmenuVisible menu. The style for vertical Menu Bars is similar, but with Vertical in place of Horizontal in the style name.

What Are All Those Menu Bar Styles About?

Most of the CSS styles that are generated to format your Menu Bar widget define the positioning and size of the menus and submenus that appear when a user hovers over a menu option. The default positioning of these menus is usually fine and does not need to be adjusted. You can customize a very unique Menu Bar by creating your own links and text, and you can create a distinctive format by customizing text and background colors.

#81 Inserting a Spry Accordion Widget

The Spry Accordion widget creates horizontal regions on a Web page that can be expanded or collapsed. Only one of these regions can be expanded at any one time. Accordion regions have the benefit of allowing visitors to your site to view or hide some but not all of your page content, reducing clutter and allowing them to focus on the content they want to see.

To insert a Spry accordion, first save your page and then choose Insert > Spry > Accordion. By default, a two-part accordion is created, with Label 1 and Content 1 on top, and Label 2 and Content 2 on the bottom. In the Document window, click and drag to select the default text, "Label 1," and enter a new label for the accordion section—this is what users will see in their browser window and what they will click to expand that accordion section. In the Content 1 area, delete the "Content 1" default text and enter new page content. That page content can be anything you would put on a regular Web page—images, text, media, and so on. Customize the second Spry accordion section the same way.

You can add or delete Spry accordion sections for a selected accordion in the Property inspector. Use the Add Panel or Remove Panel icon to add panels or to delete a selected panel. And use the Move Panel Up List and Move Panel Down List icons to rearrange the order of your panels (**Figure 81a**).

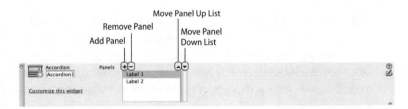

Figure 81a The Spry Accordion Property inspector.

Formatting Spry Accordion Panels

View the styles associated with the Spry accordion in the CSS Styles panel. The CSS file with the styles for the Accordion widget is SprY Accordion.css. Select and expand that style in the CSS Styles panel to see the class styles associated with your accordion panel.

- To format the tab background color for unselected tabs, edit the background-color property in the .AccordionPanel Tab style. For the selected tab, edit the .AccordionPanel Open .Accordion PanelTab style.

- To change the text color that displays when a user hovers over a tab for an unopened accordion panel, edit the color property of the .AccordionPanel TabHover style. For an opened accordion panel, edit the .AccordionPanelOpen .AccordionPanel TabHover style.

#82 Inserting a Spry Collapsible Panel Widget

Spry collapsible panels are handy ways to present optional information in a Web page. Spry collapsible panels have a clickable tab and a content area that displays or hides when a visitor clicks the tab.

The Web page that I use to check my bank balance has a number of clickable spots on the page where I can get explanations for terms or see additional detail. This information might not be necessary for a visitor and would in many cases clutter up a page. But when presented in a collapsible panel, such information is handy but doesn't take up space.

To insert a Spry collapsible panel, first save your page, and then choose Insert > Spry > Collapsible Panel. In the Document window, click and drag to select the default text, "tab," and enter a new label for the collapsible panel. Visitors will see this label in their browser window. Clicking this tab label in a browser toggles between displaying and hiding the panel.

In the Content area of the collapsible panel, delete the "Content" default text and enter new page content. That page content can be anything you would put on a regular Web page.

Like other Spry widgets, you can edit basic features of the Collapsible Panel widget in the Property inspector (see the sidebar, "Hide or Display Spry Collapsible Panels?"). To format elements of the widget like background and text color, select the CSS Styles panel (choose Window > CSS Styles), and view the styles for the SpryCollapsiblePanel.css sheet by expanding that style in the CSS Styles panel (**Figure 82a**).

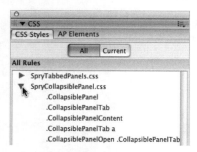

Figure 82a Viewing styles generated for the Collapsible Panel widget.

The main property of a collapsible panel that you will need to edit in the CSS Styles panel is the background color for the tab. You can edit the actual tab text in the Property inspector. But to edit the background of the collapsible panel tab, edit the background-color property of the .CollapsiblePanelTab style.

Hide or Display Spry Collapsible Panels?

When you create or select a Spry collapsible panel, the Property inspector has two menus: Display and Default State. If you choose Open from the Display menu, the collapsible panel is always open in the Document window. Independently of that, you can choose either Open or Closed from the Default State menu. If you choose Open, which is the default, the Spry collapsible panel is open when a visitor opens your Web page and only collapses if he or she clicks the tab. In my opinion, this basically defeats the purpose of a collapsible panel, and most of the time you will want to choose Closed from the Default State menu.

#83 Deleting Spry Widgets

What Are the Div Tags for Widgets?

Widget Div tag names vary depending on the particular widget and how many of that particular widget you have on a page. But the Div tags all begin with "div." followed by the name of the particular widget. For example, the tag for a Collapsible Panel widget begins "div.CollapsiblePanel," and then will vary depending on how many collapsible panels you have on your page.

Sometimes, selecting and deleting a Spry widget can get confusing, especially when you have a page loaded up with several of them or when you are editing inside a Spry widget, and you want to just start over and delete the whole darn thing.

There are two ways to select (and then delete) a Spry widget in Design view of the Document window. One is to click right on the border of the widget. This selects the widget, and you can just press the Delete key to remove the widget from your page.

The other technique for selecting widgets is more reliable, since sometimes it can be hard to precisely click on the border of a widget. If you click inside any widget, the widget Div tag displays in the Tag Bar on the bottom of the Document window. Click the Div tag for the widget you want to delete, and then press Delete (**Figure 83a**).

Figure 83a Selecting a widget Div tag in the Tag Bar.

#84 Attaching Effects to Page Elements

Spry effects are animated events that you can apply to almost anything on your page that has an ID. These are the available effects:

- **Appear/Fade:** Makes the element fade away then reappear

- **Blind:** Applies an effect similar to a window going up or down, hiding and revealing the element

- **Grow/Shrink:** Expands or reduces the size of the element

- **Highlight:** Applies colored highlighting behind an element

- **Shake:** Moves an element rapidly from right to left as if it were being shaken sideways

- **Slide:** Displaces the element vertically

- **Squish:** Rapidly reduces the size of an element until it disappears

The easiest way to apply an effect to an object is to first select the object in the Document window. Then, view the Behaviors panel (choose Window > Behaviors).

In the Behaviors panel, click the "+" (Add Behaviors) icon, and choose the Effects submenu. Choose from one of the seven displayed effects.

After you select an effect, a dialog for that effect appears. The default settings for most effects work fine.

Note
For an exploration of fine-tuning effect parameters, see #86, "Editing and Deleting Effects."

After you click OK in the dialog for the effect you assigned to an object, Dreamweaver generates JavaScript to enable the animation. Save your page and preview in a browser to test the effect. By default, effects are triggered by clicking the object to which the effect was applied. To change the triggering event to something other than a mouse click (like hovering over the image, for example), see #85, "Defining Effect Events."

Effects Are Easier to Manage If You Assign IDs to Objects

If you have an object selected when you create an effect, the effect is applied, by default, to that object. But you can apply effects without first selecting an object, and apply the effect to any object on your page that has an ID. If you do not have an object selected when you choose an effect from the Behaviors panel, you will have to choose an element on your page from the Target Element pop-up menu that appears in the dialog for your selected behavior. You choose these IDs from a list that appears of every object on your page with an ID. This ID is assigned (often by default) in the Property inspector. Objects have effects applied to them even if you left the ID (name) field blank in the Property inspector. But it is easier to keep track of what you are applying an effect to if you assign an ID to all elements on your page in the Property inspector.

#85 Defining Effect Events

By default, effects are triggered by a visitor clicking his or her mouse on the object to which the event was applied. You applied a Grow/Shrink effect? When someone clicks the object to which that event was applied, it grows or shrinks, depending on the parameters you assigned to the effect.

But what if you want something *other* than a mouse click to trigger the effect? You can change the triggering event for an effect in the Behaviors panel. Do this by first selecting the object to which the event was applied. When you do that, the Behaviors panel will display the behavior (or behaviors) assigned to that object.

If you want to change the triggering event for the effect, click in the *left* column of the Behaviors panel for a selected effect. If you have more than one behavior associated with an object, they will display in multiple rows in the Behaviors panel, so you need to select the specific behavior for which you are changing the triggering event. As you do, a pop-up menu appears. Click it to display a set of alternate triggering events (**Figure 85a**).

Figure 85a Choosing from a list of triggering events for a selected effect.

Adding Effects and Interactivity with Spry

There are a *lot* of possible triggering events, but there are a smaller number that are used quite often. Many of them have names that are intuitive. For example, onClick means an event happens when a user clicks the object to which the event is attached.

The most frequently used events for effects include onLoad, which triggers an event when a page is loaded, and onMouseOver, which triggers an event when a mouse hovers over an object.

Besides onClick, onMouseOver, and onLoad, here are some frequently used triggering events:

- onBlur triggers an event when a form element, window, or frame loses focus.

- onContextMenu triggers an event when the user right-clicks (Ctrl-click with a Mac) a form element or a link.

- onDblClick triggers an event when the user double-clicks a form element or a link.

- onFocus triggers an event when, among other things, a cursor insertion point is placed in a form field.

- onKeyDown triggers an event when the user depresses a key.

- onMouseMove triggers an event when the user moves the cursor.

- onUnload triggers an event when the user exits a document.

#**86** Editing and Deleting Effects

Once you define an effect, you might find you want to tweak the way in which the effect behaves.

With the event you want to edit selected, view the Behaviors panel (choose Window > Behaviors). In the right column of the Behaviors panel, you will see the effect you applied to the selected object. If you want to edit the parameters of that behavior, you can double-click the effect in the Behaviors panel to reopen the effect dialog (**Figure 86a**).

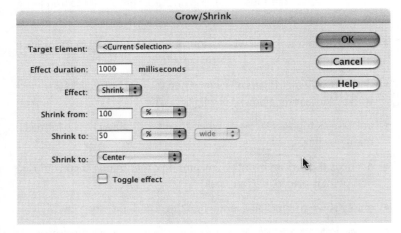

Figure 86a Reopening an effect to edit the parameters.

After you reopen the effect dialog, you can fine-tune the effect if you wish, changing the quantity, direction, and other attributes of the particular effect. There are some effect parameters that are common to all effects. Event duration defines how long it takes for the effect to happen (in milliseconds). The Effect pop-up menu defines the "direction" of an event—do you want a blind effect, for example, to go up or down? The Toggle effect check box enables the effect to work "in reverse" each time it is applied. For example, a blind effect that goes down the first time it is applied, would go up the next time it is applied.

Other effect parameters are unique to each particular effect and generally define the intensity of the effect. You can experiment with these settings and gauge the impact of any changes you make when you preview the page in a browser.

Events? Effects?

There are two main steps to defining an effect. One is defining the effect itself—choosing an effect and defining how it behaves.

The other element of an effect is the *triggering event* for the behavior. These triggering events launch the effect. I explained how change effect triggering events in #85, "Defining Effect Events."

CHAPTER ELEVEN

Adding Interactivity with Behaviors

Animated and interactive Web pages are more dynamic, more active, and often more effective than static pages. *Animation* refers to page elements moving on the page. *Interactivity* means that objects on the page react when a visitor performs an action at a Web site. A box drops from the top of the browser window informing visitors of exciting news. A button changes color when a visitor hovers a mouse cursor over it. A sound goes off when a visitor clicks a button. These and many other animated and interactive elements can be generated right in Dreamweaver.

Dreamweaver generates animation and interactivity through something called *behaviors*. These behaviors mainly use JavaScript—a coding language that enables animation and interactivity. Small (relatively small, compared to most programming) scripts become part of the page code.

Dreamweaver generates behaviors using the Behaviors panel. In the Behaviors panel, you define two elements to every action: events and actions. *Events* trigger *actions*. An event might be a page opening. Or closing. Or a visitor hovering a mouse cursor over an object on the page. An action is generated by an event. Examples of actions include an image changing, a pop-up window opening, or a sound going off.

Many behaviors are defined interactively in the Behaviors panel—you choose from a list of possible events, and then choose an associated action. Other animated and interactive elements in Dreamweaver can be generated from the main menu in the Document window.

#**87** Defining Browsers for Behaviors

JavaScript is interpreted by browsers, but some browsers don't support all Dreamweaver-generated JavaScript. For this reason, the first step in defining most behaviors is to identify the browsing environment you are designing for. Browsers like Safari, Firefox, and Internet Explorer have built-in support for JavaScript. Older browsers and older versions of Internet Explorer do not support as much JavaScript as newer browsers.

By default, Dreamweaver displays only behaviors that work in nearly all browsers. If you accept this default setting, your set of available behaviors is quite restricted. And, in most cases, unnecessarily so. Very few Web surfers are still cruising the Web with Netscape Navigator 4.0.

To change the default set of available behaviors, click the "+" button in the Behaviors panel. Choose Show Events For from the pop-up menu, and then select one of the available browsers and browser versions.

Dreamweaver's set of available browsers remains oddly out of date. However, Internet Explorer 6 is a de facto standard that most other browsers adhere to, and so behaviors that work in Internet Explorer 6 are likely to work in other browsers.

Tip
If you want to detect the browser used by a visitor, and direct that visitor to another page if their browser does not support your behaviors, you can do so with behaviors that check browser compatibility. These behaviors are explained in Chapter 12, "Testing and Maintaining Sites," #95, "Checking Browser Compatibility."

#**88** Opening a Browser Window

They're often called pop-ups—those little browser windows that open when you load a page in your browser, or when you activate the window by some action on the Web page. In Dreamweaver's terminology, they are referred to as *browser windows*, which is actually an accurate description of what most people call pop-ups.

The first step in creating a behavior that will open a browser window is to create a special Web page that will appear in that browser window. Since this page is likely to be displayed in a small browser window (you will be defining the size of that browser window as part of the behavior), you should design a page that will work well in a small browser window (**Figure 88a**).

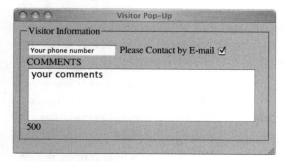

Figure 88a Defining a small Web page to use as a pop-up.

With the Web page that will open in a new browser window prepared and saved, follow these steps to define the window:

1. From the Behaviors panel, click the "+" button and choose Open Browser Window from the list of behaviors.

2. In the URL to display field, navigate to or enter the Web page that will open in the new browser window.

3. Use the Window width and Window height fields to define the size of the browser window.

4. The display options available in the Attributes section of the Open Browser Window dialog are generally *not* enabled—the new browser window that pops up is usually displayed without features like a navigation toolbar or status bar. So, leave these options deselected.

5. A window name will be helpful as you edit this behavior. Enter a name in the Window name field, and click OK in the Open Browser Window dialog (**Figure 88b**).

Open Browser
Window Trigger

By default, the open
browser window behav-
ior uses the page loading
as the triggering event.
In other words, the new
browser window opens
as soon as a visitor opens
the launching page in his
or her browser.

Figure 88b Defining an open browser window behavior.

Test your new browser window behavior by opening the page that launches it in a browser.

You can change the triggering event that opens a new browser window. For example, you can have a visitor click specific text to open the new browser window. To do this, follow these steps:

1. In the Behaviors panel, click the Open Browser Window behavior in the list. Click the "–" button to delete this behavior. You will define a new behavior that will launch the new browser window using a different event.

2. Enter text on your page that will serve as a link to open the new browser window. In the Property inspector, enter the pound symbol ("#") in the Link field to create a self-referring link. This will display the text as a link, even though the result of clicking the link will be defined by a behavior (**Figure 88c**).

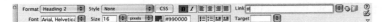

Figure 88c Preparing text to trigger an open browser window event.

3. With the text you defined as a self-referring link in Step 2 selected, define an Open Browser Window behavior just as you did in Steps 1 to 5 earlier in this technique. However, this time—because you had link text selected—the default triggering event is not onLoad (when the page opens) but onClick (when the selected text is clicked).

If onClick is not set as the triggering event, you can select that from the first column pop-up menu in the Behaviors panel. Or, if you want to use a different triggering event (such as onMouseOver—when a visitor hovers a mouse cursor over the selected text), you can choose a different event from the first column pop-up menu in the Behaviors panel.

#89 Designing a Pop-up Message

Pop-up messages present dialogs with information and require a visitor to OK them before they will go away.

To create a pop-up message that displays a dialog, follow these steps:

1. If you want the pop-up to appear when the page loads, click the <body> tag in the Tag Selector bar on the bottom of the Document window. If you want the pop-up to be triggered by clicking (or applying some other action to) text or an image, select the text or image.

2. In the Behaviors panel, click the "+" button to activate the list of available behaviors, and choose Popup Message.

3. In the Popup Message dialog, enter the message visitors will see when the pop-up message is triggered.

4. Test the pop-up by previewing the page in a browser.

5. If you want the pop-up message to be triggered by clicking (or performing another action on) link text or an image, select that image before generating the pop-up behavior. If it is difficult to tell what object you have selected, you can select the object in the Tag Selector bar, or verify that the object is selected in the Tag Selector bar. Choose a triggering event like onClick from the Events column in the Behaviors panel.

#90 Creating a Timeline

Timelines appear in a browser as an animated box that moves across, up and down, or diagonally on top of a Web page. Timelines often appear when a page opens—displaying content and providing an animated component to a page.

Timelines consist of a layer and a JavaScript that defines where and how the layer will move. The path that defines where the layer will move to and from is the "line" in timeline. The "time" element is defined by how fast (measured in frames per second) the layer moves along the line.

The first step in creating a timeline is to place a layer on the page in the Document window.

1. Choose Insert > Layout Objects > AP Div. Format the layer, and place images and/or text inside the layer. This is the content that will move on the page.

Tip
See Chapter 4, "Designing Pages with Absolute Placement Objects," for a full exploration of how to create and format AP Divs.

2. Choose Modify > Timeline > Add Object to Timeline. A warning dialog appears informing you that some features of your timeline are not supported in Netscape Navigator 4.0. Click OK. The Timelines panel appears. When the timeline is first generated, it consists of 15 frames. The keyframes define the start and end positions of the animation (**Figure 90a**).

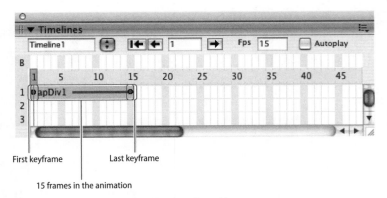

Figure 90a The Timelines panel and a selected layer.

Frames and Keyframes

Timeline animation uses an interface and terminology similar to Flash animation. Timelines use the metaphor of *frames*—referring to the way animation in movies is generated by a rapid display of frames. In a timeline, animation is generated between *keyframes*. You define the location of specific keyframes (minimum of two), and then Dreamweaver generates the content of the in-between frames to provide a smooth, transitional animation between the two keyframes.

3. With the first keyframe selected in the Timelines panel, drag the selected object (like a Div or AP Div) to the position on the page of the animation (or even off the page if you want the timeline to move onto the page from off the page).

4. In the Timelines panel, click the second (right) keyframe. With the second keyframe selected, drag the Div or AP Div in the Document window to the end point for the animation (**Figure 90b**).

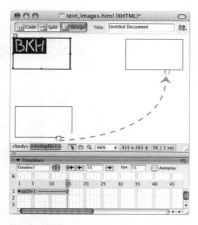

Figure 90b Placing the start point and the end point for a timeline animation.

Note
After you define the positions for the first and last keyframes in your timeline, a line appears in the Document window indicating the path the animation will take.

5. With the AP Div still selected in the Document window, you can define timeline attributes in the Timelines panel. Select the Autoplay check box to launch the timeline when the page is opened in a browser. Select the Loop check box to have the timeline repeat as long as the page is open. The default fps (frames per second) rate is 15. To slow down the animation, enter a lower value in the Fps field in the Timelines panel.

(continued on next page)

Complex timelines can include more than two keyframes. You can add a keyframe to a timeline by right-clicking/Ctrl-clicking any frame that is not a keyframe in the Timelines panel, and choosing Add Keyframe from the context menu. With a keyframe added, click that keyframe and move the layer in the Document window to the location where it will appear at that point in the animation.

However, just because pages *can* have multiple timelines, that does not mean they should have two. Generally, from an aesthetic perspective, one timeline on a page is plenty. Timelines are like hot sauce on food—they can be powerful, attention-grabbing tools when used with discretion.

6. At any point in the process, you can edit the content of the layer itself—change the background color, add or change an image, or add text.

7. Test the timeline in a browser. You can adjust timeline features in the Timelines panel.

A very complex timeline might include more than 15 frames. You can extend the length of a timeline by dragging the final keyframe in the Timelines panel (**Figure 90c**).

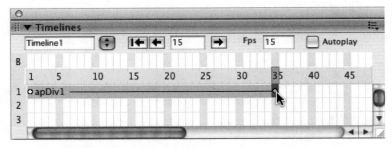

Figure 90c Extending the length of a timeline.

#91 Deleting Behaviors

Deleting behaviors can be confusing and frustrating. This is one of the things my students most often call me over to their workstations to help them with. So, let me demystify that process.

Deleting a behavior involves two things—finding the behavior in the Behaviors panel, and deleting it. The first step is the hard part. The trick to locating a behavior in the Behaviors panel is to first select the object to which the behavior is associated. Only then will the behavior be easy to find in the Behaviors panel. Once you select the behavior in the Behaviors panel, click the "−" (Remove Event) icon to delete the behavior (**Figure 91a**).

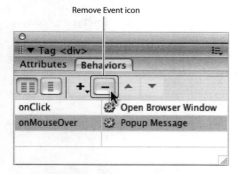

Figure 91a Removing a behavior in the Behaviors panel.

What about events that are *not* attached to any object on a page, but to the page itself? These behaviors are the ones that can be the hardest to find. But you can see them in the Behaviors panel if you click the <body> tag in the Tag Selector bar at the bottom of the Document window. Events that launch when a page is loaded or exited will likely be associated with the <body> tag.

Objects Can Have Multiple Behaviors

Objects can have multiple behaviors attached to them. In that case, you have to figure out which behavior you want to delete from the description in the Event (right) column of the Behaviors panel.

#92 Designing a Rollover

Rollover images change their display when a visitor hovers over the image. Rollover images are often, but not necessarily, used as links. There are always two images in a rollover—the original image that displays before a visitor rolls over the image, and the rollover image that displays when a visitor rolls over the image with his or her mouse.

The main work in preparing a rollover is to prepare two identically sized images. The rollover image displays in the *same box* as the original image. And if the rollover image has different dimensions than the original image, the rollover image will distort to fill the original image box.

With two same-sized images prepared, follow these steps to create a rollover:

1. Choose Insert > Image Objects > Rollover Image. The Insert Rollover Image dialog will appear (**Figure 92a**).

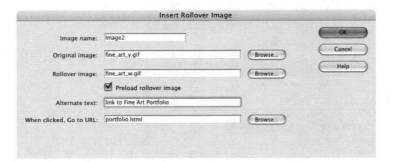

Figure 92a Defining a rollover.

2. You can accept the default image name in the Image name field; this is used for scripting. However, it is easier to keep track of your image rollovers if you define an intuitive name; for example, you can name a button after the text on that button (like "Home" or "Contact").

3. Use the Browse button in the Original image field to locate and select an original image.

4. Use the Browse button in the Rollover image field to locate and select a rollover image.

Test Rollovers in a Browser

Rollovers depend on JavaScript that cannot be previewed in the Dreamweaver Document window. Test rollovers by choosing File > Preview in Browser, and selecting an available browser.

5. Leave the Preload rollover image check box selected; this will ensure that visitors don't have to wait for the rollover image to download when they hover a mouse cursor over the original image.

6. If you want your rollover to serve as a link, enter a URL in the When clicked, Go to URL field, or use the Browse button to locate a link target in your Web site.

7. You can enter alternate text to make the rollover accessible to visitors with reader software or with image display disabled in their browsing device. When you have defined the rollover, click OK.

#93 Creating an Interactive Navigation Bar

Bring Your Own Images for Navigation Bars

For many of us, the set of navigation bar features in Dreamweaver is sufficient to create a functional navigation bar. The main drawback is that the navigation bar generator in Dreamweaver does not actually create the main navigation buttons that anchor the menu. In other words, before you can create a navigation bar in Dreamweaver, you need to have created the images that display for each state of the navigation bar elsewhere. For that, Adobe has Illustrator—the ultimate button-design package. For an extensive survey of how-to techniques like slicing to quickly generate Web-compatible images in Illustrator, see *Adobe Illustrator CS3 How-Tos: 100 Essential Techniques* by David Karlins and Bruce K. Hopkins (Adobe Press). You can also design navigation buttons in Photoshop or other bitmap editors.

Interactive navigation bars generated by Dreamweaver use four different image buttons. One button displays as a typical static button on the page. The second button displays when a visitor hovers a mouse cursor over the button. The third displays when a visitor clicks the button. The fourth image displays when a visitor hovers a mouse cursor over the button (while in down state).

This means that you need four versions of every button you use in a navigation bar. If your navigation bar has four options, for example, you need 16 buttons (four versions of each button).

To create a navigation bar, follow these steps:

1. In the Dreamweaver Document window, choose Insert > Image Objects > Navigation Bar. The Insert Navigation Bar dialog will open.

2. Each navigation bar element is a four-state button. Each button is defined separately as a four-image element. Enter the name of the first button in the Element name field, and use the four browse buttons to navigate to and select the four button states for the first button.

3. Enter alternate text in the Alternate text box to provide accessibility for visitors who will not see the button.

4. In the When clicked, Go to URL field, enter the link for the button, or use the Browse button to navigate to and select a file in your site. You can choose _blank from the in pop-up menu to open the link in a new browser window.

5. Leave the Preload images check box selected so that images that display in alternate button states are downloaded and ready to display when a visitor hovers a mouse cursor over or clicks the button.

6. In the Insert pop-up menu, choose between Horizontally (a button bar running across the top or bottom of a page) and Vertically (a button bar running down the left side of the page). The Use tables check box generates tables to lay out the navigation bar. This is generally helpful unless you have already defined a table structure for the navigation bar.

7. When you have defined the first button, *do not click OK*. You have more buttons to define.

8. After you define the four states of your first button, click the "+" button in the Insert Navigation Bar dialog to add a second button. Define the second button. Continue defining four states for each button in your navigation bar (**Figure 93a**).

Figure 93a Defining four images for the different states of a single button in a navigation bar.

9. You can use the Up and Down arrow buttons at the top of the dialog to move selected elements up or down in the list of elements. By doing so, you can change the order in which the buttons appear in a navigation bar. When you define all the buttons in the navigation bar, click OK to generate the navigation bar.

You can't test the navigation bar in the Dreamweaver Document window. To test the navigation bar, you need to preview the page in a browser. Choose File > Preview in Browser and, if you have more than one browser configured, choose from the available browsers.

Do You Really Need Four Button States?

Here's a little secret: You might not need to create four different versions of the buttons in your navigation bar. If you create three or even just two versions of each button, you can rotate or alternate buttons, so you use one or two of them twice.

You can maintain the dynamic interactivity of the navigation bar, even with just two versions of each button. So, for example, you can use one button for normal display and clicked state, and the second button for both the rolled-over and the rolled-over-when-down states.

Astute visitors will appreciate the nuance and complexity of four different versions of each button—one for each state. But in many cases, having two versions of each button is sufficient for a nice navigation bar.

#94 Editing a Navigation Bar

You can edit the navigation bar content by choosing Modify > Navigation Bar. This opens the Modify Navigation Bar dialog. The Modify Navigation Bar dialog is just like the Insert Navigation Bar dialog, and you can edit the images and links in the navigation bar (**Figure 94a**).

Navigation Bars Include Tables

Editing a navigation bar is somewhat unintuitive. What happens when you OK the Navigation bar dialog is that you actually generate both navigation bar buttons *and* a table that displays them in a horizontal row or a vertical column (depending on how you defined the navigation bar).

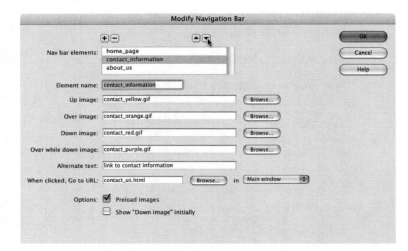

Figure 94a Modifying a navigation bar.

You edit the table that formats a navigation using the same table formatting techniques covered in Chapter 3, "Designing Pages with Tables and Frames."

CHAPTER TWELVE

Testing and Maintaining Sites

It ain't the glamorous side of Web design, but basic site maintenance like checking and fixing bad links, cleaning up bad HTML imported with text from Microsoft Word, and checking browser compatibility and accessibility makes the difference between a professional site, and—as long as we're in the vernacular here—crappy Web pages.

Dreamweaver provides a robust set of tools for making sure your site is error free, and ensuring that visitors' experience at your site is not marred with busted links. And Dreamweaver CS3 incorporates Device Central, where you can preview your Web pages in a wide variety of browsing devices.

This chapter will explore the most useful of those tools.

#**95** Checking Browser Compatibility

Does Your Site Have to Be Compatible with *Every* Browser?

It's up to you to assess your audience. If 5 percent of your visitors are viewing your site using Internet Explorer on a Mac, do you care if they see a lot of error messages? I would. Five percent can be a lot of people: the client who places the big order, the company that retains your services, family viewing your wedding photos, and so on.

At the same time, making your site compatible with all major browsers reduces the number of behaviors you can use, and some other CSS formatting is also not supported by all browsers.

One flexible approach is to configure Dreamweaver to tell you about compatibility errors in various browsers. That way, if one feature doesn't work in one browser, you can set up your page so that the nonsupported feature (like, perhaps, a CSS format applied to text) is not critical to getting content from the site.

Buried in the Dreamweaver Document toolbar is an icon that controls how Dreamweaver checks your Web pages to ensure compatibility with browsers. This icon also opens menus that produce reports on browser compatibility issues.

Dreamweaver can check your page to make sure it is compatible with any combination of Firefox, Internet Explorer for Windows, Internet Explorer for Mac, Mozilla, Netscape Navigator, Opera, and Safari. Several versions of each of these browsers are supported by this feature.

To define the browsers with which Dreamweaver will check your page for compatibility, click the Check Page icon in the Document toolbar, and choose Settings (**Figure 95a**).

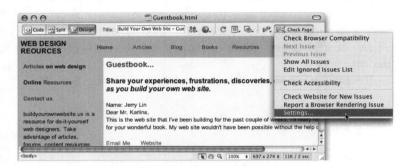

Figure 95a Accessing Browser Check settings in the Document toolbar.

Tip
If the Document toolbar is not visible, choose View > Toolbars > Document to display it.

The Settings selection will open the Target Browsers dialog. Here, you define which browsers, and which version of each selected browser, will be used to test your page. Choose browsers by selecting the check box next to the browser, and choose a version of that browser from the accompanying pop-up menu (**Figure 95b**).

Testing and Maintaining Sites

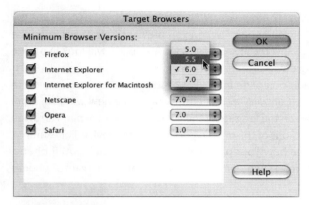

Figure 95b Defining the set of browsers for which Dreamweaver will test your page for compatibility.

After you OK the Target Browsers dialog, your pages will be tested for browser compatibility issues with the set of browsers you defined.

You can automatically check pages for browser compatibility issues by choosing Auto—check on Open from the Browser Check menu in the Document toolbar. Or, you can view a list of all browser compatibility issues in any open document by choosing Show All Errors from the menu. When you do this, a list of errors appears, telling you what features are not supported in different browsers (**Figure 95c**).

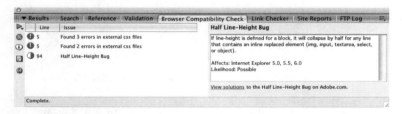

Figure 95c Viewing a list of browser compatibility issues for a page.

The list of browser compatibility issues that appears in the Browser Compatibility Check window requires some familiarity with coding or ability to decipher coding in order to interpret. The Issue column describes the support issue, and the Line column identifies the line of coding in code view. If you know some HTML, you might be able to tweak the code yourself. Or even if you don't, you can often figure out what the problem is, and delete the element in your Web page (a CSS style, for example) that shows up on the list of issues.

#96 Previewing Web Pages in Device Central

Are you curious as to how your Web page will look when viewed by various models of cell phones? When you preview Web pages in Adobe Device Central CS3, you can see how your Web page will look in a wide range of viewing devices.

To preview an open page in Device Central, choose File > Preview in Browser > Device Central. Device Central opens in a new window. From the list of devices on the left side of the window, click an expand arrow to see a list of all versions of the mobile phone or other device. For example, if you want to see how your page will look in a Motorola RAZR phone, expand the Motorola listing, and choose one of the models of RAZR phones (**Figure 96a**).

Need to Design for a Device Not in Device Central?

If you are designing for a device that is not available in Device Central, or if you are designing for a mobile browsing environment and don't know what device you are designing for, you can simply find a device that has dimensions that match your parameters. For example, if you are designing a Web page that has to be able to be viewed in a screen with dimensions of 240 pixels by 320 pixels, you can preview that page in any of the many devices that have screens that size.

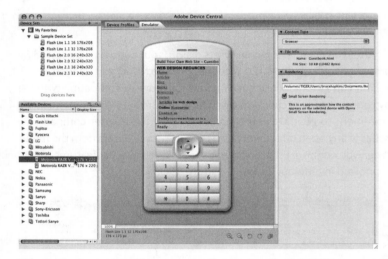

Figure 96a Previewing a Web page as it will appear in a Motorola RAZR phone.

You will see that the list of devices in Device Central also indicates the display size of the viewing area in that device. This information is listed right next to the device model.

Not only can you preview your open Web page in Device Central, but once you open the page, you can also navigate around your Web site (or around the Web if you need to for some reasons) right in the preview environment device you selected.

#97 Testing Links Sitewide

The dreaded "404 (page not found) " error is not an experience you want visitors to your Web site to go through. When visitors follow links on your site to pages that don't work—either on or outside your site—an error message appears in their browser, and—of course—they do not see the page that the link was supposed to open. Dreamweaver can easily and quickly test all the links in your site, both internal (links to files on your site) and external (links to pages and other files outside your site). Dreamweaver can also identify *orphan* pages—pages to which there is no link.

To test all links and identify orphan pages, follow these steps:

1. With or without a page open in the Document window, choose Site > Check Links Sitewide.

2. You can choose from the three reports in the Show pop-up menu in the Report window that opens after you check links. The Broken Links view shows bad links within your site. The External Links view lists links to Web sites or pages outside your site that are no longer good. The Orphaned Files view displays files to which there is no link from any page in your site (**Figure 97a**).

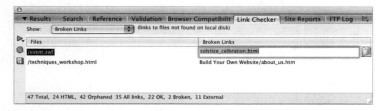

Figure 97a Viewing broken links to files outside your site.

3. You can fix a broken link by double-clicking a link in the list of either the Broken Links or the External Links reports. The page with the bad link will open, and the link will be highlighted. You can delete or edit the URL for the bad link in the Document window just as you would normally edit a page.

#98 Cleaning Up Word HTML

Frequently, text used in your Web pages is created in Microsoft Word. There are a number of ways to convert that text to HTML. You can choose to save a Word file as HTML, and then open that HTML file in Dreamweaver and edit it, or you can copy and paste text from Word into a Dreamweaver document. If you choose File > Paste Special, the Paste Special dialog provides a number of options for how to handle Word formatting when text is copied from Word to Dreamweaver.

Depending on the options you choose when importing Word text into Dreamweaver, the HTML that is generated will range from slightly flawed to really weird. If you elect to preserve all formatting from Word documents (which happens if you save a Word document as an HTML page and open it in Dreamweaver), the HTML code is full of proprietary Microsoft codes that make the page confusing to edit and format.

To clean up HTML pages with imported Word text, choose Commands > Cleanup Word HTML. The Clean Up Word HTML dialog will open (**Figure 98a**).

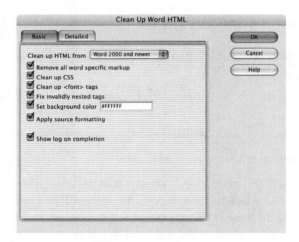

Figure 98a Cleaning up Word HTML.

Normally, you can accept the defaults in this dialog (all options are checked), and click OK. If you are using a pre–Word 2000 version of Microsoft Word, choose that version from the Clean up HTML from pop-up menu.

If you are curious as to what kind of nonstandard HTML is fixed by this process, or if you are an HTML and CSS coder and want to manage this process in detail, click the Detailed tab in the Clean Up Word HTML dialog. You can observe or change the fixes applied to Word HTML. After you click OK in the Clean Up Word HTML dialog, a dialog opens telling you what Word HTML was fixed in the process.

#**99** Adding Design Notes

If you are working on a Web site with others, or simply want to add Post-it–type notes to pages reminding yourself of things to fix, you can attach Design Notes to pages. Design Notes can be configured to open when a page is opened in Dreamweaver.

To add a Design Note to an open page, choose File > Design Notes. The Design Notes dialog will open (**Figure 99a**). Here you can define a status from the Status pop-up menu. There are eight available status settings, including draft, final, and needs attention.

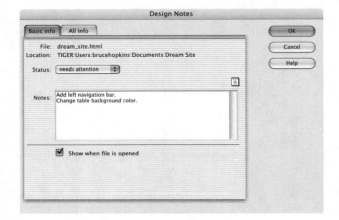

Figure 99a Defining a Design Note.

In the Notes area, enter any text you wish. Select the Show when file is opened check box to have the notes appear when you open a page for editing in Dreamweaver. These notes never appear in a browser.

> ### Note
> *The All info tab in the Design Notes dialog does not enable any additional, easily defined notes options. It displays a Behaviors panel–type environment where you can see the options you selected in the Basic info tab. It is possible to generate additional JavaScript in this tab.*

#**100** Testing Browsers for Media Support

Media files require plug-in software to be played in a browser. A large percentage of folks who browse the Web have downloaded and installed players for Windows Media, QuickTime, and Flash files.

On the other hand, not everyone has downloaded players that support all the main media file types. Dreamweaver generates a quick, easy behavior that will detect browsers that do not have a defined media player installed, and that can reroute these visitors to an alternate page in your site that does not require that particular plug-in to make the page work.

The behavior that tests a visitor's browser for plug-in support is triggered by a page loading in a browser window. To facilitate this happening correctly, select the <body> tag in the tag selection area on the left side of the status bar in the Document window generating the behavior.

Tip

By selecting the <body> tag before defining a behavior, you are allowing an action that affects the entire Web page (like loading the page in a browser) to be the triggering action for that behavior. See a more developed discussion of how Dreamweaver uses behaviors to generate JavaScript and other interactive and dynamic script and code, in Chapter 11, "Adding Interactivity with Behaviors."

Follow these steps to generate a behavior that will test browsers for plug-in support for a media player.

(continued on next page)

1. With the <body> tag selected in the open page's tag selection area, click the "+" button in the Behavior panel, and choose Check Plugin. The Check Plugin dialog will open.

2. With the Select radio button selected, choose one of the available media types from the pop-up menu (**Figure 100a**).

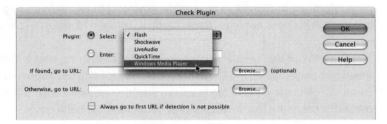

Figure 100a Choosing a plug-in to test for when the page is opened.

Tip

For all practical purposes, the plug-ins you can test for with a generated behavior are constrained to the list in the Select pop-up menu. Theoretically, you could enter the name of another plug-in in the Enter field, but this option requires knowing exactly how to formulate the name of a plug-in in a way that generated JavaScript can manage it.

3. The If found, go to URL field is optional and typically not used. If the page to which you are applying the behavior is the page with the media that requires a plug-in, visitors who do have that plug-in will stay on this page by default.

4. In the Otherwise, go to URL field, enter the (full) URL of the alternate page that contains a version of the page content that does not require the selected plug-in. If the alternate page is a file in your Web site, you can navigate to and select that file with the Browse button.

5. Selecting the Always Go to first URL if detection is not possible check box opens the current page if the script is not able to determine whether the plug-in is installed. Not infrequently, visitors have Flash or another plug-in installed, but the testing script is unable to determine this. If you select this check box, visitors will be diverted to the alternate page only if the testing script definitively determines that they do *not* have plug-in support for the selected media type. After you define the whole behavior, click OK.

Index

A

absolute links and targets, 52–53
access key support, 202
accessibility
    Alt tags for image, 132–134
    difficulties with media, 225
    Flash movies and, 231
    forms and, 200–202
    frames and, 84
    giving titles to Flash Text
        objects, 227
    link display options for, 186
    setting up text fields and text
        areas for, 205–206
    table design and issues of, 79
    text area validation attributes
        for, 218
    titles for Flash buttons, 229
Accordion widget, 242
actions
    form, 214
    triggering with events, 246–247,
        248, 249
active links, 52, 186, 187–188
Adobe applications. *See specific*
    application by name
Align pop-up menu, 139, 141
aligning
    cells vertically, 78–79
    multiple AP Divs, 99
    text and images, 139–141
Alt tags, 132–134
Animated GIF images, 146–147
animation
    defined, 249
    timeline, 254
AP (Absolute Placement) Divs
    about AP objects, 93–94
    defining, 95–101
    Div tags for, 106–111
    editing attributes of, 111
    finding invisible, 100
    formatting in Property Inspector,
        102–103
    managing, 104–105
    overlapping, 102, 103
    positioning, 109
AP Divs panel, 103
AP Elements panel, 100, 104–105
Assets panel, 162–163
attaching style sheets, 174, 175
automatic check-in/check-out
    feature, 28
autostretch column widths, 75

B

background
    color of collapsible panel, 243
    defining color of cell, 82
    setting color for page's, 179
    transparency for GIF image, 146

backing up Web sites, 14
behaviors
    creating timelines, 254–256
    defined, 249
    deleting, 257
    designing rollovers, 258–259
    navigation bars, 260–261, 262
    opening browser windows,
        251–252
    pop-up message, 253
    selecting browsers for, 250
Behaviors panel
    changing events that open
        browser window, 252
    choosing Spry effects in, 245
    designing pop-up messages, 253
    editing jump menu on, 197
    removing behavior in, 257
blank templates, 55–57
blockquote HTML tags, 118
Body tag, 178–180, 271
borders
    color of cell, 82
    defining between frames in
        frameset, 88
    showing/hiding table, 80
    thickness of box, 67
Bridge, 39
Brightness and Contrast tool
    (Dreamweaver), 136
browsers
    absolute text formatting in, 124
    access key support for, 202
    checking compatibility of,
        264–265
    defining for behaviors, 250
    designing pages readable in, 171
    ensuring borders not displayed
        in, 80
    grids, guides, and rules invisible
        in, 114
    importance of safe CSS style
        displays, 122, 123
    need consistent use of .htm/.html
        files, 12
    previewing AP Divs in, 100
    rollover testing in, 258
    testing for media support,
        271–272
    time for page opening in, 33
    unreliable support for jump menu
        Go button, 194
buttons
    check boxes vs. radio, 207
    defining images for states of, 261
    Flash, 228–229
    Go, 194
    image fields for, 213
    List Values, 211
    radio, 207, 208–209
    Reset, 213
    Submit, 213, 221

    Text Indent and Outdent, 118
    This document only radio, 183

C

Cascading Style Sheets. *See* CSS
cells
    adjusting vertical alignment in,
        78–79
    defining properties for, 82–83
    generating table to define, 71–72
    setting padding and spacing for
        table, 67–68
    splitting, 83
CGI (Common Gateway Interface)
    scripts, 198
check boxes, 207, 221–222
check-in/check-out feature, 28
classes
    periods in names of, 108
    using styles vs. HTML tags for, 182
Clean Up Word HTML dialog, 4,
    268–269
client-side scripts, 193, 194–197
Code Inspector window, 38
Code view, 38, 212
Collapsible Panel widget, 243, 244
color
    applying to fonts, 119–120
    changing tabbed panel
        background, 239
    collapsible panel's background,
        243
    defining cell's border and
        background, 82
    setting page's background, 179
Color Wheel, 119
columns, 73–76
compressing images, 5, 128, 129
connections to remote servers, 16–21
constraining
    character input in forms, 218,
        219–220
    page width display, 68
content
    collecting site, 2–5
    creating one-cell table for, 66–69
    dragging to Library window,
        161–163
    editing in Document window,
        37–38
    e-mail collection of, 199
    entering into tabbed panel,
        238–239
    generating library items from
        scratch, 163–164
    inserting into positioned Div, 111
    synchronizing local and remote,
        26–28
    templates lack, 55
    type placed in noneditable
        regions, 154–155
    viewing remote site's, 20

274

Contribute, 158
copying and pasting
    Photoshop images in
        Dreamweaver, 145, 148
    text on page, 3
creating Web sites, 1–28
    collecting site content, 2–5
    configuring remote server
        connection, 16–18
    connecting to remote servers,
        19–21
    defining local site first, 6–7
    file transfer between remote and
        local sites, 22–25
    managing site views, 10–13
    options for managing Web sites,
        14–15
    organizing local site, 8–9
    synchronizing local and remote
        content, 26–28
Crop tool (Dreamweaver), 136
cropping Photoshop images, 148–149
.css files, 172, 174
CSS (Cascading Style Sheets). See also
    external style sheets
    adding styles to existing, 176–177
    AP objects and, 93–94
    applying to links, 186–188
    attaching style sheets, 174, 175
    creating styles for individual
        pages, 183
    defining for printable pages,
        189–192
    designing pages readable in
        browsers, 171
    difficulties displaying actual fonts
        with, 226
    formatting page elements with
        style sheets, 172–177
    generating CSS file from sample,
        61–64
    global style application with, 125
    HTML text tags formatted with,
        181–183
    linked vs. imported, 64
    Menu Bar widget styles formatted
        in, 241
    page break style, 192
    periods in class and style
        names, 108
    safe browser displays of styles,
        122, 123
    setting attributes for inline text,
        121–125
    styles applied to Body tag,
        178–180
    using with Image or Table tags,
        176, 184–185
CSS Rule Definition dialog
    defining rules in, 175
    formatting options available
        in, 181
    inline text attributes defined from,
        123–124

page break style rules, 192
positioning Divs from, 109
selecting formatting options for
    link state, 188
setting page background color
    in, 179
CSS Styles panel
    collapsible panel formatting
        on, 243
    defining new style in, 122–123
    displaying, 121
    editing style attributes in, 175
    formatting Spry widgets on, 237
    formatting tabbed panels, 238
    Menu Bar widget formatting
        on, 241
    opening New CSS Rule dialog
        from, 173
    tabbed panel formatting in, 239
    viewing Accordion widget
        styles, 242
custom class styles, 182

D
dates, 45
defining Web sites
    before creating pages, 1, 48
    defining remote server
        connection, 16–18
    importance of local site creation,
        6–7
deleting
    behaviors, 257
    item on jump menu, 195
    list items, 210
    Spry effects, 248
    Spry widgets, 244
    tabbed panels, 238
Design Notes, 270
Design view
    selecting and deleting Spry
        widgets in, 244
    working in, 37
designing Web pages, 65–114
    Accordion widget panels in
        design, 242
    Body tag styles for, 178–180
    combining fixed and flexible table
        columns, 73–76
    configuring table properties,
        80–81
    creating from scratch, 48–51
    deciding on site compatibility, 264
    defining Absolute Placement
        objects, 95–101
    Div tag definitions for AP Divs,
        106–111
    embedding tables within tables,
        77–79
    features of Insert menu for, 44–47
    formatting collapsible panels, 243
    formatting framesets, 87–90

generating from sample starter
    pages, 58–60
managing AP Divs, 104–105
page margin setup, 180
readable in browser, 171
role of tables and framesets in, 65
rollovers for, 258–259
rulers, guides, and grids for,
    112–114
setting up links between frames,
    91–92
styling individual pages, 183
tables created in Layout mode,
    70–72
tables created in Standard mode,
    66–69
templates for generating new
    pages, 55–57, 157–158
using Web-safe color, 119, 120
without relying on AP objects, 94
Device Central, 266
displaying
    fonts with CSS or Flash Text, 226
    image spacing, 141
    links, 52, 186
    page width using constraints, 68
    Property Inspector, 75
Div tags
    defining, 106–111
    widget, 244
Divs. See AP Divs
Document toolbar
    about, 39, 40
    defining browsers for
        compatibility check, 264
    illustrated, 40
Document window, 29–64
    about, 1, 29
    appearance of template pages
        in, 153
    blank templates to create pages
        in, 55–57
    creating new page from scratch
        in, 48–51
    defining links, 52–54
    editing page content in, 37–38
    examining toolbars, 39–41
    features of, 30–33
    generating pages from sample
        starter pages, 58–60
    Insert menu features, 44–47
    moving or relocating AP Div in, 95
    optional display of form outlines
        in, 200
    panels and Property Inspector
        in, 34–36
    sample style sheets and framesets
        available in, 61–64
    using Insert toolbar, 42–43
documents. See also Document
    window; New Document dialog
    choosing DTD for, 49
    importing from Word and Excel, 3
    PDF, 124

saving before inserting Spry widgets, 237, 238
downloading
files from remote server, 24–25
interlacing, 146
QuickTime Player for Windows, 234
dragging content to Library window, 161–163
Draw AP Div tool, 97
drawing AP Divs, 95
Dreamweaver
background file transfer in, 23
copying and pasting Photoshop images into, 145, 148
defining forms in, 200–202
editing images in, 135–138
library items as proprietary objects in, 165
pasting Word text into, 268
Dreamweaver Exchange site, 47
DTD (document type definition), 49
.dwt files, 156

E

Edit tool (Dreamweaver), 135, 136
editable regions
adding content with Contribute, 158
defining, 152, 154
templates and, 56, 57
editing
cell content in Standard mode, 72
content in Document window, 37–38
Design Notes, 270
events that open browser window, 252
fieldset legends, 204
Flash buttons, 229
images in Dreamweaver, 135–138
jump menus, 197
navigation bars, 262
order of jump menu items, 196
Photoshop PSD files in Dreamweaver, 136
single radio button, 209
Spry effects, 248
Spry validation rules, 220
Spry widgets, 237
tabbed panel background color, 239
effects. See Spry effects
e-mail
collecting content via, 199
validating addresses for, 216
embedded pages, titles for, 88, 89
embedding. See also media
AP Divs, 100–101
CSS formatting, 179
editable regions in other editable regions, 155
Flash and Flash Video files, 230–232

Flash buttons, 228–229
images in pages, 130–131
media, 225–236
QuickTime media, 233–234
tables, 70, 77–79
Windows Media files, 235–236
enabling
page titling for embedded pages, 89
scrollbars for frame, 90
Enctype field (Property Inspector), 214
errors defining link targets, 92
events, 246–249, 252
Excel files, 3
Expanded Tables mode, 79
exporting
image files to various formats, 5
Web site settings with Manage Sites dialog, 14, 15
extensions on Dreamweaver Exchange site, 47
external style sheets
advantages of, 183
attaching, 174, 175, 176–177
defined, 172
defining in New CSS Rule dialog, 108
global application of styles with, 125
overriding with embedded page styles, 179

F

fields
about Insert Jump Menu dialog, 194
adding form, 200
collecting information in text, 205–206
FreeFind search, 198–199
hidden form, 212
image, 213
inserting updatable, 45
validating text, 215–217
fieldsets, 203–204
file field forms, 210–211
filenames
page titles vs., 50
Web page, 49
files
automatic check-in/check-out feature, 28
background transfer of Dreamweaver, 23
best formats for, 146, 147
creating print.css, 189–191
.css, 172, 174
.dwt, 156
Excel, 3
finding and uploading modified pages to server, 169–170
FLV, 230, 231
.htm/.html, 12
JPEG, 5, 126, 146

.lbi, 165
loading Flash, 227, 229, 231
naming Web page, 49
organizing local site, 8–9
placing Photoshop files in Web pages, 145–150
PNG, 5, 126, 147
PSD, 136, 145–150
saving Photoshop files in other formats, 145
selecting newer files on local site, 26–28
spacer image, 76
SWF, 226, 227, 228, 230
transferring between remote and local sites, 22–25
unlimited characters in name of uploaded, 211
uploading dependent, 24
Web formats used for images, 5
XML, 15
Files panel
choosing Local view in, 27
connecting to remote server from, 20
expanding files from, 12
generating links in, 13
menu for, 8, 26–27
selecting files for uploading, 23–24
Files window, 1, 10–13
firewalls, 18
fixed columns, 73–76
Fixed Left sample frameset, 85
fixing broken links, 267
Flash
assigning titles to Flash Text objects, 227
embedding Flash Video files, 230–232
Flash Text in Dreamweaver, 226–227, 228
formatting Flash Text, 227
using Flash buttons, 228–229
Flash Accessibility Attributes dialog, 229
Flash Player, 226, 231
FlashPaper documents, 124
flexible columns, 73–76
floating Divs, 106
FLV files, 230, 231
folders
local site, 9
saving image files in site, 131
fonts
applying color to, 119–120
displaying with CSS or Flash Text, 226
tips for absolute text formatting, 124
form actions, 214
form fieldsets, 203–204
formatting, 171–192
Accordion widget panels, 242

formatting *(continued)*
  applying CSS to links, 186–188
  Body tag with page styles,
    178–180
  defining CSS for printable pages,
    189–192
  fonts with color, 119–120
  framesets, 87–90
  global vs. local styles for, 125
  HTML text tags with CSS, 181–183
  image and page styles, 184–185
  Menu Bar widgets, 241
  page elements with style sheets,
    172–177
  setting options for CSS rules, 124
  Spry widgets, 237
  tabbed panels, 239
  text with HTML attributes,
    116–118
  tips for absolute text, 124
forms, 193–224
  about, 193
  accessibility options for, 200–202
  actions in, 214
  buttons placed on, 213
  check boxes in, 207, 221–222
  constraining character input in,
    218, 219–220
  creating jump menus, 194–197
  defining in Dreamweaver,
    200–202
  editing in Property Inspector, 36
  form fieldset definitions, 203–204
  hidden fields on, 212
  linking embedded forms to server
    databases, 198–199
  lists/menus and file field
    placement in, 210–211
  optional display of outlines in
    Document window, 200
  placing text fields and text areas
    in, 205–206
  radio buttons in, 208–209
  resources for scripting and
    hosting, 198
  Spry Validation Text Field widget
    in, 215–217
  text area rules defined for,
    218–220
Frame Tag Accessibility Attributes
  dialog, 86
frames
  borders defined between, 88
  defined, 84
  defining attributes of framesets
    and, 90
  disadvantages of designing with,
    84, 85
  enabling scrollbars for, 90
  enhancing accessibility of, 88
  links between, 91–92
  previewing in framesets, 64
  timelines and, 254
  viewing set of sample, 85

Frames panel, 87
framesets
  about, 65
  attributes of, 90
  defined, 84
  defining borders between
    frames, 88
  formatting, 87–90
  generating from samples, 84–86
  previewing sample, 64
  saving, 86
FreeFind search service, 198–199
FTP connections, 17–18

G
GIF files, 5, 126, 146–147
global style application, 125
Go button, 194
grids, 112, 114
guides, 112, 113, 114

H
Hand tool, 32, 33
headings
  assigning with HTML tags,
    116–117
  types of HTML, 181
height of tables, 69
hidden fields on forms, 212
hiding. *See* showing/hiding
hint content for commentary
  field, 219
home page
  index.htm or index.html as, 13
  viewing in Site Map view, 12
home page names, 49
horizontal Menu Bars, 240
hotspots, 142–144
hover links, 52, 186, 187–188
.htm/.html files, 12
HTML (Hypertext Markup Language).
  See also tags
  cleaning up Word, 4, 268–269
  formatting text tags with CSS,
    181–183
  saving Web text in, 3–4
  text formatting with attributes of,
    116–118

I
Illustrator
  books on, 129
  creating navigation bar images
    in, 260
  Save For Web dialog in, 128
  unable to copy and paste vector
    images from, 145
image fields, 213
image maps, 142–144
Image Preview dialog, 147–150
  about, 145
  converting Photoshop images
    in, 146

previewing four different image
  conversions, 150
using Selection and Crop tools in,
  148–149
Image Tag Accessibility Attributes
  dialog, 134
Image tags, 176, 184–185
images
  aligning and spacing, 139–141
  background tiling for, 180
  compressing, 128, 129
  defining image maps, 142–144
  displaying from thumbnails, 127
  editing in Dreamweaver, 135–138
  embedding, 130–131
  exporting, 5
  formatting, 184–185
  making accessible with Alt tags,
    132–134
  navigation bar, 260–261
  placing Photoshop files in Web
    pages, 145–150
  preparing for Web sites, 126–129
  previewing conversion options
    for, 150
  print vs. Web, 5
  reducing file size of, 127, 128, 129
  reverting to original size, 135
  sizing before importing into
    Dreamweaver, 135
  spacer, 75–76
  updating placed Photoshop,
    148, 149
  uploading dependent files for
    embedded, 24, 25
  working with, 115
importing
  sized images into Dreamweaver,
    135
  spreadsheets and Word
    documents, 3
  text into Dreamweaver, 2
  Web site settings with Manage
    Sites dialog, 14
index.htm/index.html files, 13, 49–50
inline text attributes, 121–125
Input Tag Accessibility Attributes
  dialog, 201, 202
Insert bar
  creating table from Layout panel
    of, 66
  Layout mode, 71
  showing in Windows, 96
  using, 42–43
Insert menu, 44–47
interactive navigation bars, 260–261
interactivity, 249, 260–261

J
JavaScript
  browser support for
    Dreamweaver's, 250
  defining script for image used as
    button, 213

jump menus in, 194
JPEG files, 5, 126, 146
jump menus, 194–197
   about, 193, 194
   adding and deleting items on, 195
   changing item order on list, 196
   creating, 195
   editing, 197

K

keyframes
   about, 254
   defining timeline's first and
      last, 255
   using multiple, 256

L

labels
   designing custom Submit button,
      213
   pop-up menu, 224
Layout CSS option (New Document
   dialog), 55, 56–57
Layout CSS pop-up menu, 57
Layout mode
   about, 65
   calculation of column widths
      in, 75
   Insert bar in, 71
   Standard mode vs., 72
   tables created in, 70–72
Layout panel, 66
.lbi files, 165
legends, fieldset, 204
Library Item window, 165
library items
   creating and placing, 161–164
   CSS styles of, 164
   function of, 151
   including navigation in, 167–168
   templates vs., 161
   updating, 165–166
   uploading, 167–168
linked vs. imported style sheets, 64
links
   applying CSS to, 186–188
   configuring between frames,
      91–92
   defining, 52–54
   dependent files and, 25
   Flash buttons and, 228
   generating in Files panel, 13
   hover, 52, 186, 187–188
   image maps and, 142
   providing between embedded
      forms and server database,
      198–199
   redefining file links, 9
   relative and absolute, 52–53
   states of, 52, 186
   testing sitewide, 267
   updating navigation, 167, 168
   view of prototype page, 11

lists, 210–211
local site folder, 9
local sites
   comparing content of remote
      and, 21
   defining, 6–7, 48
   organizing, 8–9
   remote vs., 16
   selecting newer files on, 26–28
   synchronizing content with
      remote sites, 26–28
   transferring files between remote
      and, 22–25
   updating templates and library
      items automatically, 169
   working without, 19
locking
   column widths, 75
   guides, 114

M

Mac platform QuickTime Player, 234
magnification for zoom, 142
Manage Sites dialog, 14–15, 16
managing Web sites
   backing up sites, 14
   defining remote server
      connection, 16–18
   managing site views, 10–13
   options for, 14–15
margins for pages, 180
master tables, 77–78
media, 225–236
   about, 225
   Flash and Flash Video files,
      230–232
   Flash Text in Dreamweaver,
      226–227
   generating and embedding Flash
      buttons, 228–229
   QuickTime movies, 233–234
   testing browsers for media
      support, 271–272
   Windows Media movies, 235–236
Menu Bar widgets, 240, 241
menus. *See also* pop-up menus
   creating jump, 194–197
   Files panel, 8, 26–28
   Insert, 44–47
   page design features of Insert,
      44–47
   placing in forms, 210–211
   Special Characters submenu, 46
Microsoft Excel files, 3
Microsoft Word HTML cleanup,
   268–269
mobile devices, 266
mouse click events, 246–247

N

names
   Flash Text, 227
   periods in class and style, 108

restricted characters for files, 12
saving Web pages before
   giving, 51
unlimited characters in uploaded
   file, 211
Web page file, 49
navigation
   prototyping site, 11
   updating links for, 167
navigation bars
   creating interactive, 260–261
   defined, 168
   defining images for button
      states, 261
   editing, 262
   including in templates and library
      items, 167–168
New CSS Rule dialog
   creating new style in, 123,
      174–175
   defining link state styles, 187–188
   opening, 173
   page break style defined in, 192
   setting up class attributes for
      Divs, 108
   using styling for Body tags, 178
New Document dialog
   selecting pages using CSS without
      AP objects, 94
   templates viewed in, 157
   viewing sample frames in, 85
noneditable regions
   about, 152, 153
   type of content placed in,
      154–155
   updating template's, 160

O

objects. *See also* AP Divs
   assigning IDs to, 245
   multiple behaviors for, 257
   selecting in Tag Selector bar, 253
onClick events, 252
one-cell tables, 66–69
onMouseOver events, 252
Open Browser Window dialog, 252
open Web sites, 16
opening
   browser windows, 251–252
   CSS Styles panel, 121
   Jump Menu dialog, 197
   New CSS Rule dialog, 173
   Table dialog, 66
   template pages, 159
   Web pages with links, 91–92
Optimize tool (Dreamweaver), 135,
   136
optional editable regions, 155
organizing local Web sites, 8–9
overlapping AP Divs, 102, 103

P

padding for table cells, 67–68
page breaks, 192
panels. *See also specific panel by name*
  collapsible, 243
  defined, 34
  elements of, 34
  Property Inspector, 36
  separating from tabbed group, 35
  tabbed, 238–239
parameters
  QuickTime movie, 233, 234
  Windows Media movie, 235, 236
Parameters dialog, 233–236
passwords for remote server
  connection, 18
Paste Special dialog, 268
PDF documents, 124
percentages for defining page
  width, 69
performance
  enhancing Flash file loading, 227,
    229, 231
  frames and improved, 84
  image compression and, 128
  time for page loading in
    browser, 33
periods in class and style names, 108
Photoshop
  books on, 129
  editing PSD files in Dreamweaver,
    136
  opening files in Dreamweaver, 126
  placing files in Web pages,
    145–150
  Save For Web dialog in, 128
Photoshop Elements, 128
pixels for defining page width, 69
placing
  library items, 161–164
  Photoshop files in Web pages,
    145–150
planning and embedding site
  elements, 151–170
  about, 151
  creating and placing library items,
    161–164
  creating template pages, 152–156
  generating new pages from
    templates, 157–158
  including navigation in templates
    and library items, 167–168
  updating library items, 165–166
  updating templates, 151, 159–160
  uploading templates and library
    items, 169–170
plug-in testing, 272
PNG files
  about, 5
  advantages of, 126
  PNG 8 and PNG 32 options, 147
Pointer Hotspot tool, 142, 144
Polygonal Hotspot tool, 142, 143

pop-up menus
  Align, 139, 141
  Layout CSS, 57
  Preview States, 217, 220, 222
  Tag, 183
  Target, 91
  validating, 223–224
  View, 20
pop-ups
  designing messages for, 253
  opening browser windows,
    251–252
Preferences dialog
  configuring form accessibility, 201
  setting Flash button accessibility,
    229
Preview States pop-up menu, 217,
  220, 222
previewing
  AP Divs in browsers, 100
  blank template, 55
  brightness and contrast
    changes, 137
  compressed images, 128
  Flash Text as generated, 226
  image conversion options, 150
  pages in Device Central, 266
  sample framesets, 64
  sharpness changes, 137
  style sheets, 61
  thumbnails, 127
print.css files, 189–191
printing Web pages, 189–192
Property Inspector
  Action, Method, and Enctype
    fields, 214
  adding and deleting Accordion
    widget panels, 242
  adjusting size of Windows Media
    file, 235
  aligning text, 139–141
  Alt tags defined in, 133
  applying HTML tags and
    attributes in, 117, 118
  assigning Menu Bars properties,
    240
  cell properties defined in, 82–83
  configuring check box states, 207
  creating CSS formatting rules, 121
  defining links between frames,
    91–92
  defining number of check boxes
    selected before submitting
    form, 222
  dimension parameters for
    QuickTime movies, 233
  displaying, 75
  enabling scrollbars for frame, 90
  Flash buttons edited in, 229
  Flash Text formatting in, 227
  formatting AP Divs in, 102–103
  hotspot tools in, 142–144
  illustrated, 36
  image-editing tools in, 136

  including hint content for
    commentary field, 219
  links defined with, 52–54
  List Values button of, 211
  object IDs assigned in, 245
  overriding style with attributes
    on, 125
  pop-up menu validation set from,
    223–224
  preparing text to trigger open
    browser window event, 252
  reverting image to original
    size, 135
  setting properties for Flash movie,
    230–231
  single radio button edited in, 209
  Spry widgets edited in, 237
  Standard mode features for cell
    formatting in, 72
  Submit and Reset buttons
    configured in, 213
  tabbed panels set up in, 238
  table column width set from, 74
  table properties defined in, 80–81
  text color assignments in, 119
  text fields defined in, 205
  using, 36
  validating zip code input, 215, 216
prototyping site navigation, 11
PSD files. *See also* Photoshop
  editing, 136
  placing in Web pages, 145–150

Q

QuickTime movies, 233–234
QuickTime Player, 234

R

radio buttons, 207, 208–209
reducing image file size, 127, 128, 129
relative links and targets, 52, 53
relative positioning of Divs, 106
remote servers
  comparing content of remote and
    local sites, 21
  connecting to, 19–21
  dangers of working only on, 19
  defining connections to, 16–18
  downloading files from, 24–25
  local vs. remote sites, 16
  signing up for, 20
  synchronizing content with local
    sites, 26–28
  transferring files from local site to,
    22–25, 170
  updating edited templates and
    library items on, 169–170
  uploading changed pages to, 159
removing sites in Manage Sites dialog,
  14, 15
repeating regions, 155
Resample tool (Dreamweaver), 136
Reset button, 213

resizing
  images in Dreamweaver, 135
  multiple AP Divs, 99
RGB color system, 120
rollovers, 258–259
rulers
  invisible in browser, 114
  selecting unit of measurement, 112
  showing/hiding, 32
  zero point for, 112–113
rules
  creating CSS formatting, 121
  defining in CSS Rule Definition dialog, 175
  editing Spry validation, 220
  page break style, 192
  text area validation, 218–220

S

sample frames, 85, 92
sample starter pages, 58–60
Save As Template dialog, 156
Save For Web dialog, 128
Save Style Sheet File As dialog, 189
saving
  before creating Spry widgets, 237, 238
  framesets, 86
  image file in site folder, 131
  pages generated from basic starter page, 60
  Photoshop files in other graphic formats, 145
  Web pages first time, 51
scripts
  CGI, 198
  client-side, 193, 194–197
  further reading on server-side, 202
  resources for form, 198
  using in jump menus, 194
scrollbars, 90
Select Image Source dialog, 130
Select Style Sheet File dialog, 63
Select tool, 32, 33
server-side services
  about server-side forms, 193
  FreeFind search engine for, 198–199
  further reading on server-side scripts, 202
Set Magnification drop-down menu, 32, 33
Sharpen dialog, 137
Sharpen tool (Dreamweaver), 136
showing/hiding
  collapsible panels, 243
  displaying Property Inspector, 75
  finding invisible AP Divs, 100
  rulers, 32
  tabbed panels, 239
  table borders, 80

Site Files view, 10
Site Map view
  about, 10, 11
  designing site using, 11–13
  remote sites not seen in, 21
site navigation diagrams, 10
snippets, 165
spacer image files, 76
spacing
  adding between text and images, 139, 141
  blue line displaying image, 141
  table cell, 67–68
special characters
  restricted for file names, 12
  using in Web page names, 49
  viewing set of insertable, 46
Split view, 31, 38
Spry effects
  attaching to page elements, 245
  defining events for, 246–247, 248
  editing and deleting, 248
  types of, 245
Spry widgets
  about, 193, 217
  Accordion widget, 242
  Collapsible Panel widget, 243, 244
  creating and editing, 237
  defining text area rules, 218–220
  deleting, 244
  editing rules for, 220
  Menu Bar widgets, 240, 241
  placing Text Field widget in form, 215–217
  saving before creating, 238
  setting up pop-up menu validation, 223–224
  using tabbed panels, 238–239
  using with check boxes, 221–222
Standard mode
  calculating column widths in, 75
  creating table in, 66–69
  Layout mode vs., 72
Standard toolbar, 39
Starter Pages (Theme) options, 58–59
states
  check box, 207
  defining images for navigation bar button, 261
  link, 52, 186, 187–188
status bar, 32–33
Style Rendering toolbar, 191
style sheets. *See also* CSS; external style sheets
  attaching external, 174, 175, 176–177
  considered dependent files, 25
  defining, 108
  global application of styles with, 125
  linked vs. imported, 64
  overriding external styles with embedded page styles, 179
  previewing, 61

Submit button, 213, 221
SWF files, 226, 227, 228, 230
synchronizing local and remote content, 26–28

T

tabbed panels, 238–239
Table dialog
  configuring table in, 66–69
  defining fixed and flexible columns in, 73–76
  opening, 66
Table tags, 176, 184–185
tables
  about, 65
  combining fixed and flexible columns, 73–76
  converting AP Divs to, 103
  creating in Standard mode, 66–69
  defining properties for, 80–81
  designing in Layout mode, 70–72
  editing in Property Inspector, 36
  editing navigation bar, 262
  embedded, 70, 77–79
  setting up cell properties for, 82–83
Tag Bar, 244
Tag pop-up menu, 183
Tag Selector bar, 32, 253
tags
  advantages of HTML, 116, 117
  Alt tags, 132–134
  blockquote HTML, 118
  Body, 178–180, 271
  defining Div, 106–111
  editing attributes in Property Inspector, 36
  formatting HTML text, 181–183
  headings assigned with, 116–117
  Image and Table tags, 176, 184–185
  text formatting with attributes and, 116–118
  using, 116, 117
Target Browsers dialog, 41, 264–265
Target pop-up menu, 91
targets
  choosing for link in frameset, 91
  relative and absolute, 52
templates
  blank templates vs., 56, 57
  creating pages from, 55–57, 152–156
  editable regions on, 56, 57, 152, 154
  function of, 151
  generating pages from, 157–158
  including navigation in, 167–168
  library items vs., 161
  updating, 151, 159–160
  uploading, 167–168
testing and maintaining sites, 263–272
  adding Design Notes, 270

testing and maintaining sites *(cont.)*
    checking browser compatibility, 264–265
    cleaning up Word HTML, 268–269
    previewing in Device Central, 266
    rollover testing in browsers, 258
    sitewide link testing, 267
    testing browsers for media support, 271–272
Testing Server view, 10
text
    aligning and spacing images and, 139–141
    applying color to fonts, 119–120
    copying and pasting on Web pages, 3
    embedding images at paragraph start, 131
    formatting with HTML attributes, 116–118
    importing, 2, 3
    pasting from Word into Dreamweaver, 268
    setting attributes for inline, 121–125
    sources for Web site, 2–3
    using Flash Text, 226–227
text areas
    defining rules with Spry widget, 218–220
    placing in forms, 205–206
text fields, 205–206, 215–217
Text Indent and Outdent buttons, 118
thumbnails
    about, 129, 138
    previewing images with, 127
timelines, 254–256
Timelines panel, 254
titles
    adding Web page, 49, 50
    defining for embedded pages, 88, 89
    entering, 51
    filenames vs., 50
toolbars
    Insert bar, 42–43, 71, 96
    Standard and Document, 39–41
    Style Rendering, 191
transparency for GIF image backgrounds, 146
triggering events
    actions, 246–247, 248, 249
    page loading as, 252

U

underlining links, 186, 188
unit of measurement, 112
unvisited links, 52, 187–188
updating
    library items, 161, 165–166
    navigation links, 167, 168
    Photoshop images, 148, 149

templates, 151, 159–160
uploading
    dependent files, 24, 25
    entire Web site to remote server, 22–23, 169–170
user interface. *See also* Document window
    elements of panels, 34
    Insert menu features, 44–47
    Standard and Document toolbars, 39–41
    using Insert bar, 42–43

V

validating
    check boxes, 221–222
    pop-up menus, 223–224
    text area rules, 218–220
    text fields, 215–217
    zip code input, 215, 216
values, 224
vertical Menu Bars, 240
View pop-up menu, 20
views
    designing site using Site Map, 11–13
    Document window, 31
    managing site, 10–13
visited links
    defining style of, 187–188
    display for, 52, 186

W

Web hosts, 19, 20
Web pages. *See also* designing Web pages; Web sites
    adding titles to, 49, 50
    attaching Spry effects to elements of, 245
    checking browser compatibility of, 264–265
    copying and pasting text on, 3
    creating from scratch, 48–51
    CSS styles of library items embedded in, 164
    defining links to open, 91–92
    embedding images in, 130–131
    generating from templates, 157–158
    importing spreadsheets and Word documents to, 3
    placing Photoshop files in, 145–150
    preparing images for, 126–129
    previewing in Device Central, 266
    sample starter pages for generating, 58–60
    saving as template, 156
    time before opening in browser, 33

updating Photoshop images on, 148, 149
    using multiple timelines on, 256
    using templates to create blank, 55–57
Web sites. *See also* planning and embedding site elements; Web pages
    collecting content for, 2–5
    connecting to remote servers, 19–21
    defining before creating pages, 1, 48
    defining local, 1, 6–7
    defining remote server connection, 16–18
    designing using Site Map view, 11–13
    determining open, 16
    managing, 14–15
    managing site views, 10–13
    organizing local, 8–9
    preparing images for, 5
    sitewide link testing, 267
    synchronizing local and remote content, 26–28
    transferring files between remote and local, 22–25
Web-safe color, 119, 120
widgets. *See* Spry widgets
width
    adjusting table, 67
    constraining page display, 68
    using Property Inspector to set table column, 74
windows. *See also* Document window
    behaviors opening browser, 251–252
    Code Inspector, 38
    defining Target window for link, 53–54
    Files, 1, 10–13
    Library Item, 165
    opening browser, 251–252
Windows Media movies, 235–236
Windows platforms
    downloading QuickTime Player for, 234
    showing Insert bar in, 96
Word
    cleaning up HTML files, 4, 268–269
    importing documents from, 3
    saving files in HTML, 3

Z

zero point for ruler, 112–113
Z-index values, 102, 103, 110
zip codes, 215, 216
Zoom tool, 32, 33
zooming to hotspots, 142